IF IT TAKES A VILLAGE,
Build One

IF IT TAKES A VILLAGE,
Build One

■

How I Found Meaning

Through a Life of Service

and 100+ Ways You Can Too

■

Malaak Compton-Rock

Broadway Books

New York

Copyright © 2010 by Angel Donyale Service, Inc.

All rights reserved.
Published in the United States by Broadway Books,
an imprint of the Crown Publishing Group,
a division of Random House, Inc., New York.
www.crownpublishing.com

Library of Congress Cataloging-in-Publication Data is available upon
request.

ISBN 978-0-7679-3170-0

Printed in the United States of America

1 3 5 7 9 8 6 4 2

This book is dedicated to my husband, Chris, who has been by my side as I have found my wings and learned to fly through a life of service and to my daughters, Lola Simone, Zahra Savannah, and Ntombifuthi Samantha.

I also dedicate this book to my South African family of Gogo Skhosana, Thusang, Crispen, Nati, Emanuel, God Knows, Wendy, Trecious, and little Chris Rock. You all have given so much to me, including love, knowledge, and even your blood.

And to the memory of Ingrid Acevedo, my friend and coworker at the U.S. Fund for UNICEF, who lost her life aboard Swiss Air Flight 111 near Peggy's Cove, Nova Scotia, on her journey to Geneva, Switzerland, to do God's work.

Contents

■

■

"Service is the rent we pay for living." I shared this lesson from my childhood in my own book, *The Measure of Our Success: A Letter to My Children and Yours*. It's a line Malaak Compton-Rock loves to quote often—but Malaak does much more than just repeat these words. She lives them every day. I have had the chance to get to know this wonderful woman through her service on the Children's Defense Fund's board. I first met her during a Child Watch visit by a group of very prominent women to New Orleans to see how children were affected by Hurricane Katrina. She did not come just for a day but helped lighten the burden of that devastation by helping establish a CDF Freedom Schools program to provide children safe havens and good books and caring adults and hope. I'm so grateful for her example of service and sharing with others. In this engaging book, Malaak passes on what she's learned about living a life of service and gives readers encouraging, practical advice on how to make service a central purpose in their own lives too.

One lesson that resounds throughout this book is that there are many different ways to serve and make a difference. Malaak has served in her own neighborhood, where she cofounded the Triple Negative Breast Cancer Foundation after a mother in her circle of friends was diagnosed with this dangerous form of the disease. Her reach extended to a neighborhood she adopted in Johannesburg, South Africa, after a first visit to the "grannies and orphans" who lived there moved her to help. She supports youth after-school programs at the Bushwick Salvation Army Community Center in Brooklyn, New York, where her husband, Chris, spent time as a child, as well as at the Children's Defense Fund's Freedom Schools program in New Orleans. Along the way, you will see that as Malaak's own life evolved, so did her ways to serve.

When her full-time work in public relations for the U.S. Fund for UNICEF became difficult to integrate with her husband's travel schedule, she fulfilled a dream of starting her own nonprofit by founding styleWORKS, an innovative program that provided salon services and accessories to women transitioning from welfare to work and going on job interviews. styleWORKS allowed her more flexibility and the opportunity to use her personal interests in beauty and style. After her children were born and her weekend commitments to styleWORKS began conflicting with family time, she adapted again. Today, as the founder of Journey for Change: Empowering Youth Through Global Service, she is combining her passions in a unique way: nurturing inner-city American children through a program that provides them with opportunities of their own, culminating with a trip to Johannesburg, South Africa. These young people, whom I have been able to meet, learn firsthand how privileged their own lives are in a global context and how much they can serve and contribute to making the world a better place for other children less fortunate than they are.

Malaak's example tells us we should not wait for the "right" time to find the time and resources to give back to others—the right time to serve is right now! She explains how service and volunteer commitments can fit every person's and family's schedule, on any budget, and provides practical advice for helping us assess and match our own talents and gifts to the needs and opportunities around us. This practical guidebook will help you research organizations, host your own fund-raising events, support products with a mission, learn to advocate effectively for causes you believe in, and more. Parents will especially appreciate Malaak's tips on how to involve and engage children. She is teaching her two beautiful young daughters and the children she mentors that their hands are never too small to help someone else.

And readers will be inspired by Malaak herself. Many people would assume that someone like Malaak Compton-Rock simply leads a very privileged and enviable life. Malaak's life does have many blessings, but she understands that from those to whom much is given, much is required. This book shows how those who have much can give and share much and have an admirable life. Read it and remember to use all the blessings, skills, and talents you have to reach out and help someone and leave the world a better place than you found it.

The Glorious Adventure of a Life in Service

■

*Dedicate your life to a cause greater than yourself and your life
will become a glorious romance and adventure.*
—MACK R. DOUGLAS

I stood in front of the crowded room at the Bushwick Salvation Army Community Center in Bushwick, Brooklyn, readying myself to speak to the seventy children who had gathered in front of me. The kids looked up at me with a wide array of expressions, some with broad smiles and eager eyes, some with curious, watchful stares, and even a few with bored faces.

We were meeting in the cafeteria of the community center that regularly feeds the homeless and elderly during the day, along with the throngs of elementary, middle school, and high school students who arrive in the afternoon after school. After serving the evening meal, the staff hurriedly cleaned up to ensure that the space was ready for the students and their families, who would soon arrive.

Some of the youths were seated at tables and others were sitting on folding chairs that had been brought in from other rooms to handle the overflow of kids, parents, grandmothers, godparents, friends, and staff who had assembled to hear me speak. I was at once excited but also very nervous. I knew what I had to offer these kids could very well change their lives. I had a sense that we were all about to embark on something very special. This was the first meeting I was having with these middle school children from Bushwick, Brooklyn, an inner-city neighborhood that consistently struggles with drug abuse, child neglect, gang violence, and poverty, and I was there to invite them to be part of a program I had recently dreamed up, the seeds of which were sown in a shack in the shantytown of Diepsloot in Johannesburg, South Africa, as I sat telling a grandmother who was raising her five grandchildren about the youths in Bushwick and my desire to impact their lives in a significant way. This program, which came to be called Journey for Change: Empowering Youth Through Global Service, was a journey for all of us in every sense of the word. By the time we were done, it would take us to South Africa; to the halls of the Capitol building in Washington, DC; to the Ninth Ward of New Orleans, Louisiana; back to Brooklyn; and to many places in between.

But now we were just beginning. I was working with the Bushwick chapter of the Salvation Army, in the very community center where my husband, Chris, came throughout his childhood for afterschool care and summer school. He even received his baptism certificate from the church here. He and I had been supporting the extraordinary work of the Salvation Army in this neighborhood, hoping to ensure that these kids got the same opportunities he had been lucky enough to get. With the support of Target, (RED), and Dell, we were in the process of establishing a new computer lab and library, and this work allowed me to spend time with the kids and get to know them; as a result, I became determined to do even more to help them overcome the many challenges they faced in their young lives.

So there I was, standing in front of everyone, telling the children that I would be selecting thirty kids to take to South Africa to meet the grannies and orphaned and vulnerable children I had come to know and love, to serve people who needed their help, to experience the world beyond their own community, and maybe come to understand some of the blessings they had at home. I wanted them to understand that it was going to be a fun, inspiring trip that would change their lives for the better. I told them about my love of South Africa, how it had changed me from the first time I went, and how I'd felt instantly connected to that extraordinary country, so deeply that I had to keep coming back.

Some of the children jumped up with joy, whooping and hollering at the thought of the trip. Some asked nervous questions, wondering whether Africa was just a big jungle, full of lions and tigers and people waving spears, not realizing that South Africa had modern and developed cities like Johannesburg, where we would be spending virtually all of our time, and even very wealthy metropolitan areas. Some were anxious about the trip itself—the thought of taking an eighteen-hour plane trip when most of them had never flown anywhere, the idea of being away from home for two weeks.

All of these concerns I completely understood. This is why I had wanted to have this meeting, so I could carefully answer all of their questions and those of their parents and family members who had come with them.

One of the children at that first meeting was LaToya Massie. La-Toya is just a little firecracker—there's no other way to describe her. She weighs maybe two pounds wet, but her spirit is huge and so is her heart. Although she didn't say much at that first meeting, she was determined to make it through the application and interview process we had set up. And when we asked her why she wanted to go on this trip, she had her answer all ready.

"I just know this trip is going to make me a better person," she told us. "This is really a big chance for me, and I don't want to miss it." She really understood the significance of traveling, and she was excited, too, about the opportunity to serve.

LaToya's mother was so supportive of her daughter. She was extremely open with us about the fact that she and her family had had a very difficult life, one that had been wracked with poverty, affected by drugs, and marred by violence. LaToya's life had been impacted negatively because of her mother's many problems, yet her mother had survived and in many cases triumphed over them and had come out stronger on the other side. Most important, she was the type of mother that we all hope to be, one who wanted her child's life to be better than her own. She told us that LaToya really deserved this trip because even after all she had been through, she was still such a positive, vibrant, and kind girl.

I appreciated her mother's honesty, and I must admit that once I finished interviewing LaToya, I had pretty much made up my mind that I wanted to take her on this trip. In fact, kids like her are why I created the program in the first place: to offer special opportunities to kids who had faced many struggles but who wanted to take a chance at something different in order to succeed in life. I thought she would make the most of it—and she turned out to get even more out of the experience than I ever imagined. I can still see her standing in the shantytown of Diepsloot, staring at the shacks that had been cobbled together from wood and scrap metal and watching the children playing in the muddy runoff from the single water spout. Despite the bright South African sun, the crowded rooms were almost completely dark, due to the lack of electricity and the fact that the shacks were often built with no windows. People depended on candles and kerosene lamps for both heat and light—though many families didn't have either. Despite the chilly weather, most had decided to wait until nighttime before using these precious and expensive commodities.

LaToya watched school-age children spending the day playing in the dust. The Brooklyn public school LaToya attended was not the best of the best, and she might not have always had the finest teachers or been in classes that had the greatest and newest materials. She did attend school regularly, and she did pretty well, though she knew she could do better. In South Africa, there is no public education, so now she was seeing children whose families couldn't afford to pay for their kids' school fees, let alone their books, pencils, notepads, backpacks, and uniforms. She was seeing children with no toys or very used and broken toys, some children barely dressed and others with no shoes, children struggling with a level of poverty she had never even imagined.

LaToya had started the day joking and laughing with her friends. After all, we were in Africa, and the journey across the ocean had been exciting and fun. But as our visit through the shantytown continued, she, like the other Brooklyn children, became quieter and quieter. And as we left the crowded warren of shacks to reach the broad, sunlit street, she began to cry.

"They don't have anything," she kept repeating. "They just don't have anything." As she took a big breath, she told me that all she wanted to do was help them.

"I want to help them and bring them some happiness," she told me through her tears. "But whatever I do will not be enough. I feel so bad and feel as if I have been selfish. I feel bad about the things that I complained about, the material things that I felt I deserved and got mad because I did not get. I am so sad."

Though my heart broke for LaToya as she tried to take in the sights of extreme third-world poverty, I knew this was the beginning of one of the biggest learning curves of her young life. And I was so glad that we had incorporated time at the end of the day to debrief one another and that I was able to take this walk with her. The personal time we had together allowed her to purge, letting all the thoughts that were jumbled up in her head pour out to me in a much-needed emotional release. And it allowed me the opportunity to speak with LaToya about the great strength of the South African people, about how proud a people they are and how they do not want our pity. But I explained that they appreciated our help and would take advantage of every blessing we bestowed upon them. It was also important for me to tell her to pay special attention to how polite the South African people are, how sincere they are when they speak to you, how they look you directly in the eyes and give you all of their attention, and how much joy they have in their lives even though many have few material possessions.

The following day, LaToya helped give out the mattresses, blankets, propane gas, food, clothes, and toys we had bought for the families based on their needs. Instead of breaking, my heart rejoiced as this sensitive girl experienced, perhaps for the first time, the true joy of helping others. Though she wasn't saying much as she handed the warm clothes, sacks of the food staple mealie-meal and beans, and packages of diapers to the grannies, older siblings, and mothers who were caring for the children she had wept over, LaToya glowed with a quiet sense of purpose. In fact, LaToya demonstrated the exact same emotional responses that I had the very first time I walked through an African shantytown. And like me, she responded with shock and sadness but quickly met the needs of the families with kindness and a fierce determination. Thirteen-year-old LaToya was taking her first few steps on the journey that had begun for me, too, in childhood: my search for a life in service. My own personal journey for change has been, in the words of motivational speaker and writer Mack R. Douglas, a glorious romance and adventure.

I have been blessed to visit many places on my journey for change, across our nation and around the world. I have also been blessed to work with a wide variety of people: celebrities helping to promote UNICEF's mission; grannies and orphaned and vulnerable children in South Africa; executives of such philanthropic companies as Target, Liz Claiborne Inc., Dell, South African Airways, JetBlue Airways, South African Tourism, and (RED); homeless families who lost everything due to Hurricane Katrina. I have spoken about HIV/AIDS with desperate mothers, teenagers, and gay men as I worked the hotline for the Gay Men's Health Crisis. I have helped to coordinate a campaign to raise awareness for the signs and prevention of child abuse and helped women moving from welfare to work feel a greater sense of confidence through makeovers as part of my work with styleWORKS. I've worked with my next-door neighbors to raise funds and awareness for triple negative breast cancer after a neighborhood mom succumbed to the disease. Where I've seen a need, I've tried to rise up to meet it. This mission has taken me not only on a journey across the globe but also on a voyage within, learning to understand myself as I struggled to understand people's needs in this world.

I've come to believe that a life in service is one of the most extraordinary privileges we can know on this earth, whether we are taking half an hour a week to spoon soup at a food pantry or spending forty hours a week running a nonprofit. Over the years, as I have grown from college student to career woman to wife and mother, my life in service has changed with each life transition. Yet I have always found a touchstone in giving back, a kind of nourishment I have never experienced anywhere else. I love my husband, my children, my family, and my friends, but I love, too, the global community I am blessed to be a part of and the family of like-minded spirits I've served, and served alongside.

So I have written this book to share my journey with you, hoping that you will find some of the same inspiration I have discovered along the way. I would also like to help smooth your path as you undertake your own journey for change. Not a day goes by that I don't get one, two, or a dozen requests from people looking to volunteer or donate funds or start their own nonprofits. So many people want to give back to this world but don't always know where to start. This book is my attempt to answer all the questions I hear every day and share the skills and information I have been lucky enough to acquire.

This book is also my attempt to show you how easy it can be to lend a helping hand to communities and people who need us. It can be as simple as giving a different type of holiday gift: say, a donation to Heifer International, where you can spend as little as $20 to buy a flock of chickens or a cow for a needy family. Maybe you'll join a giving circle, a group of people in your community that meets monthly and collects as little as $10 per month to donate to a cause you choose together. Perhaps you'll organize a carnival or fashion show to benefit your kid's school, or spend two hours a month reading to the elderly at the local senior center, or buy your kids a subscription to *Time for Kids* magazine and talk to them about becoming global citizens. Maybe there is an issue you are passionate about and you decide to advocate by passing out literature or attending a rally in protest. Or perhaps you will do something as simple as shop at Target instead of a competitor and exercise your consumer power at a store that gives away $3 million a week—your money—to philanthropic causes nationwide.

Besides sharing my own story with you, I also want you to meet some of the other inspiring people I have encountered on my journey, people serving in all sorts of different ways, of all ages, at all levels of income and experience, and in all sorts of places. You will meet a wide variety of extraordinary people, from the Brooklyn woman who collects new backpacks and school supplies for kids who would otherwise have to make do with hand-me-downs, to a popular TV journalist who uses her platform to effect change, to a woman who works for a national breast cancer foundation but started her life of service as a Peace Corps volunteer. I will also offer you as much concrete information as I can about every type of volunteering and service. You will find out how you can become an active volunteer in your local area, donate to an international relief organization, respond when catastrophe strikes, plan an event to raise money for a cause that you believe in, or check to see if a nonprofit organization is fiscally responsible before you make a donation. To make it even easier for you to serve, at the end of this book I have included a resource guide filled with additional material to help you build your own village.

In other words, there are as many ways to be of service as there are people on this earth, and part of my purpose in writing this book is to help you discover your own personal vision of a life in service. I hope that it becomes a resource that you can turn to time and time again for information and for inspiration. Sometimes we do more, sometimes less, but always, we can do *something,* however small. And from this generosity, we too reap great rewards. After all, you serve because your service is needed, yes, but also because it feels so good. Joy is what will keep you coming back. It is a joy that will fill you up and change your life.

Chapter 1

Each One, Teach One

■

Service is the rent we pay for living.
—MARIAN WRIGHT EDELMAN

As far back as I can remember, I've been engaged in some kind of service, activism, or volunteer activity, and that without a doubt is thanks to my mother, Gayle Fleming. My mother is an activist from way back—she must have gotten her interest in politics and world events from *her* mother, who was a voracious reader and writer, and she clearly decided to pass both an interest in politics and a commitment to service down to me.

What I remember most from my childhood is not so much specific issues, concepts, or causes—those came later. Instead, I remember what it felt like to be exposed to service and to be taught about volunteering. There was the thrill of getting to go somewhere with my mother, who would talk to me beforehand about the journey we were going to take for the day, whether it was a rally, a meeting with a nonprofit, or a door-to-door canvass for a candidate she was supporting. Though, like every child, I only really knew what it was like to be in my own family, I did have a sense that I was being exposed to politics and service in a way that was special and slightly different from other kids I knew. Now that I am an adult, this makes perfect sense to me because I have a mother who will get on a bike and ride from Washington, DC, to North Carolina to raise money for HIV/AIDS awareness and funding, who will plan a yoga-thon to raise money for Darfur, who will enter a book-writing competition and ask her friends to sponsor her for each word written and then give the proceeds to an orphanage in Kenya, and who will plan a fund-raiser for a local food bank to help pay off their mortgage so that they can focus on putting more food on the shelves. Now, when I take my own children to a Darfur rally, or to New Orleans to help the victims of Hurricane Katrina either through advocacy events in the lower Ninth Ward or rebuilding houses in St. Bernard Parish, or to visit the friends they've made in South Africa's shantytowns, I think of my own mother doing the same for me in our quiet Oakland neighborhood, and I feel that I, too, am carrying on the traditions of our family.

At any given moment, whether it was at breakfast, in the car, walking down the street, or at dinner, my mother and I could talk about service, volunteering, and the whole wide world. My mother found many ways to make it clear that we were citizens of the world, even if I did not have a chance to personally see the whole world up close. She often reminded me that "everyone does not have the same blessings as we do, and because of this, it's our absolute duty to give back." One of her favorite quotes was Marian Wright Edelman's saying "Service is the rent we pay for living." It is a motto that I, too, have adopted because it resonates with me so deeply. As everyone who knows me will agree, I repeat these words more than any other quote, and it remains one of my favorite sayings, a touchstone for how I view my life. As a matter of fact, journalist Soledad O'Brien recently joked that Marian Wright Edelman should start collecting royalties from me based on the number of times I repeat these words as she introduced me at an awards dinner.

Our household wasn't only service oriented; it was also very political. My mother and her friends could always be found discussing and debating local and national issues. What was the new mayor going to do to make people's lives better? Was this new policy good or bad for our neighborhood, our people, our city? Where was our country headed, and what should we all be doing about it? Now when my husband, Chris, and I talk politics at the dinner table, I feel that same connection to my past, and I hope my daughters are learning the same lesson: Family is important, yes, but family doesn't begin and end at the dinner table. We're all part of a larger family, and if any one of us is hurting, then all of us are. *If I get there before you do, I am obligated to bore a hole and pull you through—* that's what my mother lived, that's what she taught me, and that's what I try to teach my girls.

Now, don't get me wrong. I did not always want to go everyplace my mother wanted to take me. I did not really want to join her at her meditation center no matter how much she tried to convince me that it would help to make me a better person. I can remember my mom had a friend she meditated with and did a lot of service work with who also had a teenage daughter, one of my classmates. Mai and I were very similar. When our mothers went overboard (as we saw it), we were able to hang together and commiserate.

As of this writing, my older daughter Lola is only seven and my little Zahra is only five, and I do pull them from pillar to post, as my mother did with me, in order to show them the many ways people live in this world and to instill a sense of service in them from a very early age. Though I fully expect them to do their own share of teenage complaining eventually, I hope that they ultimately feel the way I do now: eternally grateful that my mother made me take part in both politics and service, because those were the experiences that helped to shape me into the woman I am today.

Certainly the issues that were closest to my mother's heart are close to mine as well. My mother attended Mills College in Oakland, a very feminist place, so she was always concerned with the rights of women, as well as with every woman's responsibility to make the world a better place. Mom was also deeply committed to civil rights and equality for African-Americans. Living in Oakland, she had the chance to become good friends with Black Panther leaders Eldridge and Kathleen Cleaver, so I remember us hanging out with them and their children while I was growing up.

Mainly, though, my mother was concerned with poverty, both here in the United States and around the world. She was and con-

tinues to be a big supporter of RESULTS, an extraordinary NGO*
that lobbies the U.S. government to allocate more resources for poor
countries and supports other groups that work directly for the poor.
As a teenager, I remember going with her to lots of RESULTS fund-
raisers and advocacy events, where I learned more about how to
effect change for the world's poor, lessons that I use today in my
work with orphaned and vulnerable children in South Africa.

These days, my mother lives in Washington, DC, where she
continues to come up with innovative ways to raise money and
awareness for the causes most important to her. She's still working
on behalf of hunger issues both in the United States and abroad,
showing special concern for food pantries, which have become a
mainstay not only for the poor but also for many middle-class people who've fallen on hard times and don't have any kind of safety net
to rely on due to our tough economic climate. As when I was growing up, my mother is still part of a vital network of friends who share
her interests, and she hangs out at DC spots like the bookstore café
Busboys and Poets, where she can talk to her heart's content about issues affecting our world, like the war in the Middle East, the genocide
in Darfur, the economy, and how to help those who are hurting because of the mortgage crisis. Times and topics have changed since I
was a child growing up in the liberal and very active cultures of Oakland and Berkeley, but one important constant has remained: *If you
have an opportunity to help, then you must help.*

On my father's side, I come from a long line of educators with a
close connection to Howard University, the historically black institution of higher learning in Washington, DC, established in 1867, two
years after the end of the Civil War and the abolishment of slavery. My
father's uncle was for many years the head of Howard's political science department. When it came time for me to go to college, Howard
University was my first choice. Not only did I want to attend a school
with a rich and illustrious legacy in terms of educating freed slaves,
I was also aware of Howard's prominent alumni, including such

---

*"NGO" stands for "nongovernmental organization." The term is used in service work
to distinguish between private groups and government agencies.

politicians and activists as David Dinkins, Vernon Jordan, and Andrew Young; author Toni Morrison; Supreme Court judge Thurgood Marshall; physician and medical pioneer Dr. LaSalle D. Leffall Jr.; and entertainers (and sisters) Debbie Allen and Phylicia Rashad. In fact, Howard University graduates more African-American doctors, lawyers, and other professionals than any other HBCU (Historically Black Colleges and Universities) institution in the United States.

I believe that by attending Howard, I was truly blessed in terms of my education. I had the great good luck to be taught by some of the most brilliant professors in the nation and to share my time with bright and ambitious classmates. To walk across such a historic campus every day filled me not only with pride but also with a sense of responsibility. Like a lot of graduates of HBCUs, I felt my ancestors' legacy, and I wanted to make them and the people who graduated before me proud—especially those first graduates, who walked to college, literally walked to Howard University, because they did not have the money for transportation, from cities all over the Deep South, seizing against incredible odds their first opportunity at higher education.

Another plus: Howard University offered me the chance to live in the nation's capital. I remember during my first semester going down to the National Mall to visit the Capitol and sitting in on congressional hearings, listening to the people who make our laws arguing and debating. I'll be honest: I usually got lost in all of the back-and-forth and the long speeches made by some lawmakers. But as the child of an activist, I understood that the laws they were talking about would have a huge impact on people's lives and even on my own life. I was thrilled to see that such life-changing debates were held in public and to be able to witness political debates by leaders who had been elected by ordinary people like my family and myself. Something about living in DC made politics more urgent—and somehow more real.

So although my major was in arts production management, I minored in political science. I even thought about going into politics for a time, though I eventually decided not to, and it's a good thing, too; I don't have the temperament for it. What I love about service is the hands-on aspect, working with people, especially children, who need my help; that excites me far more than sitting in some conference room hammering out policy. Plus I think I would be far too impatient—as in bite my arm off!—with the slow pace of creating policy when I can serve in a hands-on way on behalf of critical issues that need immediate attention. I understand, though, that politicians, administrators, and especially advocates are a crucial part of service. Howard was where I first began to understand that each of us has to find our own path, our own particular way to serve.

I was also conscious of the fact that Howard, like so many well-known institutions of higher learning—such as the University of Southern California, Yale, and Columbia, to name a few—was located smack-dab in the middle of a low-income, primarily African-American neighborhood struggling with crime and drug abuse. I felt a sense of responsibility to serve where I lived and attended school. Since I was close to the Washington, DC, headquarters for RESULTS, the organization my mom had long supported, I ended up working on its special events, volunteering to help set up rallies, street fairs, and even a huge gathering on the Mall. I also have fond memories of mentoring a little girl who lived in my neighborhood, a child who was being raised by her grandmother. To protect her privacy, I'll call her Jasmine M. Over the three years that I mentored her, Jasmine M. and I became very close, and I got a huge lesson in how far a little bit of time can go in someone else's life.

I also saw that "it takes a village to raise a child," since I soon had pretty much everyone I knew involved in mentoring Jasmine M. as well, including all my girlfriends and my then boyfriend. Whichever one of us was available would spend time with Jasmine M., sometimes just hanging out with her or maybe taking her to museums and exhibits. I had a weekend job as a concierge at the Embassy Suites Hotel, and soon Jasmine M. was sitting behind my desk for my entire shift, coloring or reading. After a while, she became everybody's child. And isn't that how it should be?

After graduation, I tried to stay in touch with her, and on my trips back to DC, I often took Jasmine M. out to lunch. Though I do not know where she is or what she is doing all these years later, I can only hope that I had a positive influence on her life. I know that she had an amazing influence on my life and I still think of her to this day.

Bright Lights, Big City

But despite the satisfaction I felt with Jasmine M. and my calling to change the world, I had other goals as well. As a child and young adult, I'd wanted to be an actress, even to the point of spending my summers at theater camp in Minneapolis. But somewhere along the way, I understood that I had only a tiny chance of becoming a working actress. The people who succeeded in this demanding profession lived and died by their desire to do that work. I just didn't want it that much, which I was wise enough to realize meant that I probably wouldn't succeed at it.

So instead of majoring in theater, I got a degree in the business side of the arts and set my sights on going into public relations. I'd been inspired by an article about Terrie M. Williams, who headed the largest public relations firm owned by an African-American woman at the time. Over the course of her impressive career she has represented such clients as Eddie Murphy, Janet Jackson, Johnnie L. Cochran, Essence Communications, Time Warner, and HBO.

I was especially intrigued to read that Terrie had been a clinical social worker before she'd become a publicist. After giving it her all in this field and feeling like she needed a change, she became a successful public relations professional, and when she began her new line of work, her first two clients were Eddie Murphy and Miles Davis. Talk about starting at the top!

Terrie had gotten her start by convincing Murphy and Davis to give her a chance, so I thought maybe I could persuade her to do the same for me. My senior year at Howard, I wrote to her, expressing my desire to work for her, and she actually called me personally. Later I learned that Terrie treated every single letter or phone call the same way, whether it came from the head of HBO or some college student she'd never heard of. No matter who it was, she responded promptly, either in person or by having someone on her team follow up (and if you were the one who was supposed to follow up, you had to prove to her that you did!). That was an important lesson that has stuck with me to this day.

Terrie was kind enough to offer me an internship with her company in New York. There was no pay, only a small stipend, but to me it was the opportunity of a lifetime. At the same time, I got a "real" job offer from a fashion merchandising firm in another city, with a substantial salary that would have had me living pretty well as a new college graduate.

Still, whatever the cost, I had to choose Terrie. As a college student, I was no stranger to living on a budget, and I was used to working hard. Choosing the route of greater opportunity seemed worth the challenge of struggling in order to live as my more authentic self. And as luck would have it, Terrie promoted her assistant a few months after I got there. I got to move up into the assistant position, which paid better than the internship had—but just a bit!

Terrie was busy, as always, and she believed in delegating responsibility. She was and continues to be a dynamo who whirls in and out of a room and in and out of town like a tornado. She also judges people by what they can do, not by their age, how long they have been in the business, or what is on their résumé. She just wants to know whether you can do the job. So when the time came for the premiere of Eddie Murphy's film *The Distinguished Gentleman,* she said to me, "You know what? I really need you to do some serious work on this, so I am going to give you as much to do as you can handle. But you are going to have to work hard."

It was an extraordinary opportunity. I ended up coordinating a lot of the press relations for the premiere with Terrie, doing far more than any assistant would normally have been allowed to do. I loved the work leading up to the premiere and especially loved working the night of the premiere, which was held at a theater downtown that I always went to on the weekends to see movies. All went well, and from there, I just kind of moved on up. Terrie hadn't been lying—I *did* work hard! I often slept at the agency, but if you are given a chance to be taught by the best and given opportunities that most do not receive, and you are learning a lot to boot, you better take advantage of it!

Of course, I also had a lot of fun. I was invited to amazing events;

met interesting and inspiring people; went to great parties with Terrie, or without her when she told me to go in her place; and got to be a part of New York City in a way that I would have never been able to had I not taken the chance to move up there and work for the Terrie Williams Agency. And, just as icing on the cake, it led me to meet my husband, the comedian Chris Rock.

A Turning Point

Terrie was demanding, hardworking, and generous to a fault. As hard as she worked for all her high-profile actors and executives, she worked just as hard for her pro bono clients, and she was able to give nonprofit agencies access to resources that they never would have had if not for her influence. So I saw firsthand how you could have a successful business while mentoring young people and helping nonprofits. What an inspiration!

I spent three wonderful years working with Terrie, but then I realized that it was time to begin a new chapter in my life.

I've always loved makeup, so when I heard about a job opening at Elizabeth Arden's media department, I thought it would be perfect for me. Because, okay, I'll admit right now, I don't just love makeup—I'm a product queen! What I had liked about public relations was the chance to convince somebody that a person with talent was worth being talked about or that the world should take note of a particular new TV show, movie, or CD. Promoting a creative person or product required all *my* creativity, which I found both challenging and fun. And it was a terrific high to read the article I had helped to place or to watch the talk show I'd managed to get my client on. I liked knowing that I had helped talented people—especially new talents—achieve their dreams or get the chance to promote a project they were proud of. That said, as much as I liked wearing makeup and perfume, I just didn't get the same thrill from promoting them. I very quickly realized that what I really wanted was to take my love of public relations, along with all the skills and experience and connections I had acquired working for Terrie, and use it to promote something worthy that I believed in.

What happened next seemed like fate—I came across an ad in the *New York Times* that seemed to have my name on it. The U.S. Fund for UNICEF was looking for a public relations person with a background in entertainment, specializing in celebrity relations and special events, someone who could start a new division within the public relations department at the U.S. Fund to help raise the organization's profile. As soon as I knew the job existed, I wanted it, and though it took a lot of patience and persistence, I got it!

UNICEF, of course, is the United Nations Children's Fund. It's supported by contributions from member organizations around the world. The U.S. Fund for UNICEF raises money and awareness in the United States to support UNICEF's critical lifesaving work worldwide.

My job at the U.S. Fund for UNICEF was to build up the celebrity relations department, plan special events, and work as part of the public relations team to promote the U.S. Fund's and UNICEF's major initiatives and reports. UNICEF had traditionally had a very successful relationship with celebrities who worked very hard as UNICEF Goodwill Ambassadors. Past Goodwill Ambassadors whom we all know and love include the glamorous and caring Audrey Hepburn and the extraordinary actor Peter Ustinov. Current and longtime Goodwill Ambassadors include Roger Moore and Harry Belafonte, who are still hard at work traveling the world raising awareness for UNICEF.

But now the U.S. Fund was looking to expand the program. They wanted to bring in younger celebrities and well-known people of all colors and backgrounds. They also wanted to make better use of the Ambassadors they had and find new ways that celebrities could help promote UNICEF's mission.

Since I came to UNICEF from the entertainment field, I knew firsthand that there were many celebrities who already had a deep commitment to helping their fellow man. I decided to concentrate not so much on collecting big names as on finding an authentic connection between the celebrity and the cause that he or she was promoting. Usually—not always, but usually—you don't want just someone's name; if at all possible, you want their heartfelt commitment and genuine passion. You want the person to be knowledge-able, so that when he or she talks to the media, the interview has some real content. And you want them to care—really care—about the facts and figures and stories that they share about your issues, so that even to the most cynical reporter, their words ring true.

Given the kinds of in-depth celebrity relationships I hoped to develop, I was looking not just for famous people but for down-to-earth individuals who just happened to be celebrities because of their gift of talent and good luck at having us all enjoy what they do. I wanted stars who would be willing to come to events, do media interviews, and also take UNICEF-assisted trips: going into the field, learning about the situation on the ground, and then talking about the nitty-gritty needs of that particular area.

Luckily, I had a great roster of people to start with, including actors Edward James Olmos and James Kiberd and actress Jane Curtin. These three phenomenal people were so kind to me, welcoming my ideas with open arms, telling me freely what they were passionate about, and working so hard for the U.S. Fund for UNICEF. I was especially moved by the work of Edward James Olmos, who is known as a spectacular actor with great intensity and who took that same intensity and used it as he traveled throughout Latin America, so he could advocate in the United States for the needs of Latin American women and children. Within months, I was free to call Edward, James, and Jane at home with my requests, and they called me, too, sharing their ideas and telling me how they wanted to help. It was a true partnership that I hoped to extend to other celebrities, making it the model and not the exception for the U.S. Fund for UNICEF.

That's why I developed what you might call a niche approach to celebrities while I was at the U.S. Fund for UNICEF, seeking ways we could link our organization to something they already cared about and that made sense for them to speak about. Once you let people find their own platform, they become so much more committed. They do their homework, deepen their involvement, and speak so much more passionately. Celebrities with a genuine personal connection to an issue will not only do a much better job of communicating with the public, they will also be excited to take part in innovative approaches to promoting their cause and will go above and beyond to make themselves available for whatever is needed.

For example, I read that the actress Sarah Jessica Parker had trick-or-treated for UNICEF as a child. I immediately hoped we could use this early UNICEF connection to involve her further.

Trick-or-Treat for UNICEF is a Halloween tradition that began in 1950, when five kids in Philadelphia decided to collect money to help the children in postwar Europe, using milk cartons that they had decorated themselves and raising $17, a considerable sum at the time. The tradition took off, and soon, children across the United States were collecting money in official orange UNICEF boxes. Over the years, U.S. kids have collected more than $150 million for UNICEF, while Canadian children have raised more than $96 million in Canadian dollars, and Hong Kong kids have contributed more than $5 million in Hong Kong dollars—figures that I bet would have astounded those first five kids in Philly.

Sarah Jessica Parker was one of the many U.S. children who grew up participating in this tradition, so in 1996 I contacted Michelle Kydd Lee, a wonderful woman who is the executive director of the CAA Foundation. CAA is one of the leading talent agencies in the world. Its foundation exists to help the agency's clients and employees serve. Michelle was so cool and immediately liked the idea of the future *Sex and the City* star being that year's Trick-or-Treat for UNICEF spokesperson. Sarah Jessica also liked the idea and agreed to appear at our annual kickoff event. She has gone on to support the program—and UNICEF—in numerous ways, as she is now a Goodwill Ambassador. I owe a debt of gratitude to Sarah Jessica Parker and Michelle Kydd Lee, because my thought that you should find a celebrity who had a genuine connection to the cause proved true very early on in my career at UNICEF and set the tone for my work at the agency.

Likewise, TV journalist Katie Couric and poet Maya Angelou stand out in my mind for the level of dedication and commitment they brought to their roles as Ambassadors. Katie in particular was very good at communicating to the public an overall sense of

UNICEF's goals: universal access to clean and safe water, immunizing every child against major diseases, ending child labor, improving health care, and decreasing mothers' mortality rates. Part of her ability to be such a passionate and effective spokesperson was that she was so well informed about the organization's work and the hot-button issues that affected the global communities UNICEF supported.

To make sure all of our Ambassadors were as well informed, one of my most important responsibilities was to plan UNICEF-assisted field trips, official visits that allowed our celebrity spokespeople to tour a particular region and meet with field-workers, doctors, volunteers, other UN staff, and members of partner NGOs, as well as, of course, the communities receiving UNICEF aid. These visits let our spokespeople see UNICEF's achievements for themselves as well as what problems still remained to be solved.

During these trips, I needed to publicize the celebrity's activities, using his or her fame to gain attention for the people living in the countries where UNICEF worked, while also making sure that the trip reflected the celebrity's interests. We needed to know both what we needed to get out of a trip and what our celebrity spokesperson wanted to get out of it. To this end, I generally worked with our Ambassador's publicist and manager while also communicating with our field offices, helping them put together a trip that would speak to the celebrity in question.

I think back to a particularly successful trip I helped plan for Claudia Schiffer to visit Bangladesh. Claudia actually called us, inspired by learning that the glamorous and dedicated Audrey Hepburn had been one of UNICEF's most respected and beloved Ambassadors. We met with Claudia, but I remember that there was a little bit of trepidation in our offices about whether to move forward with her. I think some people might have been skeptical that a stunningly beautiful supermodel could also be a serious person, or maybe they were just afraid that she wouldn't be taken seriously.

I was really clear, though, that working with Claudia would be a terrific plus for our agency, and I lobbied for her acceptance. At the time, Claudia Schiffer was one of the hottest supermodels in the industry. She had a huge fan base, and that's exactly what we wanted. I knew that any time she opened her mouth, reporters would be eager to publicize what she had to say.

Claudia was eager to go into the field. I was thrilled, of course, but wanted to make sure that she had firsthand information that would help her to be a credible spokesperson. Her first stop then was an orientation program we set up for our Ambassadors to visit UNICEF's international headquarters, across the street from the United Nations, and meet with every single department head at UNICEF as well as with certain UN officials who helped UNICEF do its work. This orientation was always a wonderful day that proved very helpful to our spokespeople.

After orientation day, it was time for Claudia to visit a developing country so she could see UNICEF's work on the ground. Her first trip was to Bangladesh, one of the poorest countries in the world, hard to navigate and harder still to find any comfort in. Claudia was used to traveling first-class and staying in luxury hotels, and as a model, she obviously wore designer clothing for a living. Yet she was so understanding of the fact that as a nonprofit we did not fly first-class and that she needed to dress down not only because of the poverty-stricken environment but also out of respect for the country's culture, the people's religious affiliations, and the simple need for comfort!

We needn't have worried. Claudia was wonderful on her trip to Bangladesh. She was generous with her time, kind and gentle to the women and children she met, full of energy, and extremely inquisitive, everything you need to be an effective Ambassador. She continues to be one of UNICEF's most valuable spokespeople.

Celebrities Pay Their Rent

*T*here are many celebrities who speak out for important causes every day. There are also many well-known people who have started nonprofit organizations to raise money for a particular need. Here are some of my favorite admirable celebrities. If you share my appreciation, you might consider volunteering with or donating to one of the groups listed below.

Celebrity Activists

- Drew Barrymore, World Food Program Ambassador, dedicated to making sure all people have access to nutricious food
- Beyoncé, supporter of Feeding America, dedicated to aiding the hungry by delivering more than 3.5 million meals a year to local food banks nationwide
- Don Cheadle, raising awareness and aid for the genocide in Darfur
- George Clooney, raising awareness and aid for the genocide in Darfur
- Sheryl Crow, raising awareness of breast cancer and environmental issues
- Ted Danson and Mary Steenburgen, activists for environmental issues, especially clean and safe oceans
- Mia Farrow, UNICEF Goodwill Ambassador, serving children and women in 160 developing countries, especially involved in the campaign to end the genocide in Darfur and in protests against China's sale of arms to Sudan
- LaTanya and Samuel L. Jackson and Deborah and Carlos Santana, board members and founders respectively of Artists for a New South Africa (ANSA), working to combat HIV/AIDS
- Wyclef Jean, founder of Yéle Haiti, which provides aid to Haiti
- Angelina Jolie, United Nations High Commissioner for Refugees Goodwill Ambassador, raising awareness for the world's most vulnerable displaced people
- Lucy Liu, U.S. Fund for UNICEF Ambassador
- Jay-Z, supporter of Water for Life, a UN initiative for clean and safe water worldwide

Celebrity Nonprofits

- Andre Agassi: The Andre Agassi Foundation, supporting youth educational development, www.agassifoundation.org

- Lance Armstrong: The Lance Armstrong Foundation, supporting cancer research, www.livestrong.org

- Bono: The One Campaign working to end extreme poverty and preventable disease and to establish debt relief in developing nations, www.one.org

- Michael J. Fox: The Michael J. Fox Foundation for Parkinson's Research, www.michaeljfox.org

- Mariska Hargitay: The Joyful Heart Foundation, founded to help heal those who have faced sexual assault, www.joyfulheart foundation.org

- Elton John: The Elton John AIDS Foundation, funding direct-care services for those with AIDS as well as AIDS prevention programs, www.ejaf.org

- Alicia Keys: Keep a Child Alive, providing lifesaving antiretroviral treatment to children and their families with HIV/AIDS in Africa and the developing world, www.keepachildalive.org

- Madonna: Raising Malawi, supporting orphans in Malawi, www .raisingmalawi.org

- Alonzo Mourning: Alonzo Mourning Charities for youth educational development and mentoring, www.amcharities.org

- Paul Newman: Newman's Own, a for-profit company that donates all profits and royalties after taxes to educational and charitable projects; the Hole in the Wall Gang Camp, which provides seriously ill children with a camping experience, www .holeinthewallgang.org

- Brad Pitt: Make It Right Foundation, providing Hurricane Katrina relief through building sustainable green houses, www.makeitright nola.org

- Christopher Reeve: The Christopher and Dana Reeve Foundation, which develops treatments and cures for paralysis caused by spinal cord injury and other central nervous system disorders, www.christopherreeve.org

- Marlo Thomas: St. Jude's Children's Research Hospital, a hospital for children with cancer, www.stjude.org

- Lee and Bob Woodruff: The Bob Woodruff Foundation, helping to heal the physical and psychological wounds of war, www .remind.org

Boy Soldiers and *Apocalypse Now*

I had many wonderful experiences working with all of the Ambassadors at the U.S. Fund for UNICEF. But the one person who made a really lasting impression on me was the actor Laurence Fishburne.

I didn't know Laurence at the time, and I don't even remember whether we approached him or he came to us. All I know is that at some point, he said, "Maybe I'll get involved with you guys—let's talk," and I came in on the talking part. I bonded with his publicist, a phenomenal media guy named Alan Nierob, the first time we chatted, and Laurence also got along really well with the U.S. Fund's then president, Charles J. "Chip" Lyons.

Laurence proceeded to tell us a remarkable story. He'd begun filming his breakthrough role in *Apocalypse Now* when he was only fourteen, a grueling two-year stint in the Philippines. Like many of the actors in that film, Laurence found the experience both inspiring and traumatic because of the subject matter. And like any great actor, he'd taken to heart the experiences of the character he played. Even though he hadn't actually been a child soldier, he'd been a fourteen-year-old who played a soldier—a soldier involved in a particularly brutal war—and it had left a deep impression on him.

When Laurence came to meet with us, the issue of child soldiers was very much in the news—and very much on his mind. Because of his experiences filming *Apocalypse Now*, he wanted to help raise awareness of this painful issue and to join in UNICEF's mission to end the illegal and atrocious practice of using children as soldiers in the military.

In response, I set up a trip for him to the Ivory Coast and then on to war-torn Liberia, a West African nation then notorious for having abducted and drugged many children whom it had involved in its recent seven-year war. The war had just ended and UN peacekeepers were still stationed in the battered nation. I accompanied Laurence on that trip and I'll never forget landing in the country's capital of Monrovia, where the vast majority of the people still had no lights, no electricity, and no running water. We who stayed on the UN base were able to benefit from generators and a rudimentary plumbing system, but our use of lights, showers, and even toilets was highly restricted.

With UNICEF field-workers as our guides, we traveled through the city and some of the countryside, learning how UNICEF was helping the young victims of that war. One of the main issues was reuniting the former child soldiers with their parents. Many of these children had been kidnapped during the night, often with their villages burned and families tortured. Stolen as young as fourteen, twelve, and even nine, they had often been given drugs by the warlords who had induced them to kill—and kill horrifically.

When the war finally ended, UNICEF was there to reunite these children with their parents or a family member who had survived the war, as well as to provide counseling for the traumatized youths, and eventually job training. It was a daunting task. Imagine a boy stolen from his parents at age nine, drugged, and made to kill. Now the war is over, he's sixteen, and by his culture's standards, he's a full-grown man. He's lived through too much to go back to school, but he's not trained for any kind of productive work. Nor does he have any idea how to live within a family, a community, and a country attempting peace; all he knows is traveling through a war-torn city or a devastated countryside, scavenging for food with his fellow soldiers, also young boys, and committing the atrocities he's been trained to undertake. How does a young man like this return to any kind of normal life?

UNICEF had a three-part program: reunification with families, counseling, and job training. It seems miraculous that it could be successful—but in many, many cases, it was.

Both Laurence and I were shaken by what we saw, and he

emerged from that first trip fully committed to UNICEF and its extraordinary work. He helped promote the agency's goal of eradicating the practice of using child soldiers as well as its three-part mission to help the children. Sadly, UNICEF's work has had to continue in Africa today, where the problem is most critical in countries such as Sierra Leone, the Ivory Coast, Chad, Sudan, Uganda, and Congo. Children are also used as soldiers in various south Asian countries and in parts of Latin America, Europe, and the Middle East, in countries such as Sri Lanka, Colombia, Russia, Afghanistan, and other nations. And Laurence Fishburne continues to be a staunch supporter of former child soldiers and is also the chairperson of the U.S. Fund for UNICEF's campaign against HIV/AIDS. For more information on the plight of child soldiers worldwide, visit the Coalition to Stop the Use of Child Soldiers at www.child-soldiers.org.

UNICEF for Life

The fascinating thing about both the U.S. Fund for UNICEF and UNICEF itself is that almost everyone who works there becomes in some sense a lifer. Most employees simply work there forever, and if I hadn't married a man whose career took him all over the world, I certainly would have stayed there, too. (More on that life-changing decision in the next chapter!)

But even those of us who have left still consider ourselves UNICEF people. We identify with the organization and seize every chance to support its work. I am personally blessed to have been on many UNICEF-assisted trips to developing countries since I left the organization. That's how I first visited South Africa, which opened up a whole new world to me.

So in one way, I don't feel that I've ever left the U.S. Fund for UNICEF. But since I'm no longer with that wonderful agency officially, I'd like to take a minute to acknowledge all the extraordinary ways in which it transformed my journey for change.

First and foremost, working at the U.S. Fund for UNICEF cemented for me that advocacy and service were indeed what I wanted to do for the rest of my life. It was one thing to sit at my desk at Elizabeth Arden and dream about working for a nonprofit; it was another thing entirely to get out into the world and realize that my dream actually had some substance. We've all had dreams that didn't quite fit us and made moves that weren't quite right for us. Working at the U.S. Fund for UNICEF showed me that this was one dream that had enough staying power to last a lifetime.

I think the U.S. Fund for UNICEF also opened up my ability to think globally. Working for an organization that helps children around the world, how could I help but develop a broader view? I consider myself to be a smart, aware person, but there is no way I would have known about the problems facing most of the world's people had I not worked at the U.S. Fund for UNICEF. In fact, that's why I took so much pride in working so hard to promote the organization, so people could learn about the problems it was trying to solve. Thanks to the U.S. Fund for UNICEF, I've seen with my own eyes and felt with my own heart the plight of the world's children, and painful as that often is, I know it makes me a better mother, friend, wife, and world citizen.

In particular, I'm grateful to UNICEF for my first trip to the continent of Africa, which was that journey to the Ivory Coast and Liberia with Laurence Fishburne. That experience, the opportunity to hug and kiss former child soliders, to watch UNICEF field-workers work so diligently at child reunification, and to hear a group of schoolchildren taught in a bombed-out church singing, "We want peace, not war," to us, created in me a lifelong commitment to Africa and a lifelong respect for that troubled but inspiring and enriching continent.

Last but not least, I think my time at the U.S. Fund for UNICEF taught me that field-workers—no matter which government agency or NGO they work for—are the angels who live on this earth. I'm not a field-worker—I do some hands-on work, yes, and that grounds me and nourishes me to a remarkable extent, but most of my work is in creating and supporting programs. Those heroes who live every day in the shantytowns of Johannesburg or the refugee camps of Sudan or the homeless shelters of New Orleans are the people I most admire. I don't think that I'd have truly appreciated the work they do if I hadn't had the chance to meet the UNICEF staff and to see for myself just how much difference they make in the lives of the people around them.

So I spent three wonderful years at the U.S. Fund for UNICEF—and then it was time to leave. But UNICEF holds a special place in my heart as the agency in which I really discovered my inner humanitarian. Of course, you don't have to find a full-time job at a nonprofit, but I hope my experience shows you how rewarding this sort of work can be.

However, there are as many ways to contribute as there are causes that need your help. One of the most basic forms of service and a way to begin to make a connection with an organization is a simple charitable donation. If a journey begins with a single step, a journey for change can begin with a single check.

Finding Your Authentic Self in Giving

Finding just the right place to make a charitable donation can be daunting. After all, there are so many different groups that need money, and often you are bombarded with direct mail from many of them. How do you decide whom to give to—and how do you say no?

Whether you're thinking about donating five dollars, five hundred, or five thousand, this is an issue that requires some consideration. No matter how much or how little money I have to work with, I always try to think it through and make smart choices based on research and my personal giving platform.

Although my commitment to making careful choices hasn't changed, what has changed is my attitude. As I've found my authentic self in giving, discovering which causes and issues mean the most to me, I've simply had to get over my guilt at not being able to donate to *everything*. I respect a wide variety of causes, so much so that I promote them on my website and speak about them a lot, but I may not personally donate to them because they are not a part of my personal giving platform. Examples include the symphony, the opera, large museums, and institutions with large endowments and a lot of donor plaques all over the buildings.

I won't give you rhyme or reason for my preferences; they're just the issues that I happen to care most deeply about. And if you're going to make donations of your own, you need to develop your own preferences—and then get comfortable with them, too. This way, not only will you feel extraordinary when you write your check for $10, $100, or $1,000, you will also soon begin to feel the fruits of your giving, because you are focused on a cause or an organization and will be able to follow up and know that your contributions are making a difference.

Now, one thing I always do is read what is sent to me and listen when people explain to me why their cause is important. I cannot tell you how many times I have learned something new, have met someone whom I find interesting and want to stay in touch with, or have even been convinced to give a donation I thought I would not give.

Take the organization Opus 118. At first glance, it is a symphony, and I do not normally fund them. But Opus is a symphony for children living in Harlem. And because programs for at-risk youths are at the top of my list, Opus 118 fits my giving platform. Most of the time, though, I use my own gut instinct to decide how I'm going to allocate my resources and which causes I connect with. After all, when it comes down to it, you can't force somebody to care about something that you care about.

Look, hard as he's tried, my husband can't force me to get interested in baseball—I just think it's boring! I just cannot make it through a game, especially one that goes on and on into extra innings. I am always like, "Can we go home?" But that's another thing I can't feel guilty about. We are who we are, and we give how we give. The most important advice I can ever give you is to be passionate, smart, and educated about your choices.

Deciding How Much to Give

Now that you've decided *to* give, how do you decide *how much*? Again, this is an area where a lot of people come unglued. They often start feeling guilty about how small their gifts seem, not realizing that every cent counts to a nonprofit organization. They turn what should be a joyous, positive, self-affirming experience into something that causes them guilt or sadness. And no one should be feeling either of these emotions when they have decided to serve by giving.

Again, the first thing to remember is that a donation of any amount, no matter how small, means a great deal. When I was putting together Journey for Change: Empowering Youth Through Global Service, for example, I went for the big grants and corporate sponsorships because I needed to raise a large amount of money in a short amount of time. But I was also heavily dependent on the private donations I received, both large and small.

Truth be told, the individual contributions are what made it possible for thirty at-risk youths from Brooklyn, NY, and thirty college-age mentors to go to Johannesburg, South Africa. I'll never forget the time I received a $10 Wal-Mart money order from someone who heard me on the radio. She was so moved by the idea of my taking children who had never traveled to South Africa that she just up and sent me a donation—she found the address on my website. And when we came back and she read about how the children were preparing to become Global Ambassadors, continuing to raise money and advocate for change in South Africa and at home, she sent me an additional $20. Those two gifts mean the world to me, and they stand as a tribute to the power of giving, no matter what the amount.

Having said that, I suggest that you sit down and figure out what's a comfortable amount to give based on *your* budget. Remember, everyone has a limit, so be generous, but be realistic, too. You should also figure out how you're going to give: Monthly? Yearly? At certain times of the year?

When Chris and I were first married, we'd set aside some money every month and sit down together to think about how to spend it. I'd bring him four or five organizations to choose from and we'd talk about which one we wanted to support. These days, what I do is target about three-fourths of our charity budget for groups that I'm already committed to, which leaves one-fourth for people who come to me for funds. If their project fits my platform—at-risk children worldwide, breast cancer research, HIV/AIDS, women's issues, and education—and if I think the group is legitimate, I send a donation. I may not make my involvement with this group a long-term thing, but I'm thrilled to support them once, twice, or yes, maybe long-term if it works out that way.

A Little Goes a Long Way

*O*ne of the things that is hardest for people to understand is how impactful even a small donation can be. So often I've had people tell me that they'd like to give but that they can only afford to contribute $50 or $10 or even $5 to an organization. Surely, they say, such an amount is far too tiny to make any difference, so why bother to give? In fact, when it comes to giving, no donation is too small. Here a few examples of just how far your dollars can stretch:

- A $5 gift to Table to Table (www.tabletotable.org), a hunger-relief organization in Bergen County, New Jersey, helps the group deliver lunches to fifty children, while $10 given to the same group would help feed a family of four for a month.
- A mere $30 a month—that's only a dollar a day—could help UNICEF (www.unicefusa.org) test twenty children for malaria, perhaps saving their lives from this treatable but potentially fatal disease.
- A $50 donation to Free the Children (www.freethechildren .com), an international group whose goal is to end children's exploitation, would buy textbooks or sports equipment for a school.

So the next time you consider making a donation and catch yourself thinking that it's too small, picture the children in Malawi or Thailand or even Bergen County, New Jersey, who are receiving lunch, or malaria shots, or textbooks. Think about the difference you're making in their lives. Think about them growing up happy, healthy, and strong because you took the time to send in a donation that, at the end of the year, you will hardly miss—but that they will remember forever. And then, click on that website icon or fill out that check, secure in the knowledge that you are truly making a difference.

Investigating Charities

So many people tell me that they'd like to give money to a charity but that they get scared about where their money is *really* going. I totally identify with this concern. What I'm not in favor of is deciding *not* to give because of this uncertainty, especially when it's now so easy to find out more about a charity.

The main thing you're concerned with is whether the organization is allocating enough of its income to actual services rather than spending money on overhead, fund-raising, events, or savings for the future. You're going to be most interested in the percentage of funds that goes to administrative costs, since those are the dollars *not* going to the people whom the charity is intended to benefit.

Basically, a group should be spending no more than 25 percent of its income on overhead, with at least 75 percent going to actual services. Anything more than 75 percent is really, really good. Anything between 50 and 75 percent should make you wary and want to ask some questions before donating, e.g., why is so much money going to expenses *other* than the work of the charity?

Most nonprofits list this information in their annual report, which you can find on their website. You can also ask any group to send you this information by mail or e-mail. Smaller groups may not produce a formal report and may not even have a website. Don't hold that against them, though, since they, too, should be able to send you financial information by mail or e-mail if you request it.

Groups That Can Help You Research Charities

You don't have to do all the work by yourself. The organizations listed here can help you determine whether a charity is legit—and whether it is operating efficiently.

Independent Charities of America (www.independentcharities.org)
One of the most respected charity-rating organizations in the country, this group awards the Independent Charities Seal of Excellence to member organizations that meet the group's highest standards. Of the 1 million charities operating in the United States today, fewer than two thousand have been awarded this seal.

Charity Navigator (www.charitynavigator.org)
Charity Navigator provides information on more than five thousand charities, evaluating the financial health of each group it rates. The ratings are based on organizational efficiency and organizational capacity. If a charity spends less than a third of its budget on the programs and services it exists to provide, then Charity Navigator gives that charity a score of zero for organizational efficiency. Under "Tips" on this website you'll also find a very useful list: "The Top 10 Practices of Savvy Donors."

BBB Wise Giving Alliance (www.bbb.org/us/charity)
The BBB Wise Giving Alliance awards the BBB national charity seal to groups that meet its standards. Don't expect small, local charities to have a seal; only national charities are eligible. Among other requirements, the BBB expects charities to spend at least 65 percent of their total income on program activities and to spend no more than 35 percent of contributions on fund-raising. It also expects charities to avoid accumulating funds that could be used for current activities.

Simple Gifts: Five Fun Ways to "Pay Your Rent"

If you're interested in making a donation, you can feel great about writing a check. But if you have more time and want to try something different, there are lots of ways to make giving more fun—and to get your family, friends, and neighbors in on the good times as well! Here are seven simple ways to "pay your rent for living" while also providing you and your loved ones with a good time.

1. Have a Party!

Who doesn't enjoy spending time with family and friends—and this way you can do it in the name of a good cause. For example, you could choose a local charity and send an Evite to your family and friends to come over for a fun get-together complete with appetizers and cocktails or a playdate for the kids. Include information about the charity on the Evite and ask each guest to bring a prewritten check in a sealed envelope. Collect the checks as guests arrive and proceed with your event. This is a cool way to raise money without your guests feeling any pressure as well as a wonderful way to enjoy your friends' company! Or perhaps instead of asking guests to bring a check, ask them to bring designated items such as winter coats, shoes, professional work clothes, baby items, canned goods, and the like. Or you may consider asking guests to bring an assortment of travel-size toiletry items, such as toothpaste, deodorant, shampoo, soap, razors, and so on. Have baskets, cellophane paper, ribbon, and scissors available for your guests so that they can create care packages while they enjoy your appetizers and cocktails. Then donate the items to such venues as a local homeless shelter, domestic violence shelter, food bank, welfare-to-work organization, or teen support center, or send them to our soldiers overseas. Remember that people who are going through a life transition often don't have even the very basics, including diapers for their children, coats, shoes, and blankets. Your small gift can mean a great deal to someone in need.

2. Blessed Blooms

Whenever you host a special event, consider donating the floral arrangements from your special day to a local hospital. Just contact the community relations office of your local hospital and they'll help arrange for transportation. You can also ask your florist to transport the flowers—often, they'll say yes. The flowers are usually arranged in public areas where families and patients gather, but sometimes they're delivered to actual patient rooms. What a great way to share your special day with others!

3. Bowling for Dollars

Invite your friends and family to go bowling. Ask each person to bring along a check of any amount along with an idea for a charity to support. You bring pens, envelopes, and a basket to the bowling alley. Then whoever wins the game will have the honor of choosing the charity to which the basketful of checks will be given. Have the guests make out their own checks and seal them into individual envelopes. When you get home, slip all the little envelopes inside one large manila envelope and drop it in the mail.

4. Spring-Cleaning Block Party

Send out flyers inviting your neighbors to join you for a spring-cleaning block party. Together you can decide on a date for the event and choose a charity. Then make up more flyers and distribute them all over town. You might even convince a local newspaper to write a profile of your charitable neighborhood! This idea not only raises money and brings you closer to your neighbors but also helps you get rid of the items in your household that you no longer need.

5. Knit and Crochet for Good

Do you belong to a knitting or crochet circle? Why not designate a month where you knit or crochet for good? You might make hats and booties and donate them to a homeless shelter, domestic violence organization, or teen-parenting center. Or you could make shawls and blankets for the elderly. Use your creativity and enjoy the company of your fellow crafters while you make beautiful items for those in need.

Giving of Yourself

I hope I've given you a sense of all the ways you can pay *your* rent for living, making a difference just by doing simple things. In the next chapter, we'll take it a step further. I'll show you how to find groups right in your own area to volunteer with—and I'll share with you my own experiences of doing just that.

MY JOURNEY: AUTHOR AND ADVOCATE
TERRIE M. WILLIAMS

It was really such a pleasure to conduct an interview on volunteerism and service with Terrie M. Williams, my first boss, social worker by training, public relations guru, inspirational author, mental health advocate, and founder and president of the Stay Strong Foundation.

Q. When was your first volunteer experience? What did you do?
A. My first volunteer experience was actually as a Girl Scout—and later it was being the president of the Keyette Club at Mt. Vernon High School. We were a community service organization founded to participate and engage in activities, such as volunteering at local nursing homes and tutoring children, that would uplift our town.

Q: Who influenced your life, in terms of giving back and serving others?
A. My parents sowed the seeds for and influenced my philanthropic spirit. My sister and I were taught to always share with others—and to remember that we are all one. "The best and the blessed of us must take care of others."

Q. What has been one of the most meaningful ways that you have given back to society?
A. Connecting with an individual's spirit, acknowledging, smiling, and saying hello to people who we meet in our travels who are often ignored and considered "nobodies," literally transforms both spirits. Founding the Stay Strong Foundation in 2001, an organization serving youth, whose motto is "If we don't give our kids time, the system will." Finally, the outpouring of e-mails and letters from people responding to my work in the field of mental health has been *the* most inspiring—waking people up to naming our pain and explaining what depression looks like, sounds like, and feels like in the black community is gratifying. My book *Black Pain: It Just Looks Like We're Not Hurting* and the Stay Strong Foundation's Healing Starts with Us

campaign has transformed thousands of lives and has begun the healing of so many of our distressed communities across the nation.

Q. What makes you choose to support a particular initiative or service project?
A. There is an overwhelming sense of need in humanity. We must share ourselves with one another. We must guard ourselves from overload; therefore, I match my involvement based on whether I or someone I care for has been touched by a cause.

Q. Since you are a very busy career woman, how do you balance your professional and service obligations?
A. Terrie "Plus One," an "outside the office" opportunity for young people to join me and other professionals to attend black-tie fundraisers, corporate and private dinners, movie premieres, sports events, awards shows, speaking engagements, and special events. We have fun and introduce our young people to others and new situations. Since there are other people at these events, we encourage them to interact with the kids . . . and it's not solely on our shoulders. Our youth have to be at the table with us if they are going to hope, dream, aspire.

Q. What is your advice to someone who wants to serve and give back but does not know where to start?
A. There are many websites available that will match your talents with a local not-for-profit organization that is seeking volunteers. Also, I encourage individuals who are passionate about a cause that is not being addressed to form their own organization or coalition. Watch, look, and listen—everywhere you go.

Q. Though I know you support many endeavors, your passion is the Stay Strong Foundation. Can you tell us about this foundation and its mission?
A. The Stay Strong Foundation is a New York–based 501(c)(3) not-for-profit organization that works to support, educate, and inspire America's youth through a series of programs and events that are

designed to raise awareness of teen issues, promote the personal well-being of young people, and enhance their educational and professional development. The foundation encourages corporate and individual responsibility and develops educational resources for youth and youth organizations. We launched in July 2009 a campaign in partnership with the Ad Council, SAMHSA, and the Grey Group to address the issue of mental health in the black community. Our message is "Share ourselves . . . Healing starts with us."

Q. What can the average person do to help your platform of raising awareness and funding for mental health issues?
A. Visit our website at www.thestaystrongfoundation.org and www .healingstartswithus.net to find out what the signs of depression are in everyday language—what it looks like, sounds like, and feels like—and spread the word.

Chapter 2

Me to We:
Finding Myself by Serving Others

■

The best way to find yourself is to lose yourself in the service of others.
—MAHATMA GANDHI

While I was working at the U.S Fund for UNICEF, Chris and I got engaged and then married. I continued working with the organization I loved, but after about a year, it became really difficult to keep up with my demanding job given Chris's unusual schedule as an entertainer. Each of us had been living in Brooklyn when we met, and he'd mainly been doing stand-up, which made it easy for us to live on the East Coast. But then his career began to include a lot more movies. Soon he was filming almost exclusively on the West Coast, doing projects like *Lethal Weapon 4* and—one of my favorites—*Nurse Betty.*

My job was consuming, but his schedule was even tougher. In order to see him at all, I found myself leaving work at four P.M. every Friday, dashing to the airport, getting into Los Angeles at nine, spending two days with Chris, and then coming back on the Sunday-evening red-eye. On Monday morning, I'd go straight to work from the airport, and my hectic week would begin again.

We lived this way for months, and eventually, it got to be too exhausting. When I had to travel somewhere on a UNICEF-related trip, I saw even less of my husband and even more of airports. Finally, I started to think, "This job might not work."

My supervisors at the U.S. Fund for UNICEF did everything they could to help. Long before it had become common to offer employees flextime, they worked out a plan where I could work two weeks in the Fund's L.A. office and two weeks in our headquarters in New York. For a while, that was really helpful, because at least Chris and I got two straight weeks together. But sometimes Chris's schedule would change—maybe his movie would go on location or he'd get a stand-up gig somewhere. So as the gods would have it, even when I *was* in L.A., he might be someplace else!

At some point in everyone's life there comes a time when you have to be honest with yourself, and when I finally was, I found myself facing a difficult reality. I had married a creative man whose work might take him anywhere in the world, whether he was doing TV, shooting a movie, touring, making a special appearance, or writing. If I wanted to be with my husband, the two of us living like a regular married couple, I would need to be free to travel.

I dearly loved my job at the U.S. Fund for UNICEF, and if I'd married a nine-to-fiver, I'd probably be there still. So if I had to leave, I was determined to move on to something equally fulfilling and challenging, work that would allow me to have a direct impact on the people I was trying to help. I started thinking about which population I wanted to work with, what skills I could bring to the table, and how I imagined my new role.

Around that time, the news was full of then-president Clinton's efforts to end welfare as we knew it. Clinton's focus was on helping women and men move from welfare to work, and I could just imagine how difficult that could be.

Of course, President Clinton knew that many of the people on welfare needed education and job training. In fact, he mandated that the states fund job-training programs, though some states discharged that responsibility better than others. But I felt that many people would also need help with the mechanics of job seeking: how to conduct themselves on a job interview, how to dress for an interview in a way that was appropriate to the job, and how to groom themselves to look and feel good. As someone who by this point had worked for several different employers, I knew how hard it could be to look for a job, even when you've had plenty of experience doing just that.

One evening, I happened to see an interview on *60 Minutes* about a wonderful organization called Dress for Success. This groundbreaking group was started by a farsighted woman named Nancy Lublin who understood that in our looks-conscious society, women reentering the workforce or working for the first time needed to look like they belonged at their new jobs. She knew that even if you could type ninety words per minute, you wouldn't make a good first impression on your first interview if you came in wearing inappropriate attire. So she took some money that she inherited from her grandmother and started Dress for Success, a nonprofit organization that provides women with the clothes they need to . . . well, to dress for success! I was so inspired that this young women used her inheritance to help others when so many people would have spent it on themselves. She was selfless—and she started a movement!

The *60 Minutes* episode featured a woman who had recently been released from jail, where she'd been lucky enough to get some job training. They followed her to Dress for Success, where she picked out a suit. I saw that whether the clothes were used or new, they all seemed to be in fantastic shape and that the whole atmosphere resembled not a charity but a store. I admired the way the Dress for Success volunteers helped their clients figure out which suit was best for them, based on the job they were applying for as well as on their body type and general appearance. But I also saw that the clothing might not be enough. This woman, who had just left prison, was still sporting the traditionally African and easy-to-care-for hairstyle of cornrows, and she wore large rings on each of her fingers. I looked at her hopeful face and thought, "I'm so glad she had job training, I'm so glad she has a suit, but she is going to have a hard time getting hired anywhere until she has a complete look that is accepted in corporate America and takes off every single one of those rings. Who's going to tell her that? More important, who is going to tell her that with kindness, with an understanding of the culture of her hairstyle, but with the simple and honest truth of what is expected in the working world?"

So maybe there was a place for my sense of service *and* my sense of fashion. Hadn't I learned at the U.S. Fund for UNICEF that when you help the mother, you help everyone else—kids, husband, relatives, community? I'd seen it time and time again: When the mother is working and healthy, everybody reaps the benefit; when the mom stumbles, everyone around her seems to stumble, too. If women could get their clothes from Dress for Success, maybe they could get their overall style—accessories and hair and makeup—from me. So I did my homework and discovered that no one else was focusing on that particular area. And that's how styleWORKS was born.

Sharing Your Gently Used Clothes

Dress for Success has grown into a national organization that has inspired many other groups to offer a similar service. I wholeheartedly encourage you to donate your new or gently used business attire to one of the following organizations:

- Dress for Success, www.dressforsuccess.org. The website will link you to a chapter in your area.
- The Bottomless Closet, www.bottomlesscloset.org. Our clients at styleWORKS relied on both Dress for Success and this organization.
- The Alliance of Women's Business and Professional Organizations, www.womensalliance.org. The website will link you to local organizations in your area.
- Career Gear, www.careergear.org. Unlike the other groups, which focus on women, this organization offers interview attire to men. It has several chapters across the country, so check the website to find out the closest place for you to donate.

A Passion for Fashion

I envisioned styleWORKS as a kind of one-stop fashion destination for women who had completed their job-training programs. They would go to Dress for Success or the Bottomless Closet to get their suits and then they'd come to us for everything else: hairstyling, makeup application, waxing services, and those all-important accessories to complete a look: handbag, jewelry, scarf, and shoes. I wanted us to pamper our clients, teach them how to keep up their new business-oriented look, and then send them home with everything they needed, from the perfect belt and a new pair of shoes to a gift bag full of cosmetics. Most important, I wanted each woman to leave the salon feeling and looking great so she could walk into her interview the next day with a renewed sense of confidence, her self-esteem lifted, and the ability to look the interviewer in the eye with her head held high! I knew that my first key step was to incorporate as a nonprofit so that I could go after corporate sponsors for product donations. Believe it or not, I found all the information online just by searching for the phrase "how to start a nonprofit." I quickly realized that every state has different rules for nonprofits, so I had to look up and then follow the guidelines for my own state of New York, which is where my permanent residence was at the time.

My next step was to secure donations from a hair-care company and a makeup company. I knew that we were going to need a lot of product, and I wanted to be able to give our clients product to take home as well. I did what I always tell others to do: I called everyone I knew, told them about my idea and asked them to let me know if they had any contacts in these areas. Terrie M. Williams knew someone who worked for Clairol's parent company, and a friend had a friend who worked at Black Opal. So I was lucky enough to land two corporate sponsors right away. And this is truly because I told everyone I knew about my new venture.

Black Opal is no longer in business, but when I started styleWORKS, it was a major New York–based mass-market makeup company for women of color. They donated a wide variety of products, including foundation, powder, blush, lipstick, eyeliner, and eye shadow. And the wonderful thing is that their color palette worked for women of all skin tones and ethnicities, whether they were Caucasian, African-American, Asian, or Hispanic.

My second sponsor, Clairol, produces a multitude of brands. As it happened, when styleWORKS began, they were just launching a new one: Textures & Tones, specifically intended for women of color.

They gave us every kind of hair-care product you can imagine: shampoos, conditioners, hair color, relaxers. As a result, I became a big fan of this product line and continue to color my hair with its Cedar Red Brown!

I still needed to provide our clients with shoes, belts, jewelry, and all the other accessories that go into creating a put-together look. But with my two sponsors on tap, I felt ready to start approaching salons that might let us bring women in on a day that they were closed.

At some salons there were people I knew personally or had contact with through friends; at others I just walked in and asked for the manager. It almost didn't matter: As soon as people heard what my plan was, they were eager to help. Maybe as stylists and salon owners, they understood why our women needed this service. Or maybe as hardworking women—or as men who worked with women—they identified with our clients. Either way, they pitched in to a remarkable extent.

At the same time, I was looking for hairstylists, makeup artists, and facialists who were willing to donate their services. I was committed to making this a good experience for both them and the salon, and I didn't want either party to have to spend a dime of their own money or give up an ounce of their own products. Once again, I was moved almost to tears by how eagerly people signed up to help.

My search for corporate sponsors hadn't stopped, and I continued to be blessed with a terrific response. Liz Claiborne donated thousands of fashionable business-style handbags; Carolee gave us lovely jewelry, including faux pearl earrings and necklaces that were perfect for work; Kenneth Cole supplied our women with classic shoes in tones that would complement any suit—dark brown, black, tan, and navy—with various heel heights.

These donations were wonderful—but they weren't enough. Even after we began providing services, I had to keep approaching companies for more donations. Eventually, I received makeup applicators and other products for the hairstylists to use from Sally Beauty. I also got tweezers and nail clippers from Tweezerman, which made it possible for us to send the women home with everything they needed to keep up their look.

Even with the tremendous response I received, I had a huge organizing job because of the wide range of women coming through the program. By this time, I'd made connections with a number of job-training agencies in the city, and they agreed to send their students to me as the women graduated from their programs. But a stylist who's used to doing African-American hair may not be as skilled with white folks' locks, while a makeup artist who's a whiz with Latina skin tones may not have the same expertise with all African-American clients. I also had to make sure that we had the right products available: the right shades of makeup, the appropriate hair relaxers, the correct accessories, and all the other items geared to a wide variety of women. Some of our clients had additional special needs due to homelessness, physical abuse, or past drug dependencies, or just as a by-product of everyday life. Some had scars, bruising, inappropriate tattoos, or facial piercings that might keep someone from hiring them. Some had unprofessionally long fingernails or intricate fingernail art, while others had elaborate and colorful braids or other hairstyles that are perfectly fine in the neighborhood on weekends but would not be considered appropriate for the workplace. I had preinterviews before each woman's scheduled makeover day and personally explained to each client in private why I felt we needed to make a change in her appearance while at the same time giving her a look she would feel good about and could keep up on her own. I also gave the women handouts with the date of their makeover, the salon location, subway information, emergency contact information, and anything else they needed to know. Finally, I made sure that every woman went to Dress for Success or the Bottomless Closet to get her suit before she came to us. That way, we could make sure each of our clients got a handbag, shoes, and jewelry that would match her new suit perfectly.

The fun really started when the clients arrived. We'd typically have a group with anywhere from six to twelve clients, and though it was a real challenge moving them from hair to facials to waxing to makeup, it was a fun challenge. The energy in the salon was always fantastic. We would play music, have coffee and muffins in the morning, and then stop and serve lunch. We'd told the women to make child-care plans, so we could both work properly and give them a day dedicated totally to them—a real gift to a busy mother. We always had volunteer coordinators to keep things moving throughout the day, and except for the rare occasions when I was traveling, I was always there, too, making sure everything went smoothly.

When each woman arrived, the stylists would consult with her about her hairstyle: Cut? Color? Straighten? Perm? We knew that our clients didn't have a huge amount of time to get ready each morning, and we didn't want them to have styles that had to be kept up with expensive products or equipment. The goal was for them to feel empowered, to have a businesslike look that they could maintain while handling all the new challenges of the job search or the job and all the old challenges of keeping the family together.

While the client's hair was drying, we'd give her some literature about job-interview skills, which included major points such as researching the company you are interviewing with and knowing the correct pronunciation of your interviewer's name. Then we'd move her on to a facial and waxing. Though we would wax all facial hair, our most popular service was to wax eyebrows. It never ceased to amaze our clients how much a well-groomed eyebrow improved her entire face. Afterward, every woman had her makeup applied while receiving a lesson on how to repeat at home what the stylist had done in the salon.

After hair and makeup, we got each woman the accessories she needed to set off her smart new suit, and finally, she was ready! Typically, we were finishing our last client by about five P.M, and though a few women had to rush off before then to take care of children or other responsibilities, many wanted to wait until we were all done so they could savor the joy of everyone else's makeover together. As each client said good-bye, one of our volunteers made her up a goodie bag with whatever makeup and implements she needed to sustain her new appearance based on what was used by the stylists. And of course, she received whatever accessories she needed to complete her new look.

Our clients often left the salon at the same time and strutted down the street together looking fabulous. Each woman's self-confidence was through the roof! You could see in her eyes and her face and her whole way of walking how good she felt about herself. We always took "before" and "after" pictures so I could show our current sponsors how much difference their donations had made while successfully soliciting new sponsors, salons, and stylists. (Keeping your sponsors informed and showing your gratitude is critical—I'll say more about that in chapter 8.) I'd also stay in touch with our referring agencies so I could find out what percentage of our clients actually got jobs. Sometimes it took one interview; other times, a client needed four or five interviews. I'm proud to say that some 70 percent of the women who came to styleWORKS eventually found jobs!

Finding Myself by Serving at styleWORKS

You know how you meet certain people and they somehow help you understand yourself better? Well, that's how it was for me at styleWORKS. I learned something from every single one of our clients, but there are some who stand out more vividly, perhaps because I was so moved by their courage and cheer.

One client I'll never forget is Charlotte. (I've changed all the names and some identifying details to protect these women's privacy.) She was far from your image of the typical welfare client: She actually had a master's degree and had been a stay-at-home mom in a beautiful New York City neighborhood. After about fifteen years of marriage, she finally left her abusive husband—but because she had no recent job experience, she couldn't get a job. As a result, she'd been on welfare until she got into a job-training program. After she came to us she went off to an interview with a professional New York sports team, where she was hired and then rose quickly through the ranks.

When I think of Charlotte, I think of how important it is never to take your lot in life for granted. One day you can be on top of the world; the next day you can lose it all. We had many, many clients who had had good jobs but then something went wrong:

They were laid off, or had to stop working to care for ailing parents, or were struggling with domestic abuse. You never know what might happen in your life; you can only hope there will be some kind of help for you when you need it. That's why I support welfare, especially having traveled to countries with no welfare system at all. That safety net is really crucial. And yes, sometimes it might be abused, but you then have to think of a person's children and be thankful we live in a country where there is public housing and food assistance so they don't have to live in a shack, as some children do when there is no form of governmental assistance. And in fact, contrary to popular belief, most people do not abuse the system and most people do not want to be on welfare for long periods of time. In fact, more than 70 percent of women on welfare stay on the rolls for less than two years and only 8 percent stay for more than eight years, although sometimes women who have left welfare do need to return to it within five years due to a renewed family crisis or job loss.

Despite her impressive background and education, Charlotte had not an ounce of self-importance, no sense that she was somehow more deserving of attention than any other woman in the salon. She was in the same boat as everyone else and just as appreciative of the help she was being given. When I want to work on my own humility, I remember Charlotte, thinking of how abuse can cause a person's life to take a turn for the worse. But Charlotte's story also helps me to remember that if you have the courage to leave and can take steps to help yourself, someone will assist you in return.

We also had clients who'd been on welfare for a long time. These women were for the most part untrained and all too well aware of how limited their options were. After all, a job at McDonald's—even if you're lucky enough to get it—won't cover your bills, your child care, or your health insurance. At least being on welfare guarantees you and your children medical care, and being at home means your children get some kind of supervision. But even the "typical" welfare client was an individual, someone who might turn out to be far from typical.

Annette, for example, was a Frenchwoman (again, name and details have been changed) who was totally devoted to her kids. She'd come to New York on a student visa, married an African-American man, and ended up living and raising kids in Harlem, of all places.

Annette never expected to be on public assistance, but she and her husband had had some financial problems, and she needed the money to continue raising her kids. Again, she needed the safety net. But once she was over the hump and knew that she and her family would continue to have a roof over their heads, she realized she needed to go to work and get off public assistance as soon as she could. To that end, she enrolled in a training program and ended up at styleWORKS.

I loved Annette as soon as I met her. But she was not my typical client and I remember having to go out and purchase cosmetics for her skin tone. Many Caucasian women who came through the program could use Black Opal, which had shades for the lightest of African-American women as well as Asian and Latina women. But the product line had no shades that were right for Annette. I was happy to go to the drugstore and purchase many shades of foundation and powder for her so that the makeup artist could find the perfect match.

At least I didn't have to worry about her hair. Being French, even on a limited income, Annette had a strong sense of style and wore a chic black bob. Our stylist just worked to take out the gray, put a nice shine to it, and trim it to perfection. And of course, this classic Frenchwoman knew which accessories were the right ones for her.

Beautiful as she was—especially by our society's standards—Annette was unsure of herself and even more insecure about her skills. Her career had been motherhood. She spoke fine English but she had a very strong French accent. It took everything she had to leave the full-time mothering she loved and reenter the workforce. In that way, she was like millions of other U.S. women who once thought they could live on their husband's salary and who now find that their families are unable to survive on a single income.

Finally, though, Annette got a job as a teacher's aide and, to her own surprise, discovered that she actually loved helping to teach kids. I kept in touch with Annette for a long time after she found work and we had wonderful conversations about her kids, her job, her life, and how far she had risen from the threat of being evicted. Even better, she found herself in the process. When I want to remind myself that even the most beautiful woman, who seems so confident and empowered, can actually feel like a timid outsider, I think of Annette. And when I want to summon my own courage to take risks, approach an unfamiliar challenge, or muster the courage to ask for help, I think of Annette then, too.

styleWORKS Ends—and Lives On

styleWORKS didn't end when the women left the salon. We had also arranged a mentoring component for the program, so our clients could stay in touch with women who were already working in business. Sometimes we gave seminars to help women think about such topics as financial literacy, maintaining a bank account, getting a foot in the door of a new field, taking the right steps to gain a promotion, figuring out how long before you could ask for a raise, and coping with the distress of losing your job. We'd invite working women—sometimes our own graduates!—and our clients would eagerly show up, excited to see how the others had fared and thrilled to share their own news.

We also started a book club, which, believe it or not, is still meeting monthly to this day. Our clients choose the books, we buy them, and we find a place for everyone to meet. Every couple of months, we go out to dinner together or maybe see a play or a movie, especially if one of the books we read is turned into a film. Once a group of nervous clients, our styleWORKS ladies have become a real community of women who have successfully moved from welfare to economic independence. After all these years, they support one another—through new financial crises, one woman's bout with Parkinson's, another woman's difficulties with her children. They support one another through the triumphs, too, the new jobs and promotions. I am so moved that even when I went on to other projects and had to stop offering direct services, these women insisted on staying together. It's a real tribute to the power of community—and to the difference that each of us can make in the lives of others. And truly not a day goes by that someone does not e-mail me, write me, or stop me on the street asking about styleWORKS. They want to know if I still run that amazing organization for women. I tell them no, but I always tell them that if they want to do something similar in their area, they should, and that I will be there to offer support and guidance.

What's Your Inspiration?

I started styleWORKS because of an episode of *60 Minutes* that made me realize I could link my passion for fashion to my desire to serve. As you can see, there is no shortage of ways to discover your own personal inspiration or to find ways that you can use your particular skills.

What if you're not sure *what* kinds of volunteer work you'd like to do? If so, you're not alone: People are constantly sending e-mails to me to ask how they can figure out how to serve. My first response is to ask, "Is there an area that already interests you?"

If a satisfying answer comes immediately to mind, take that ball and run with it. But if you're still searching, here are some questions that might help trigger an "aha" moment!

1. What Kind of People Do You Like to Spend Time With?

Do you enjoy children? Boys, girls, or special-needs children? Or maybe senior citizens—do you have fun hanging out with your grandparents and their friends? Would you enjoy working with babies, kids, teens, seniors, or people with special needs? If so, think about what you would like to do with them.

2. What Issues Get to You When You Hear About Them?

When you watch the news and you hear the latest statistics about HIV/AIDS, do you find yourself saying, "I can't believe we haven't found a cure for that yet!"? Does hearing about poverty make your blood boil—or your heart ache? Does someone in your family struggle with a disease such as cancer, multiple sclerosis, Parkinson's, or autism, moving you to want to help? When you learn that children around the world work for a living instead of attend school, does this boggle your mind? When you see someone sleeping on a park bench, do you wish you could just bring them home? What issue makes you want to raise a ruckus?

3. What Are Your Hobbies?

As we've seen, there are a hundred different ways to turn your interests into a kind of service, from photographing a group's events, to leading a poetry night, to cooking for the homeless. Think about what you love to do and who else might benefit from the activity that brings you so much pleasure. Along with the other hobbies mentioned, think sewing, knitting, boating, skiing, reading, hiking, or even jogging. There is a wonderful woman named Anne Mahlum who on her morning jog used to run past homeless people. She went on to start the organization Back on My Feet and turned it into a nonprofit running club for homeless people! Working with shelters, Mahlum shares her joy for running with the homeless, believing that the activity she loves will help others develop the skills they need, including "discipline, respect, leadership, teamwork, and goal setting." To learn more, visit her website at www.backonmyfeet.org.

4. What Type of Person Are You?

Are you the type who wants to work directly with the people you're helping? Or are you happier behind the scenes, answering phones, handling paperwork, or helping to plan services or events? Do you see yourself handing out literature at a rally or talking to people on the street about an issue and getting them to sign a petition? What's going to feed your soul in terms of what you're actually doing for this organization or cause?

5. What Do You Do in Your Profession?

We've already looked at ways you can donate specific skills—accounting, design, writing. Now think about the meta-skills you use: working with people, organizing systems, arranging spaces, putting together events. Would you like to use any of these types of skills to benefit a group? Does that give you any clues about where you'd like to serve?

Are You Good At...

*W*hile you're taking inventory of what volunteer opportunities are out there, don't forget to ask yourself what skills and resources you have to offer. Here are some of the kinds of help for which volunteers are often needed:

• **Accounting:** If you can work with numbers, you will be the most in-demand volunteer in town! Consider sharing your book-keeping skills with one or more local groups that could use your help.

• **Advertising:** If you work for an advertising firm or consult in the field, offering to design a pro bono PSA (public service an-nouncement) print or TV campaign would be a huge and amazing gift to a nonprofit. Most organizations cannot afford to pay an ad agency, so the only way that they can get the promotion of a big campaign is if one is designed free of charge. Employees of small local ad agencies can do this as well as the big guys.

• **Art:** Can you teach art classes? Organize a group of kids to paint a mural with a theme that would mean something to them or their community? Or maybe you can teach a weekly or monthly class for adults and/or children at a community center, a YMCA/YWCA, or a local shelter.

• **Books:** Do you have library skills? So many groups receive do-nations of books that they don't have time to catalog or even to shelve them in any organized fashion. You can also help by choosing books for the population using them or helping to secure titles that are greatly needed.

• **Clothes:** Are you good at organizing your own closet? Thrift shops are often overwhelmed with donations of used garments, coats, and shoes. Could you be the one who can make the local thrift shop look like an appealing boutique? Or can you use your skills at a welfare-to-work organization like Dress for Success?

• **Computers:** Can you teach computer skills? Program a com-puter? Fix a computer? For organizations that receive used computers, this would be an awesome gift. And if you are good at useful programs like Word and Excel, many job-training programs could use your help.

• **Driving:** Do you enjoy being behind the wheel? Giving rides to people, transporting equipment and supplies, and doing other car-related errands is something that agencies *always* need, especially those that serve the hungry and the elderly.

• **Florist:** Are you a florist or do you own a flower shop? Consider donating free flowers to a local nonprofit's event. This will both cut costs for the group and promote your business. Also consider teaching flower-arranging classes to a group, such as the elderly in a retirement home or teens in a community center.

• **Food:** Soup kitchens need people to serve—and also to shop, cook, and clean up. They might also be able to use an enterprising person who can convince grocery stores, restaurants, corporate cafeterias, and catering services to donate leftover food to hungry people.

• **Graphic design:** If you are a graphic designer, you already know how important a strong visual presentation can be for just about any project, event, or issue. Think about sharing your skills at drawing, designing, or laying out text with a group that couldn't afford to pay your regular rate. (And to learn more about the graphic designer who has saved *my* life more times than I can count, read the feature on Richard Menage later in this chapter.)

• **Photography:** Hiring a photographer can cost a lot of money for a nonprofit. You can make a significant contribution to a nonprofit organization by donating your photography services and shooting an event or PSA campaign for free. And of course, you can also share the magic of this art form by teaching photography to kids or the elderly. I am personally indebted to the photographers Timothy White, Lynda Sheeler, and Julie Skarratt for their pro bono support of my philanthropic endeavors.

• **Promotion and publicity:** Can you write a press release? Call reporters? Offering to do ongoing public relations or to make yourself available for a single event could be invaluable to a local group.

• **Writing:** If you are a talented writer, you can help an orgnization to draft a leaflet or pamphlet or write for their website. Or you can teach a writing class at a community center, organize a poetry reading, or lead a book group.

Getting Started

Now that you've got some idea of the kinds of volunteering you might like to do, how do you figure out where? Here are some suggestions for finding the right place to pursue your interests.

If You Want to Work with Seniors . . .

• Call your local senior day-care center, nursing home, or assisted/ independent-living facility. These places offer friendship, fellowship, fun, and meals for the elderly, and they often provide a wide range of activities as well, such as book clubs and classes in gardening, arts and crafts, singing, yoga, tai chi, and tennis. They're usually very grateful to anyone who wants to teach a class or lead an activity.

• Adopt a grandparent: Find an elderly person who could use some visitors and spend some time each week or month reading to them, doing errands, or just hanging out. Little Brothers: Friends of the Elderly is a wonderful organization that helps you find an elderly person who wants to make new friends. Look them up at www.littlebrothers.org.

• Organize a performance: If you're a singer, dancer, actor, or musician, consider organizing a group or solo performance at a senior facility. You may discover the joys of performing for a grateful audience!

If You Want to Work with the Poor or Homeless . . .

• Check out your local soup kitchen. Most places need not only people to serve but also kitchen staff who can chop, stir, season, and clean up! Or call your local food pantry and ask, "What are you going to need to get through the coming winter [or summer]?" Now more than ever, our food pantries nationwide are suffering from shortages of donations and an increased clientele due to our distressed economy. Visit Feeding America at www.feedingamerica.org to look up local food pantries and soup kitchens.

• Visit homeless shelters, where there is a huge need for a wide variety of services. You might ask the shelter director what the facility needs. The director will let you know if there is a class you can teach or a service you can offer, or if the shelter needs volunteer hours in a particular area. Or if you have a particular interest, it is fine to bring that up as well. Here are a few ideas you might be interested in asking about:

- Do a "beauty night" by bringing in beauty products and a few friends so you can offer residents facials, manicures, and other treatments.
- Set up a movie night and take a group to the movies. Or bring in the movie, along with popcorn and drinks for whoever signs up.
- Organize a clothing drive. Make sure to ask the shelter director exactly what is needed and fulfill only those requests. A shelter has no room for items that it cannot use.
- Teach an exercise or yoga class. Try to engage women, men, and children in this healthy and necessary activity.
- Contact your local thrift store, such as those run by the Salvation Army and Goodwill. These organizations always need volunteers to work in the stores and to organize the donations that are made to them on a regular basis.
- Volunteer with a local welfare-to-work organization. Your knowledge of computer programs, accounting, or another field may come in handy. These organizations are also in constant need of people to answer the phone, run errands, and file.

If You Want to Work with Children . . .

- Mentor. As I learned in college, there is often no better way to help a child than by mentoring. Today's children are so often growing up in either one-parent families or in busy two-parent families, and we have a generation of latchkey kids in a very different society. Cuts in schools and after-school programs mean that children are spending even less quality time with adults who can guide them effectively, making mentoring more important than it's ever been. Call a mentoring agency in your area, go to www.mentoring.org, or just look for a local Big Brothers or Big Sisters program.
- Volunteer at an orphanage, hospital, or library. You can be so

useful if you like playing with children, holding and rocking babies, or reading to groups of kids.

If You Want to Work in the Arts . . .

• Call your local museum, theater, or other arts-related group. They all need volunteers for a wide variety of tasks, everything from ushering and answering phones to leading tours and building sets. Even if you have no special experience or skills, you'll often have a chance to learn. And if you have skills you'd like to share, so much the better!

• Volunteer to help give tours at a museum.

• Start a book group, poetry group, or writers' group at your community center or homeless shelter, or perhaps at a shelter for women escaping from domestic violence.

If You Want to Work for the Environment . . .

• Get involved in a local cleanup effort—or perhaps organize one yourself.

• Contact your local zoo, which can often use volunteers to help with environmental education.

• Contact the Sierra Club at www.sierraclub.org and click on "Get involved locally" to find environmental volunteer activities in your area.

• Advocate at your local school board for your school district to become green.

• Host a party at your home and give your guests tips on how to go green. You might also consider selling green products at your party and donating the proceeds to an environmental organization.

• Build a community garden in an urban area. You can really help to make a big difference because of the great need for urban greening. Your contribution will allow people who do not have direct access to fresh vegetables to plant sustainable gardens right in their own neighborhoods. Find more information by visiting the American Community Gardening Association at www.community garden.org.

If You Want to Work for Women . . .

• Get involved with a women's rights group, such as the National Organization for Women (www.now.org), the National Council of Negro Women (www.ncnw.org), the Feminist Majority Foundation (www.feminist.org), or Women for Afghan Women (www.women forafghanwomen.org).

• Volunteer for a rape crisis hotline.

• Help women recover from domestic violence. Contact a social-service agency in your area to learn about battered women's shelters or other support groups for domestic-violence survivors.

If You Want to Work for Justice . . .

• Volunteer for your local chapter of the NAACP, the National Urban League, or the American Civil Liberties Union. (See the resource guide for contact information.)

• Become active in Amnesty International. Go to www.amnesty .org for a multitude of ways that you can become part of a worldwide movement of people who campaign for internationally recognized human rights for all.

Virtual Volunteering: Websites That Can Help You Find Your Niche

If you'd like a quick overview of all the volunteering opportunities in your area, the computer is always a good place to start. Here are some extraordinary websites that can hook you up with a range of choices faster than you can say "Where do I begin?" You can find even more resources in the resource guide at the back of the book.

The Angelrock Project, www.angelrockproject.com

My own website lists lots of organizations where you can find volunteer listings, information on volunteer vacations, and valuable tips on volunteering. I also list organizations that you can donate to based on your own giving platform. After going to the site, just click on the tab called "Angel Service" or "Angel Giving."

1-800-Volunteer Org, www.1-800-volunteer.org

This site is as easy as one-two-three. Under "Keywords," you choose your area of interest. You then put in your city and state, or your zip code, and then specify how far you are willing to travel from your home. Hit search and voilà! A list of nonprofit organizations will come up, along with all of the pertinent contact information.

Volunteer Match, www.volunteermatch.org

If you want to find out what volunteer opportunities match your skills, interests, and location, this is one of the best websites out there. Go to the site, choose "Opportunities," and then enter your location and any keywords that might define the kind of volunteer experience you're looking for, such as "homeless," "pets," or "environment." The site will provide you with a list of groups that fit your specifications, allowing you to browse before you choose.

CharityFocus, www.charityfocus.org

This website is a great resource; it requires a bit more commitment, but it's worth the effort! You fill out an application and they get back to you with information about opportunities.

Network for Good, www1.networkforgood.org

Choose either "Donate" or "Volunteer" and enter a state. A list of groups comes up, allowing you to choose among the options "Donate," "Volunteer," and "Research." The "Research" button is especially helpful, since you can find out all about each group.

Idealist, www.idealist.org

You have the option of filling in a keyword or choosing a term from a preexisting list of areas of focus. You can specify the state, city, and country, and you can also ask for opportunities that are appropriate for children of different ages, for families, or for groups. You can further sort opportunities by "skills needed," "language needed," and "dates available." The site provides you with a list of organizations so you can read a bit about them.

Making the Most of Your Experience: Eight Tips for Volunteering Wisely

1. Think About the Issues That Are Important to You

It's really important that you find deep satisfaction in your volunteer work—if you don't, you'll have a hard time keeping up with it, and you'll also be cheating yourself out of a great experience. The first step is deciding which issues are important to you so that you can volunteer with an organization that shares your concerns.

2. Consider Your Skills and Interests

Do you want to donate your career skills, maybe computer programming, graphic design, accounting, or legal services? Nonprofit groups often can't afford to hire people to do these important jobs, so you could have a huge impact on the success of some organization by donating these useful skills. Or maybe you'd rather do something based on your hobbies, such as reading, knitting, drawing, yoga, or studying a language? Perhaps you could donate your time and have fun doing it by teaching your favorite activities at community centers, homeless shelters, or retirement homes. Take this opportunity to think outside the box and give back something to society that you really love.

3. Research the Groups That Might be Right for You

Once you know what you'd like to do, find the groups that are looking for your services. There are lots of suggestions in this chapter for how to find out more about charities and service groups; you can also just make an appointment with a group that interests you or sometimes even drop in unannounced.

4. Don't Overcommit

Think about how often you can or want to volunteer. Know that you are doing a wonderful service even if you volunteer only once a month or six times a year. If you have more time than that—*great!* But don't push it, or you won't have the great experience that you deserve. Also, make sure you volunteer on days that work for your individual, job, and family schedule: On weekends? After work? On a weekday morning? If you work from home or from your own office, perhaps you'd prefer to do your volunteer work from there. Take some time to figure out the schedule that will be best for you.

5. Be Open to Suggestions

You might have an idea of what you want to offer, but the organization you approach might have other immediate needs. If you can be open to the needs of the organization, two wonderful things can happen for you: You will know that you are truly giving back what is needed at the time, and you can be pleasantly surprised by how much you like learning a new skill or serving in a way that is foreign to you. And guess what? If you're really not happy doing a particular job long-term, you're free to move on to something else knowing that you've already made a huge difference for the organization.

6. Consider Volunteering as a Family

Volunteering is an awesome experience and sharing it with the people closest to you can be an amazing and rewarding journey. By volunteering as a family, you can share important time together that you might not have if you were to serve solo—and you're teaching an incredible lesson to your children as well.

7. Be Willing to Do Your Homework

Some volunteer jobs require training before you start. If your group wants you to do some training, please know that it's for your own good and for the good of the people you are going to help. No good nonprofit wants to spend money on training if it doesn't have to. And if you have to take a test after the training? No worries—you'll never fail. The group will just provide you with the correct answers!

8. Give It Your All

When you find the right organization and the right schedule, go into your new volunteer job with an open mind and a willingness to have fun. Few things can make you feel as good as connecting with a person or a group and knowing that you are positively effecting change. Go for it! Give it your all! Be the best volunteer that you can be! You'll be glad you did.

When It's Time to Move On . . .

*I*t's fine to do a volunteer job for a while and then move on to something else. You may choose to do another job in the same organization or volunteer someplace else doing something completely different. Or you may need to take a break from volunteering for a while. Don't feel anxious or guilty about stopping. Volunteering is about doing something to help someone else while fulfilling your spirit and soul at the same time. So, if you feel that you need a break or find you are no longer feeling fulfilled, do *not* feel guilty. Take some time off and move on to the next experience when you feel ready.

Finding Your Niche, Finding Yourself

The beauty of volunteering is that there's something for everyone—you just have to figure out what it is. In the end, it's not about money or making a donation; it's about helping yourself to find the joy of giving through serving in the ways that are right for you.

MY JOURNEY: GRAPHIC DESIGNER RICHARD MENAGE

Richard Menage, a New York City–based graphic designer, offers an array of design services to a wide variety of companies. Richard is also an avid world traveler and a generous humanitarian who gives back regularly by offering pro bono design services to a multitude of small nonprofit organizations. Like most self-employed people, Richard needs to work long hours for his own business.

Yet whenever I start a project, Richard is always there, somehow finding the time to e-mail me design ideas and respond to my concerns. He's an extraordinary example of how you can donate your skills without ever leaving your desk—and make a world of difference doing so. Here's an interview conducted with him for my website.

Q. Please tell us a little about yourself. Please also talk about your family and your career.

A. I am a native of New York City who grew up in Queens. I am the son of an airline executive and a high school French teacher, and my neighborhood gave me a rich, diverse experience from the public schools and the many colorful characters on my block. A childhood friend of mine bemoans the overly protective and scheduled life his kids have in contrast to the free-form urban life we led then. But of course that was a different era.

Q. As a graphic artist, you have so generously donated your talent to many nonprofit organizations and causes. Why have you been compelled to do so?

A. I feel an inner impulse that one cannot go through life only for the betterment of oneself or even immediate family. Your fellow human beings need your help. And somehow that good karma comes back to you: Good luck comes your way often!

Q. How do you feel knowing that your service helped to establish new grassroots organizations like styleWORKS and the Triple Negative Breast Cancer Foundation and projects like Journey for Change?

A. I feel really, really good to add to those efforts. The challenges are immense and frightening but we must persevere. It was by chance that I met you when you were with the Terrie Williams Agency. Our paths must have crossed for a reason, and I believe you were the catalyst to interest me in getting involved in many other volunteer projects in addition to yours. Our relationship started with a fund-raiser for the United Negro College Fund, a kind of food festival called Flavor of New York with top chefs cooking foods of all kinds. I designed the journal, invitations, etc., and that led to working for many other causes and events.

Q. Please talk about how your upbringing influenced your spirit of giving.
A. I had an amazing exposure to the vastness and diversity of this world. We had a discount on airfares through my dad. From an early age, I went with my family . . . on trips throughout Europe and the Middle East. . . . Later I went on my own to Africa, South America, and India. That really instilled a tremendous perspective. My travels have included the third world, and I have seen some very poor people and places as well as extraordinary beauty.

Q. You have shared stories with me about your sister and her work in Africa. What does she do and how has that affected you?
A. Nicole Menage has been with the UN World Food Programme for more than twenty years, working and living in Malawi, Burundi, Togo, Zimbabwe, and Tanzania. I visited some of those countries as a result and became more aware of the history and current events in Africa. The opportunity to see and meet people abroad connects all of us.

Q. What global issues concern you today?
A. I believe population explosion is near the top of my list. Our species is ever closer to outstripping our natural resources. Then the climate crisis, which stems from that—don't get me started!

Q. You have traveled a lot around the world. What are your favorite countries and why?
A. Well, I would say the Tanzania trip was pretty unforgettable. The chance to go on safari in the Serengeti plains and the Ngorongoro Crater ranks right up there. The Taj Mahal seemed surreal. I am quite fond of Paris and also Positano on the Italian coastline.

Q. Last question. You offer your services so generously and work so hard. Why don't you ever ask for credit?
A. Oh, I guess it's my self-effacing nature. I reluctantly draw attention to myself. I think of the boy in front of the dam that was springing leaks. He just instinctively went to plug the holes, no questions asked.

Chapter 3

Raising Children Who Give

■

It is easier to build strong children than to repair broken men.
—FREDERICK DOUGLASS

When I think about the kind of mother I want to be to my girls, I always go back to the kind of mother my mom was to me. I remember all the ways she showed me that living a life of service was not something you did to impress people or to be "good" or to overcome your guilt—it was just what you did. She showed me, too, that besides serving others, you can and should do something to stand up for causes that you believe in. Some of the earliest memories I have are those of my mother taking me to rallies. I don't even remember what the rallies were for—but I remember the passion, the excitement, and the joy that swirled around me as so many people came together to take a stand. And I wanted to re-create that experience for my own daughters, who were then three and five, when I began taking them to the rallies against the genocide in Darfur. I had no intention of trying to explain such a horrible set of events to children of that age. But what I could tell them was what my mother told me: that there is power in numbers, power in a lot of voices coming together to talk about what needs to be changed.

From styleworks to Motherhood

About two years after I started styleworks, I got pregnant with Lola. I worked the entire time I was pregnant, organizing several fund-raising events for the group. One of my favorites was a tea that we gave at the Plaza Athénée honoring Iman, the Somalia-born super-model, successful businesswoman, and committed humanitarian. We toasted Iman's dedication to not only styleWORKS but also to the countless other organizations for which she works tirelessly. As a special show of appreciation for her commitment and a testament to her heritage we served only African tea, and for the gift bag, we presented each guest with a beautiful satchel of "Iman Tea," a mixture of African teas I had personally selected and blended at a teahouse a few days before the event. Iman loved the whole event but especially that touch, and so did I. Sometimes, even when you are raising money for an important cause, you can be fun and creative. And to be fair, I must thank my good friend event planner Dwight Johnson of Dwight Johnson Design for donating his ideas and time to this great event.

Then I had Lola. styleWORKS was still going strong, and for the whole first year of Lola's life, I kept up with the group as though nothing had changed. Our salon days were almost always on Sunday and Monday, since that's when most salons were closed. During the week, I'd make visits to referring agencies, conduct preinterviews, book my stylists, and keep working those corporate sponsorships. I also handled all the other things you must take care of to keep a nonprofit running: keeping the books, following up with my donors, getting those grant proposals in on time.

So far, so good. After all, an infant does sleep a lot during the day! With only one child, I was able to work my schedule around Lola's. When my daughter was very young, I could even bring her to the salons. Since I was coordinating, not styling, I could have her on my hip or in a sling when she wasn't sleeping in her bassinet. It wasn't all that difficult to stop whatever I was doing in order to feed her or change her or play with her a little when she was awake. The stylists loved her, of course, and so did the clients. So for that first year, I felt as though Lola was really a part of the team. Sure, I could combine work and motherhood! Why not?

Then Lola got older and started to walk. And as every mother and father knows, that's when everything changes.

A Big Decision

For almost every minute of my children's lives, I've been blessed to have wonderful child care during the week. The only exception was during the year after Lola turned one, when for several months I was without child care.

Even with help, every hands-on working mother who enjoys being with her family and knows the importance of spending time with them has to make adjustments to her work schedule. Soon it became apparent that Sundays in the salon just weren't going to work anymore. My angelic infant had become a mischievous toddler whose overwhelming curiosity and adventurous spirit were taking her all over the place. Clearly, she was going to get into every bag, jar, and rack of clothing she could reach—except, of course, when she was asking to be fed or read a story, or when she came to me for a cuddle or hug.

Under those circumstances, how could Mommy concentrate on the clients? Leaving my child at home was an option only if my husband was in town and not working. Plus, I truly was not ready to be separated from my child. I also began to want Sundays to be family days. Since both my husband and I worked so hard during the week, I wanted us to be able to share Lola on Sundays as well as Saturdays when Chris was in town.

For a while, I had my assistant or one of my salon volunteers coordinate the Sunday sessions, leaving me with only the Mondays to worry about. But most of our stylists and clients preferred Sundays, and no one enjoyed the coordinator's role quite as much as I did. So instead of doing twice-weekly sessions, we cut back to once a week. That didn't seem like *so* much time to be away from Lola, and either Chris or my babysitter could handle the child care.

Then, when Lola was fourteen months old, I got pregnant again. And when Lola was twenty-three months old, Zahra was born.

As for many mothers, my second pregnancy was far more tiring. After all, you're pregnant and running around after a toddler, trying to do all the things that you do for the child you already have even while you're going to the doctor, getting a nursery ready, and coping with the exhaustion of being pregnant. Then, when the baby is born, you suddenly have an infant *and* a toddler to take care of. Between Lola, Zahra, and my weekends in the salon, it got to be really, really difficult.

So I had a choice. I could find someone to take over the coordinator job and delegate myself to working in the office. But the salon days were the most satisfying part of running styleWORKS, the part that made all the fund-raising and paperwork worthwhile. More important, I felt a real commitment to the salon owners who were lending out their spaces to ensure that the day was run perfectly, safely, and according to each owner's rules. I liked to see the last piece of trash thrown out, make sure that we never mistakenly used product that belonged to the salon, and then lock up if I had been entrusted with the keys to the space.

So eventually, I decided to stop offering direct services and only referred clients to one salon in Harlem on a case-by-case basis. This particular salon was very giving and all of the regular stylists were volunteers, which meant that I could send over the "emergency cases" who needed a makeover on the very day of their interview. I also kept running our job-retention programs and the book club, which did not require me to be away from my family.

Beyond these accommodations, however, I let styleWORKS disband and set out to find another type of hands-on work that fed my soul in a similar way. Sometimes it still nags me that this feels like a selfish decision. To this day, people call me about styleWORKS, hoping to volunteer their time, come in for a makeover, or refer clients. I am happy to refer them to other organizations though. And I have been told by my old volunteers that they have found satisfying ways to serve at other organizations, some even at Dress for Success. It warms my heart that people found their niche in volunteering through styleWORKS and that they made the decision to include volunteering as a permanent part of their lives. But eventually, we all need to move on, and so I had to accept that the time had come for me to do so, though of course, I still see my book club ladies monthly!

Raising World Citizens

In the wake of styleWORKS, I longed to find some other way to feed the "service" part of my soul—but meanwhile, I had kids to raise. And while I didn't want to raise them *exactly* like my mom raised me, I did want them to grow up with the same spirit of world citizenship that I had been surrounded with.

So, as I said, I took them to rallies. And I tried to think of the other ways my mom had brought me into her world and to come up with my own version of doing them, like making sure we had time carved out to have discussions at the dinner table. For most families, I think, that dinnertime with the kids is so important, no matter what you talk about. To share food and conversation at the end of the day really cements the idea that your family is a team and your home is a haven. Kids are reminded every day that you're interested in what they have to say, what they did that day, and what's going on with them. And they get a daily lesson in relationships, life skills, and, if you're so inclined, world citizenship, just by watching how you and your partner treat each other and by listening to what you talk about. If you're a single parent who relies on other caregivers, that time may be even more important, a chance for the kids to remember how much you love them and that you'll always be there for whatever they need, even if it's something as simple as a listening ear and a few words of praise. But besides the warmth of family time, my childhood dinners were occasions for me to listen to my mother and her friends or sisters talk about civil rights, Oakland politics, South African apartheid, and famine in Africa. My own kids have heard Chris and me getting into intense conversations about the genocide in Darfur, world hunger, the plight of children orphaned by HIV/AIDS all over the world, the lack of resources in the inner city, the bad economy, and of course, Barack Obama's historic campaign and election as president of the United States. As I was working on this book, I realized that my children have been hearing about politics, service, and world issues since the day they came out of my womb. Long before they were old enough to volunteer in their own right, they were surrounded by people who care about local, national, and world issues. For them as for me, it seems natural to participate in both service and advocacy. When I actually introduced the acts of volunteering and giving, their early childhood experience had already set them up to understand why I think those things are important.

Another way my mother brought me into her world was by reading to me, and that's definitely something I'm doing with my kids. Lola, who's now seven, has started saying that she wants to read to me, which of course warms a mother's heart. Still, my answer is always, "Honey, you can read to me while we're doing our homework, but at night, Mommy reads to you!"

About a year and a half ago, we were at the Alex Haley Farm in Clinton, Tennessee, where I was speaking on behalf of the Children's Defense Fund's Freedom School initiative. The farm is now owned by the Children's Defense Fund, and there is a wonderful library and bookstore on the property where the kids and I picked up a copy of Marian Wright Edelman's book *I Can Make a Difference: A Treasury to Inspire Our Children* (Amistad, 2005), a wonderful anthology of proverbs, fables, affirmations, and Barry Moser's illustrations that has become one of our favorite bedtime books.

Reading this treasury with my kids gives me the bittersweet sense of having truly come full circle, since when I was a young woman, my mother gave me another Marian Wright Edelman book, *The Measure of Our Success: A Letter to My Children and Yours* (paperback edition, Beacon, 1992). As the title suggests, Ms. Edelman wrote that book for her children, and when I first read it, I felt as though it were written for me. Of course, that was Ms. Edelman's intention!

As I've already said, Marian Wright Edelman has been one of my heroines ever since I can remember. She grew up in the Jim Crow South, was the first African-American woman to be admitted to the Mississippi bar, worked with Martin Luther King Jr., and went on to found the Children's Defense Fund—on the board of which I am now privileged to serve. Recently, I was able to host a book party for her latest book, *The Sea Is So Wide and My Boat Is So Small: Charting a Course for the Next Generation* (Hyperion, 2008)—a party to which the Journey for Change kids from Bushwick were invited.

My Lola sat with rapt attention at Ms. Edelman's feet during her reading and conversation with the guests.

Watching my childhood heroine graciously asking those children about our trip to South Africa, seeing her hug my kids and greet my mother, who had flown up for the occasion, and knowing that Ms. Edelman had honored me by asking me to help promote her remarkable book filled me up with gratitude. By giving that earlier book to me, my mom had been able to connect a lot of the dots, showing me that service and advocacy and family life and pride in yourself were all part of the same thing. And now both my mother and Ms. Edelman were there in my living room, along with my biological kids and my Journey for Change kids, all of us part of the family I had somehow managed to create.

So thank you, Mom, for everything you did to instill in me a sense of service and advocacy at such a young age. Now, as an adult, I can see that it did work and that you can teach your children at a very young age that we all have a responsibility to one another. Sometimes it's not so easy to know how to communicate that message; sometimes it's not so easy living up to those ideals yourself. But that night in my living room, I knew it for sure: The rewards more than make up for any hardships along the way.

The Elephant in the Room

One word: guilt. In my experience, that's the elephant in the room when it comes to raising children, especially for us busy moms, whether we're working full-time, part-time, or mainly in the home.

I don't think there's a mother alive who doesn't feel guilty at least some of the time about having not spent enough time with her kids or about having possibly failed them in some other way. I do hear mothers say occasionally that they *don't* feel guilty or that they have somehow managed to make the perfect choice, and I have to tell you, it just drives me crazy. Whether you're a stay-at-home mom or a full-time career woman, it's *hard* raising children and it's even harder coping with all the many demands on your time, your emotions, and your commitment. You give some things up when you let your career go, and you give other things up when you try to work full-time *and* raise a family; however you manage to work it out, you're always painfully aware of what you're missing, unless you just suppress those feelings or pretend that you don't have them. We all have to do the best we can with an extremely difficult set of choices—but at least we can be honest about how hard it is!

I do believe that what kids need most is a happy mom, which is why it's so important for each of us to know what truly makes us happy. A happy mom is a fulfilled mom. So even with a busy home and work life, it's okay to take time out to care for others. I know: easier said than done.

I have my fair share of guilt. I still feel bad sometimes, as a working mother who's lucky enough to have child care and a very involved co-parent, that my own work often takes me away from home to care for *other* people's children. I spent the first two years of both my children's lives focused completely on them, and I'm so glad I did, but now I need a balance among work, parenting, and family life. So as my children got older, I started adding work hours to my day and began to focus more on service work.

I'm definitely a very hands-on mom. But I also spend a lot of time cradling somebody else's child or setting up programs that will help somebody else's family. I try to explain to my daughters that this is important work for Mommy to be doing, helping other people who need it. But I also want them to understand that I do it for me, so I can say to them, "I hope one day that you find something that *you* love as much as I love this work."

At their ages, it's hard to know what they understand. But I remember things my mother told me that I didn't understand at the time, and even now, something will come back to me and I'll say to myself, "Oh, so *that's* what she was talking about!" As with every other aspect of parenting, you're going on faith a whole lot of the time. But at least I have my own childhood experience to go by.

One thing I've been blessed to be able to do is to bring my kids with me on a lot of my projects. Soon after they returned from South Africa, the Journey for Change kids held a car wash in Brooklyn to raise money for children in South Africa. Our Brooklyn kids might have thought of themselves as disadvantaged before they went to South Africa, but the poverty they saw gave them a whole new appreciation for how much they actually have here. They all pitched in to raise funds—and Lola and Zahra came and worked at the car wash, too. My kids are also familiar with the shanty houses, so telling them that the car wash was intended to raise funds for South Africa was all they needed to know. At the fund-raiser, I watched proudly as my girls pitched in to help their friends by washing whatever parts of the cars they could reach.

My kids have friends in South Africa, too, children they've met in the shantytowns who come stay with us in our hotel when we visit there. It's important to me that my children understand what Mommy does so that when I do leave them at home, they can at least imagine why I've made that decision. Whenever possible, I want them to know the people I'm serving and picture what I'm doing when I'm gone.

Some people have questioned me about making my children aware that they have so much while other people have so little. "Don't you think they're a little young for that?" is a question I'm frequently asked.

Well, no. I don't. I'd rather they come with me to the shantytown neighborhood of Diepsloot, South Africa, or walk through Soweto so they can understand poverty and the need to help orphaned and vulnerable children than allow them to watch some of the kids' programming on TV that in my opinion often features sassy, spoiled, and rude kids who talk back to their parents in ways that I don't think are always appropriate. Personally, I think there are lots of things that our kids see on TV, hear in music, and view online that are far more devastating than the fact that most people are poor in this world and it takes a village to help them.

Talking to Your Kids About the Tough Issues

People also ask me how I talk to my kids about the big issues, especially since my girls are still so young. In my opinion, there is no magic age that you wait for; you just figure out how to gear the topic to the age they are. And it is your personal decision. Just because someone else talks about something with her or his child at one age doesn't mean you have to if it does not feel right for you.

I personally find it very difficult to talk about race with my kids. They are so oblivious to it and have never experienced anything hurtful because of their skin color. They have friends of all colors and religions and access to everything a child could want.

However, race relations are a factor in our country's history and in our society. I felt very fortunate that when my kids heard their parents and everyone else talk about how historic Barack Obama's run for the presidency was and asked me why, I was able to answer their question honestly and teach them about our country's issues with race at the same time. Likewise, I was able to talk to them about apartheid when they saw the haves and have-nots living so close together in South Africa.

Of course, there are other things that as parents we might have a hard time talking about with our kids, such as sex and drugs, and we may dread the day when we have to have those conversations. But I don't think that any age is too young to start talking to your children about service, giving, and responsibility. There are many ways to introduce these themes at a young age, and the concepts will resonate with your children for the rest of their lives.

The thing I think we want to remember is that giving and service just plain feel good. In our individualistic society, with such a focus on looks and consumerism, we can all come to feel that buying things for ourselves or pampering our bodies is the highest pleasure. And sometimes as parents, we want nothing more than to be able to give our children whatever new gadget they want because it makes us feel good to make them happy.

But children can also feel the ultimate sense of happiness and fulfillment while doing service of some kind. Kids love goals and a lot of service projects are goal oriented. I will confess that there are a few things my mother wanted me to do as a kid that I haven't kept up with as an adult. But a life of service *did* feel right, and I'm grateful to have been introduced to it so early. That's why it's instinctive for me to do the same for my kids.

Spirituality, family togetherness, and education were very important in my childhood home, and they're crucial to my children's lives as well. I was taught early on that manners are important and so is respecting your elders, and I teach my children the same. To me, service and volunteering work in exactly the same way: You start your kids with what they understand and bring them along as they get older. And just as some learn about going to church, synagogue, or the mosque each week, being polite to Grandma, and not eating their spinach with their fingers, they learn that there are other people in their neighborhood and in their world who might need help—and that it will feel good to help them.

Keeping Kids Informed: Some Useful Resources

Part of helping your children develop an interest in service and advocacy is teaching them about their world. Here are some kid-friendly publications that can help your children become informed and caring world citizens.

Scholastic News Nonfiction Readers: Community Helpers

Intended for first- and second-grade children, this boxed set of readers includes plenty of full-color photos. Since the series is designed to be sold to schools, it also includes a teaching guide. I've enjoyed going over these readers with Lola, however, and maybe because she knows I'm interested in the material, she likes reading from them to me. In our house, they're a great opportunity for mother-daughter bonding *and* for learning. You can find them in most large bookstores, or go to www.scholastic.com and put the series title in the search box.

Time for Kids

This weekly classroom news magazine provides news and features to children at a reading level they can handle and with a focus on stories of special interest to children. Our own Journey for Change kids have been featured in this publication, along with many other children doing interesting and sometimes extraordinary things. It's available at three levels: K–1, 2–3, and 4–6. It's a fantastic classroom resource, so encourage your children's school to subscribe or buy your own subscription to share with your kids at home. For more information, go to www.timeforkids.com.

We the Kids

Available at three levels—K–1, 2–3, and 4–6—the *We the Kids: Young Citizens in Action Skills Books* are designed to inspire children to become engaged citizens. Besides in-depth articles, the sets include such kid-friendly features as plays and interviews, and of course, plenty of maps, charts, and graphs. Check out your local bookstore, or go to www.scholastic.com and put the series title in the search box.

Highlights

This grandmother of all modern children's magazines was founded in 1946, and it's still one of the best resources you could ever find for your children aged six through twelve. According to the company website, the magazine is dedicated "to helping children grow in basic skills and knowledge, in creativeness, in ability to think and reason, in sensitivity to others, in high ideals and worthy ways of living—for children are the world's most important people." The same company puts out a publication called *Highlights High Five* for children aged three through six. You can learn more or buy a subscription at www.highlights.com.

Moments in America for Children

When I am thinking about my lucky children and ways to inspire them, it often motivates me to think about all the kids out there who aren't as fortunate. The following statistics from the Children's Defense Fund, dated March 2008, make clear how many U.S. children are in crisis.

Every 35 seconds a baby is born into poverty.
Every 36 seconds a child is confirmed as abused or neglected.
Every 41 seconds a baby is born without health insurance.

Every minute a baby is born to a teen mother.

Every 2 minutes a baby is born at low birth weight.

Every 5 minutes a child is arrested for a drug offense.

Every 9 minutes a child is arrested for a violent crime.

Every 18 minutes a baby dies before his or her first birthday.

Every 3 hours a child or teen is killed by a firearm.

Every 6 hours a child is killed by abuse or neglect.

Every 14 hours a woman dies from complications of childbirth
or pregnancy.

Visit the Children's Defense Fund's website at www.childrens
defense.org for more child research data on poverty, health, welfare, education, juvenile justice, housing, hunger, and violence.

Raising World Citizens: Ten Activities You Can Share with Your Children

Like most of us, children learn more from example than from instruction, and they learn more from doing than from talking. So if you
want your children to become world citizens, they need to practice
what you preach—and you need to practice it with them! Here are ten
suggestions to get you started as a family on ways to make a difference.

1. Talk About the News with Them

As parents, you have to choose wisely what kinds of news you share
with your children, depending on their age and temperament. But
certainly if there's a disaster—a typhoon or tsunami, a Hurricane
Katrina or Gustav, a famine in Ethiopia or Somalia—your kids are
likely to hear about it, so why not take some time to help them
process the event?

Often, especially for younger children, looking at the images of
a disaster is very difficult, so you might want to steer your child
toward talking and listening rather than watching. You might go
online, for instance, and print out reports from news agencies. It
can actually be inspiring to visit disaster-relief sites (I suggest some

useful ones in chapter 5) and talk with your kids about what people are doing to help.

2. Let Your Children Know that No Matter Where You Live, There Is Somebody in Need Right in Your Own Neighborhood

If you live in a major city, of course, your children can see this for themselves. It's rare in any big city never to pass a homeless person or someone in obvious distress. We all have the impulse to look away, at least some of the time, but you can use even this impulse to open up a conversation with your children about why people become homeless and what needs to happen to help them.

In a suburb or rural town, poverty may be harder to spot, but I promise you, it is there, and you can find out more about it. Go online or visit the local library to get statistics on the percentage of people living in poverty in your area. Find groups addressing local poverty, like Table to Table in affluent suburban New Jersey, which in 2008 delivered 5.5 million meals to local people struggling with hunger. Talk with your kids about how many children in your area are living in poverty or struggling with other types of need.

3. Volunteer Together in an Area Soup Kitchen or Shelter

Even if you don't want to make this a regular commitment, it's a great thing to do around the holidays. You can work in the facility or contribute in some other way. That's what I do with my kids: Every Thanksgiving, Christmas, and Easter Sunday, we make extra food. Then, before we eat, the girls and I go drop it off at a salon in Harlem that we know feeds the homeless. Or you can collect turkeys by asking your friends and family to drop off the birds on a day close to the holiday. On the day of or the day before the holiday, load the turkeys in the back of the car and donate them to a soup kitchen together.

4. Do a Family Walkathon

You can participate in an organized event or start one of your own. Either way, this is an activity you can share with the whole family, as the adults reach out to their friends and the kids reach out to theirs.

Every member of the family can set a goal, and then you can all coach and encourage one another as you try to reach it. Choose a cause that all of you care about—or let your kids take turns picking the cause. Now that most kids are computer-savvy, the kids can even send out their own fund-raising appeals!

5. Find Ways to Protect the Environment, Including Recycling

When it comes to environmental issues, service definitely begins at home. Make a list with your children of all the ways that you can help protect our planet, right there in your own house. Children definitely get the concept of recycling if it's explained to them, especially if you show them how to sort the trash and most especially if you can make a family field trip to a recycling plant, a waste-disposal site, or some other place where your kids can see with their own eyes how materials get reused.

You can also make a family list of ways to save energy. Even a very young child can understand when you say, "Look for lights or a TV that someone has left on when there's no one in the room—and turn them off." And if you decide to switch to energy-efficient lightbulbs, let your kids get in on the action. My children love to tell me when a regular lightbulb burns out so we can replace it with the energy-efficient kind. They've learned to help Mommy and the planet, too!

6. Sponsor a Child

In these days of phony Internet solicitations, we all fear being taken advantage of, but there are lots of legitimate nonprofit organizations that have been around for years helping you to sponsor a child for a small monthly donation. Consider one of the following wonderful agencies:

- World Vision, www.worldvision.org
- Save the Children, www.savethechildren.org
- ChildFund, www.childfund.org

If you've found another group and want to make sure it's legit, see chapter 1 for information on how to check out charitable organizations. Remember to check if the organization has a charity star rating or a rating from the Better Business Bureau and also check how much money goes to the children and programs as opposed to overhead. The organizations I've suggested all meet those standards.

For as little as $35 each month, you can make sure a child in a developing country gets food, clothes, medicine, and an education—and your children can have the satisfaction of knowing that they've helped to make this possible. Find ways that everyone in the family can contribute at least some money to the monthly donation. If your children don't get an allowance, consider hiring them to do some extra chore each month and then encouraging them to donate at least part of their "salary" to the cause.

7. Make a Family Donation Through Heifer International

I have a friend who visits this wonderful organization's website every Christmas and Hanukkah so that she and her children can pick out gifts together. For as little as $10, you can buy a share in an animal or development project that can help sustain a family or community in a developing country. Think how much fun your kids will have choosing a cow, a goat, an ox, or a flock of baby chicks to give to a family who really needs the help. You can look at a map or globe to identify some of the fifty-three countries and twenty-eight U.S. states that Heifer serves, or you can give to a family in a country that your kids are learning about in school or who speak a language that your kids are learning. You can also make Heifer your gift registry for a wedding or birthday party.

A Heifer present is truly the gift that keeps on giving. First, people can use the animals for extra income, selling the milk or eggs they produce. Then they can combat hunger by eating the animals. And in an effort to build community, Heifer's policy requires recipients to become givers: If you receive a cow and she calves, you're required to give the calf away. Find out more at www.heifer.org.

8. Organize a Canned-Food or Winter-Coat Drive Together

This is a project in which you can involve your kids every step of the way. Decide together on the group you want to donate to—maybe a local soup kitchen or homeless shelter. Then get every family member to solicit donations of winter clothes or canned goods from friends, classmates, and coworkers.

The work—and, hopefully, the fun!—doesn't stop there. Together, you can sort and pack the items you receive and then go together to give them away. Your children can see firsthand what a difference it makes to serve—and what a joy it can be.

9. Give Money Together

If you're looking for a low-maintenance way to make service a part of your kids' daily lives, make a "donations jar." Decide how much you'll each put in every week—Mommy may contribute $10, while the kids give a portion of their allowance—and decide together who'll get the money. You can pick one charity that you support long-term or, as Chris and I did when we were first married, choose a different one to support each month.

My mother has come up with a nice variation on this idea. Every birthday and holiday, besides giving my kids presents, she gives each of them a check for $25 and has them fill in who they want the check to go to. She usually gives them a choice among a few groups she's picked out. I do something similar, but with yet another twist: I give my kids checks to donate, but I start by asking them who they want to help. Then I go online to find a group involved in that particular cause. As the kids get older, they'll be able to look online for themselves.

10. Introduce Your Children to Activism by Taking Them with You to Rallies, Protests, Demonstrations, and Meetings

As you've heard, that's what my mom did, and it's what I do now, too. Of course, you have to use some judgment, depending on your kids' ages. When I took my kids to their first Darfur rally, three-year-old Zahra had no idea what it was all about, but five-year-old Lola did. Both kids were thrilled to be running around on the National Mall with thousands of other people amid all the excitement, but only Lola understood that we were there because people were suffering and we needed to show the world that we cared.

When Lola was a baby and we had first moved to our New Jersey home in Alpine, I remember I took her to some neighborhood meetings about restarting a local electrical grid. This grid had been dormant for years—and lots of big houses had been built in its vicinity—but after 9/11, there was talk about firing it up again to make sure we had plenty of power. In the end, we prevailed and the grid remained inactive, but Lola was an infant and she didn't understand any of that. Luckily, she slept through most of the meetings, or else I couldn't have taken her (and maybe couldn't have gone). I'd never bring a six-year-old to a meeting like that—but a ten-year-old might well be able to follow and even enjoy the discussion.

Another great place to take kids to when they are old enough is your local school board meeting, especially if you are advocating for something that your kids are passionate about, such as getting new computers in their classrooms, keeping an after-school program from being cut, or creating a new playground. These meetings are open to the public and I can assure you that if your kids stand up and advocate for what they want, they will be heard!

Children for Charity:
Ten Activities for Kids of All Ages

Even when your kids are eager to help, it can be hard to know how to get them involved. These "starter" activities are appropriate for children of all ages. Your kids will find them fun—and empowering.

1. Get Your Kids' School Involved in Fund-Raising

You can ask your principal to let you send a fund-raising letter home with each kid requesting that they each bring in $1 to donate to a particular cause. A friend of mine at a school with 2,000 kids raised $2,000—and the kids were enormously proud of themselves for making such a big donation. I'm planning on having my kids do something similar for Journey for Change. You might also choose a kid-related cause, such as supporting a school in a third-world nation. That way, you can teach your children how fortunate they are, educate them about another country, and really make a difference in the lives of schoolchildren who truly lack the basics. A good way for your kids to do this is for them to become O Ambassadors, a program *The Oprah Winfrey Show* supports to help kids in the United States raise money to build schools in third-world nations. Go to www.oprah.com for more information. Another option is available through Invisible Children's Schools for Schools initiative. U.S. students can help raise money to build schools for former child soldiers and other vulnerable children in Uganda. For more information, visit www.invisiblechildren.com. And a completely different option is to participate as a school in Locks of Love, where children can cut their hair and donate it to the organization that makes wigs for kids with cancer, alopecia, or other autoimmune diseases. What a powerful statement for a group of schoolchildren! More information is available at www.locksoflove.org.

2. Organize a Birthday Giveaway

A great way to instill a sense of service in your children is to encourage them to turn their birthday party into a service-related event by letting their friends and friends' parents know that any gifts received will be donated after the party. Let the birthday kid choose the beneficiary—maybe a community center, an orphanage, a group home, or the children's ward at a local hospital—and then encourage guests to give appropriate presents. After the party, choose a day for you and your children to make the donation together. And, of course, as the proud parent, you can then allow your child to pick out a special, personal birthday present for being such a giving and wonderful human being. (At the end of this chapter, you can read about how twelve-year-old Jack Hausmann decided to turn his birthday party into exactly this kind of event!)

3. Playdates for Charity

Identify a children's charity to donate to and have your kids invite their friends to a little party. (You'll probably want to be in touch with the parents.) Arrange for every child to bring a toy, book, or check to the gathering that can then be donated to a local organization that helps kids. At the party, the children can make cards to go along with their gifts. If your donations go to a local group, the kids could actually pay the place a visit if they wanted to.

4. Encourage Your Kids to Combine Performance and Service

If your children perform at recitals, gymnastics meets, or other events, they can make these occasions do double duty as fund-raisers. Ask the owner of the dance studio or gymnastics center to allow your group to donate a portion of the yearly recital ticket sales to a local charity. Or ask if you can give an extra performance for free and invite special guests like residents of an assisted-living facility or a home for the mentally or physically challenged.

5. Practice "Get a Toy, Give a Toy"

Like many children these days, my kids seem to have more toys than they have time to play with. So we have a rule in our house: "Get a toy, give a toy." If you get a new toy, you have to choose an old toy to give away. For younger children, the toys might be stuffed animals and little cars; for older children, we might be talking video games and cool gadgets. Either way, the goal is to keep from drowning in playthings without ever thinking about the children who don't have as much as they do. By the way, this isn't a bad rule for grown-ups, too. After you've accumulated all the "stuff" you need, maybe start thinking about giving away some of it.

6. Made with Love, Donated with Kindness: Making Things to Sell

I know one extraordinary little girl who crochets different-colored bracelets and sells them all over her community to raise money for various causes. She makes pink bracelets for breast cancer, red for heart disease, and red, white, and blue to support our troops. I spoke with her recently to interview her for my website, and I was simply blown away. Although she was only nine, you'd swear she was thirty-nine, she is so thoughtful, giving, and aware of the world. I talked to her mom, too, and told her, "Your daughter didn't get that way on her own. That came from you!" If you have craft-oriented children who are looking for a way to contribute, encourage them to make and sell their own gifts as well.

7. Lemonade Stand

It's a classic for a reason, people! I did it as a kid (though I no longer remember what I was raising money for). And when I started working with a group called the Triple Negative Breast Cancer Fund (which you'll hear about in chapter 4), some children in Massachusetts somehow heard about our group, ran a lemonade stand—and sent us a donation! I recently learned about a nine-year-old girl on Twitter who is raising money for autism by selling lemonade. Her Twitter name is lemonade4autism. Your kids may already know a group they'd like to help, or you can go online with them and help them find a local, national, or international nonprofit to support.

8. Trick-or-Treat for UNICEF or Another Cause

Go online in September (www.unicefusa.org) if you want to order those classic Trick-or-Treat for UNICEF orange boxes. Or you and your kids can make your own collection boxes out of milk cartons and collect for either UNICEF or a cause of your choosing. When my kids do it, after we come in and count the change, I write a check to UNICEF for the amount they raised and then put the change into their savings accounts. The kids love saying, "Trick or treat," for candy and then holding up their orange carton and adding, "Trick or treat for UNICEF!" To date Trick-or-Treat for UNICEF has raised more than $150 million.

9. Share the Wealth

Now that Lola is old enough to have regular visits from the tooth fairy, we have a deal: She saves one-third, spends one-third, and gives the last third to charity. We go online together and pick out a group, or she chooses one she remembers from another activity. You can do this with birthday money, holiday money, allowances, and other kinds of monetary gifts that your kids receive. You and your child can decide how much you want to save before you divvy up the money.

10. Join or Organize a School Club

Your kids can take the action one step further by joining or organizing a school club in support of a topic that they're passionate about. I've known high schools with groups that advocate for peace, human rights, and equality for women and girls, as well as groups that started antipoverty campaigns. Let your teenagers express themselves through a group or start a new one on a topic that they are passionate about. It's never too early to take a stand! For teens who are more interested in service than advocacy, a giving club might be a good idea, with a focus on either volunteering at local agencies or raising money for various causes. Check out Do Something! at www.dosomething.org with your child or teen to be inspired by other youths who are doing something.

Bringing My Kids on the Journey

As a mom, I want the world for my kids. I love the fact that my kids are able to get lessons in tennis, dance, and skiing. As I write this book, we've taken or are planning some wonderful family vacations: We took a cross-country RV trip visiting U.S. landmarks and national parks at the end of the 2009 summer season and have planned a February 2010 ski trip to a kid-friendly resort in Colorado. Later that summer we will rent a villa in Florence for a month as a home base from which to explore other parts of Italy. I love being able to give that to my children, because I'm trying desperately to raise global citizens and I am also hoping that they will catch my travel bug. Of course, I was a lot older before I was able to travel as they are, so the globe, books, and my imagination were my best friends.

But I also love that my children are aware of the world for another reason. When they act spoiled, as all kids do sometimes, I can say, "Oh, so you don't want to eat your vegetables? Well, you know you must be grateful for the food you have—because you've met kids who don't have anything to eat." When my little fashionista Lola, who has as many shoes as her mother, complains that she doesn't have a pair to match one of her outfits, I can say, "Maybe we should have you wear the same pair of shoes for a whole week, so you can feel what it's like for some children who have only one pair. Some of the very kids you've met don't have a choice about which shoes go with which outfit." This settles the situation real quick.

Sometimes I wonder about how my children will handle having a childhood with so many more advantages than either Chris or I had. Chris jokes that everything his kids did by age two he didn't do until he was at least eighteen. But both of us want our children to realize the hard work we've done to give them this life. And we both want them to know that they must give back. But I do worry about how to balance their privilege with a sense of responsibility.

I remember the first time I took the kids to Diepsloot when Lola was four. We were visiting many families that day on an official UNICEF visit, but we stayed especially long at one particular house, and after about twenty minutes, Lola got hot and bored.

I was proud of my little girl, because instead of nagging me to leave, she just asked if she could go outside and play. We were in one of the many little shacks cobbled together along a dirt alleyway and I admit I had a moment's trepidation about letting her go out there. But I knew that the field-workers, my security team, and the women of the township would keep an eye on her. So I let her go and returned to my conversation with the family.

About twenty minutes later, I stepped outside and saw Lola sitting on the ground with a few other little girls her age, drawing pictures in the dirt with a rock.

"Come on, honey, it's time to leave," I said, thinking she would be relieved that I was finally ready to take her someplace more interesting.

But my daughter surprised me. "No, Mommy. I don't want to go!" she said without even looking up.

"Why don't you want to go?"

" 'Cause I'm having *so much fun.*"

"Why, Lola? What are you doing?"

And then my four-year-old daughter looked me straight in the eye and in her father's deadpan, slightly disgusted tone she said, "*Mommy.* I'm playing in the dirt with a rock!"

So there was my four-year-old girl from one of the most affluent suburbs in New Jersey, a child who has every comfort imaginable, sharing a playdate with two little South African girls from some of the poorest homes you can imagine. They had no toys, no clean clothes, not even a decent place to play. But children are children and they can play with anything. So they were drawing in the dirt with a rock. And my daughter was having the time of her life.

MY JOURNEY: TWELVE-YEAR-OLD PHILANTHROPIST JACK HAUSMANN

Jack Hausmann is only twelve years old and in the sixth grade, but through his family and his own initiative, he's already been involved in a wide variety of service projects. When you ask Jack why he donates his time and sometimes his birthday gifts to other kids, he smiles and says, "Because I like making people happy."

With his family, Jack has been involved with various causes, including a 5K run raising money for food allergies and family donations to such organizations as Heifer International and Kiva, whose websites allow you to buy animals for needy families or make microloans to struggling people in developing countries. Actually, Jack has been giving money to charity since he was five and his mother invited him to pick out a group to which he could donate. The lesson sank in, and Jack has been involved in service ever since.

For his twelfth birthday, Jack decided that since he was getting a few big presents from his family, he didn't really need any gifts from his friends. Instead, he asked them to make donations to Journey for Change, my program that brings at-risk U.S. children from Bushwick to serve in South Africa. Jack's mother, Annie, had gone with us to help chaperone our first South African trip, and Jack helped out at a fund-raising car wash we held a few weeks after we returned. Jack's generous decision is a great example of the ways kids can choose to serve if we only give them the chance. Here's an interview with him about why he likes service so much.

Q. Tell me about what it was like being at the car wash that was raising money for Journey for Change.
A. Everyone was very happy. . . . I made a lot of new friends. . . . It made them feel good to help people that have even less than they do living in the inner city.

Q. What charity did you first donate to?
A. The Make-A-Wish Foundation, which grants wishes to sick children. The reason I picked Make-A-Wish was because . . . I thought it . . . would be the most effective. The kids in Make-A-Wish are going to die, and if they haven't had an experience, I think it would be nice to let them have that.

Q. What advice would you give to parents who want their kids to get involved in service?
A. First I would say to try to be a real model, like get involved yourself, 'cause kids follow their parents a lot. They can also give them the choice, for a birthday, like, if they want to donate money or their time . . . to kids that don't have a lot of time to . . . make friends 'cause they're always helping their families out.

Q. What advice would you give to kids who might want to get involved in service?
A. I would say do it, because it makes you feel very good, seeing other kids that don't have a lot, they aren't very happy a lot—seeing a smile on their face makes you feel good. I'd tell other kids to try it and it will probably make them feel good and want to do it some more.
   The first time I did it, I saw a picture of these kids and they were smiling and happy. It made me feel good.

Q. Do you think you'll keep doing this kind of work when you grow up?
A. Yes. Instead of growing up and just stopping, I'd like to keep doing this for as long as I can. As long as it makes other people happy, that will keep me happy. . . . 'Cause if everybody just stopped doing this, it would make a lot of people sad, and they wouldn't have a lot of happy moments in their life. . . .
   Another reason I do this is I give a lot, but I get a lot more than I give. I get so many things, I think I could at least give a little back . . . and it makes me feel very good.

Chapter 4

When a Cause Finds You:
One Person at a Time Changing the World

■

To the world, you may be one person—but to one person,
you may be the world.
—ANONYMOUS

Sometimes you go out looking for a cause. But sometimes, a cause finds you. That's what happened with the Triple Negative Breast Cancer Foundation, not just for me but for a whole group of us. Our friend Nancy Block-Zenna was only thirty-five, with a loving husband and a little girl, and suddenly she was diagnosed not only with breast cancer, but with *triple negative breast cancer,* a little-known and very aggressive form of the disease. More "typical" breast cancers are fueled by the presence of estrogen receptors (which bind with estrogen), progesterone receptors (which bind with progesterone), and human epidermal growth factor 2 receptors (which bind with HER2). No one who gets breast cancer is lucky, of course, but women who get a form of breast cancer fueled by the female hormones estrogen and progesterone or by HER2 are a bit luckier than other cancer patients because they're able to benefit from the many new forms of hormonal treatment, such as the drugs tamoxifen and Herceptin. These treatments are generally less debilitating than chemotherapy, and for many women, they're quite effective.

But triple negative breast cancer gets its name from the fact that the women who suffer from it don't have any of these receptors. In med-speak, their tumors are "estrogen receptor–negative, progesterone receptor–negative, and HER2-negative"—hence, "triple negative."

I first heard about Nancy's illness from Sharon Fredman, whom I'd met in a Mommy and Me music class when Sharon's Margo and my Lola were about six months old. Though they don't go to the same school they still share playdates and go to the same summer camp.

Sharon was a very close friend of Nancy's—she knew Nancy far better than I did—but I did know Nancy, because her Jolie and my Lola had gone to the same camp as well. And of course, Sharon knew that I'd done a lot of fund-raising, event planning, marketing, and public relations for philanthropic causes as well as founding my own nonprofit.

One day, when Margo and Lola were three, Sharon and the kids were over for a playdate, and Sharon told me about Nancy's diagnosis. At the time, all we knew was that Nancy had breast cancer.

I was heartbroken, of course. As I watched a bunch of three-year-olds run happily around my house, I shuddered to think of Nancy leaving her little girl and said a silent prayer that she would be okay. As a mother, I cannot think of anything more terrifying or painful than to have to leave your children before you are done raising them.

About a year later, we had all learned something about triple negative, and we had also discovered that Nancy probably had very little time left. Nancy's friends began to raise money for what they thought were going to be Nancy's unpaid medical bills. When it turned out that her insurance policies covered most of the cost, Nancy quickly shifted gears and told her friends that she wanted to start a foundation. "I don't want anyone else to go through what I went through," Nancy told us. "I want people to have information and hope." So we started a foundation to raise money for research and to promote awareness among women and the medical community.

It all began with towels. Our friend Sharon called me one day to say, "We are selling towels that have three pink ribbons on them representing triple negative; will you buy some?"

I took $1,500 worth of towels and made good use of them. They were huge beach towels, so when I gave them out in the South African shantytowns I was working in, they were much appreciated by the residents. I kept about ten of them. Lola, Margo, and Jolie attended the same summer camp, and Lola came home one day saying, "I want to take a Triple Negative Breast Cancer Foundation towel to camp. Everyone has one, even Jolie!" The towel, which was the first way the foundation ever raised money, was the hottest beach towel at camp! I just loved it!

When I told Sharon I would buy all those towels, she laughed and said, "That would be great. But what we really need is your advice on starting a nonprofit and then raising money for the foundation."

Between family and my other projects, I had more than a full plate. But this was a cause that had found me, right here in my own community. How could I possibly say no?

"If there's anything else I can do," I told Sharon, "count me in."

Triple Negative: Targeting Young Women and African-American Women

Before Nancy was diagnosed, I had never heard of triple negative breast cancer. I soon learned, as previously mentioned, that it was one of the many subtypes of breast cancer, with its own specific risk factors and treatments.

Triple negative tumors often *do* respond to chemotherapy, so if a doctor catches the condition quickly enough and prescribes the right treatment, a woman has a decent shot at beating the disease. The problem is that until recently, the disease was so little known that many doctors didn't recognize it. If a woman came in with a diagnosis of breast cancer, they were likely to prescribe a hormonal treatment, which left the disease free to rage unchecked within her body. As in Nancy's case, by the time the disease is correctly identified, it may be too late.

The problem is compounded by the fact that triple negative is an unusually aggressive form of cancer, so it works fast. If you don't start the chemo early, you may have missed your window of opportunity. Worse, the disease is especially prevalent among two groups of women who are even less likely to be diagnosed correctly: young women, whom most doctors don't expect to have breast cancer, and African-American women, who we know are far more likely to receive substandard health care or who don't have access to health care in the first place. The disease is also more likely to reoccur than other types of breast cancer.

One thing that was very important to our foundation was to identify an advisory committee of medical experts who could help give us direction and whose research we could learn from and support. Two board members cold-called three of the leading doctors in the field: Dr. Lisa Carey, Dr. Edward Winer, and Dr. George Sledge. I'm still awestruck that men and women of this caliber agreed to give their time to some unknown group of women in New Jersey. It says a lot about their character—and about the power of service. Once you start a group's momentum, it's amazing who joins in along the way.

These three doctors advised our foundation to host the first-ever symposium on triple negative breast cancer. They told us whom to invite and helped us choose the date—a day before another major conference was being held—and the end result was that we had thirty-four of the world's leading doctors attending the inaugural Triple Negative Breast Cancer Symposium in December 2007, and its follow-up in December 2008. We are currently planning the 2009 symposium, and by the time you are reading this chapter, we will have jointly sponsored the Susan G. Komen for the Cure $6.4 Million Promise Grant, cofunded by the Triple Negative Breast Cancer Foundation.

The other important initiative of our foundation was to create a website that would serve as a virtual community for women who suffer from triple negative. Nancy's original vision had been to start a research foundation, and that was still our main focus. But I knew that women who had this disease needed a place to come together, where online users from around the world could talk to one another about their experiences, sharing both their medical knowledge and their personal stories. We now all agree that this website is one of our finest contributions, a space where thousands of women from all over the world can chat with one another about all sorts of topics.

Building from the Ground Up

There are so many things to do when you want to start a new nonprofit. You have to build a board of directors, file for incorporation and tax-exempt status, figure out how to raise funds, and pitch your group to the press. These were all areas I'd had varying amounts of experience with, since by this time I'd been in the nonprofit field for twelve years, one way or another. Based on my experience, I was able to advise the group that was slowly forming, though I wasn't really a big part of it yet.

By the time I did get involved, Nancy was really struggling. The cancer had spread to her spine and she was in a lot of pain. She was a trouper, though, and continued to take Jolie to school and all her other activities in between her own doctor's appointments. After being asked by our mutual friend Sharon if I would help, we planned to meet at my home to organize a fund-raiser, a cocktail party that I would host at my home that would hopefully spark the real start of this important organization. Nancy came to the first meeting at my house, along with maybe a dozen other Bergen County women, only about half of whom I knew. One of the women I didn't know was Annie Hausmann, who through this work became a good friend and ended up coming with me as a chaperone on my first South Africa trip for Journey for Change: Empowering Youth Through Global Service.

At the first and only meeting Nancy attended, she lay on my carpeted floor in my TV room because that was how she could be most comfortable. Though she was in pain, she was lively and contributed a lot to the conversation. She kept thanking me over and over, but I already knew that we were onto something special and life-changing and I could not thank *her* enough for letting me be a part of it. And I continue to thank Sharon for calling me in the first place.

Because Nancy was so sick, we agreed that we should have the cocktail party soon. Though normally I never want to allow less than six months for creating an event—and eight is better—this time, we all felt it was important to make an exception. With help from our entire community, we held the first annual Peace, Love and a Cure Fundraising Cocktail Party just a few weeks later, on June 10, 2007, and raised a whopping $270,000 from an event that cost us less than $7,000.

How did we do it? We begged, borrowed, and all but stole. I asked my florist, Saundra Parks, who owns a wonderful flower design firm called the Daily Blossom, to donate the flowers, as she often does to my nonprofit work. My wonderful graphic designer, Richard Menage of Menage Graphics, worked his usual pro bono magic with our invitation and program. (You read an interview with Richard in chapter 2.) My local caterer, Food for Thought Catered Events, gave us the food at cost, and their rental company gave us a discount. Several of the women in our group now hire this company regularly for personal parties at their homes, so the company did a good deed *and* benefited from it. Someone else asked a local liquor store to give us a price break on the liquor, which was wonderful because, after all, we were throwing a cocktail party! We had three former lawyers in the group who were now stay-at-home moms, and they took care of getting us our nonprofit and tax-exempt status and any other legal business we needed.

The contributions didn't stop there. Sharon, the friend who had gotten me involved in all of this, worked with her husband to build our website so we could promote our event online. Another friend, Claudia, whose son Aaron had also been in the Mommy and Me music class with Lola and Margo, put together our gift bags.

One of the highlights of the event was our silent auction and raffle, organized by Annie, the auction queen. She got local merchants to donate beautiful gifts and then added her special creative touch in organizing the auction. Many of us also called in favors to get some really exciting gifts—VIP tickets to *Saturday Night Live*, for example, or a shopping spree at Saks Fifth Avenue with a personal stylist and lunch. We ended up raising $60,000 from the auction alone!

Throughout the whirlwind of planning and organizing, I kept

rediscovering how personally I took this whole issue. First there was Nancy, a young suburban woman who reminded me of me: She had changed her career and moved to the New Jersey suburbs from Manhattan to raise her child and to create a whole other kind of life for her family. Whenever I thought of Nancy, I said to myself, "There but for the grace of God go I."

Then there was the disease itself, which strikes disproportionately among young women and African-American women. I could not help but think that if I were to be diagnosed with breast cancer, there was a high chance of it being triple negative. Because of my work with this foundation, I have had many heartfelt moments with women of all races but have been particularly touched by my exchanges with African-American women—for example, when ABC's *Good Morning America* cohost Robin Roberts announced to me that she had triple negative breast cancer while I was on the show promoting *Oprah's Big Give.* This was the first time that Robin told America the exact type of cancer she had, and it made all her sisters with the same disease feel as if they had a champion, a beautiful champion who was living proof that you can live a full life during treatment and go into remission. I was also contacted by journalist Tavis Smiley when his beloved business partner Sheryl Flowers died of the disease, and Helen Sugland, who manages the actor Laurence Fishburne, when her sister Barbara was diagnosed with stage 4 of the disease. As of this writing, the family of Sheryl Flowers has set up a memorial fund in her honor to join our efforts to find a cure. I must say, it makes me proud that I am able to help anyone who comes to me for resources and support.

Even though the organization is growing by leaps and bounds and we are so proud of our ability to effect positive change as it pertains to finding a cure, I continue to think how lovely it is that it remains a grassroots community effort.

In so many ways, this issue was very close to home, and it reminded me that sometimes we're moved to act not by something that we've heard on the news, as happened for me with styleWORKS, or by something that was a very conscious decision, as happened for me when I decided to go into the nonprofit field and ended up at the

U.S. Fund for UNICEF, but by something that simply gets us where we live. We were moved to start the Triple Negative Breast Cancer Foundation by the wish of a dying friend, and we remain as committed to it as ever.

Exercise Your Consumer Power: Gianna Rose Atelier Pink Ribbon Soap

Stacy Klein was a former lawyer and current stay-at-home mother of two. A friend of Nancy Block-Zenna's, she was part of that first group of us who founded the Triple Negative Breast Cancer Foundation. As it happened, her sister-in-law was a public relations consultant for a very successful company called Gianna Rose Atelier that specializes in making beautiful soaps and bath items.

Stacy had the brilliant idea of asking her sister-in-law to go to the company and ask them to create a specialty soap for our first annual fund-raising event as a special giveaway to our guests. Gianna Rose Atelier produced a lovely pink soap embossed with three breast cancer ribbons representing triple negative. The soaps looked beautiful, smelled wonderful, and were luxuriously packaged. We were thrilled.

After the event, the company wanted to promote the soaps for Breast Cancer Month in October. They asked if we would approve a press release saying that they had created the soap for the Triple Negative Breast Cancer Foundation's Peace, Love and a Cure event and that the event had been held at the home of Malaak and Chris Rock. Since they were offering our group a percentage of their sales, we said, "Of course!"

The story was picked up by numerous magazines, including *People, Us,* and *Glamour.* And now, when you visit the company's website (www.giannarose.com), you'll see on the lower left-hand corner a pink ribbon and the slogan "Support the Triple Negative Breast Cancer Foundation." Click on the words and check out the soap. If you like, browse through the rest of the website as well. I firmly believe in supporting any company that gives back to society, and Gianna Rose Atelier certainly does a good job of that!

Finding Funds: Your Fund-Raising Options

We at the Triple Negative Breast Cancer (TNBC) Foundation chose to give a cocktail party, but when you're raising money for a good cause, you have lots of options. Here's a quick look at the pros and cons of each:

• *Fund-raising letter.* This is the simplest choice and often the most effective. You write a letter to people you know, asking them to donate money to your cause. If you have tax-exempt status, you're offering them both the chance to do something good *and* a tax donation, so it's often best to send this kind of letter toward the end of the calendar year. Whatever you do, *don't* send one in January, when people are feeling spent out after the holidays and when the tax benefits won't kick in for another eleven months. For your donors to receive their tax deduction, for any contribution under $250, they must keep their canceled check, bank statement, or credit card statement. For contributions of $250 or more, your donors must have a written acknowledgment from you.

PROS: Easy, inexpensive, and often effective.

CONS: You're limited to people you already know and people who already care; you don't really have the chance to educate people about the issue or to get people to pull in their friends.

• *Sell something.* Does someone in your circle have a gift for producing handmade cards? Do you know someone, as one of our TNBC women did, who makes handmade towels? Do you like the idea of creating T-shirts, or buttons, or some other relatively inexpensive item to sell at a profit? Do you have a member who is able to create a unique product for your group? If the answer to any of these questions is yes, you might be able to raise money by selling something, either as your main fund-raising effort or during a party, walkathon, or other occasion.

PROS: You can educate people and make money at the same time; you can reach people who aren't familiar with your cause or even interested in it; offers a chance for all your members to do outreach and education as they sell.

CONS: May require an initial investment of time and/or money; may not be cost-effective if you can't make enough to justify the money and time it takes to produce and sell the items.

• *Walkathon.* Like the bake sale and the lemonade stand, this fund-raising method has become a real classic. You sponsor a walk—or, if you've got a lot of young, athletic members, a run—and people collect pledges from family, friends, and coworkers to be paid if they stay the course. You can also solicit donations from local merchants, such as refreshments or other items to sell at the beginning or end of the event. Walkathons often work well in conjunction with a raffle, as you sell tickets to win prizes donated by local merchants.

PROS: You can reach a wide range of people, as your members explain their cause while soliciting pledges or selling raffle tickets; each member can collect small donations from lots of people, which might add up to a big sum; the walk itself is often a really fun and inspiring event; you can involve local merchants.

CONS: Some people who would do other types of work for your group won't feel comfortable asking others to sponsor them or to buy tickets from them; you need a certain "critical mass" of people to participate or the walkathon/raffle may feel like a failure.

• *Fund-raising event.* This term is a huge umbrella covering many different types of gatherings, including a breakfast, lunch, dinner, cocktail party, golf outing, theater party, carnival, shopping day, or some other type of entertainment. Holding a fund-raising event can be extraordinarily effective if done correctly, pulling in people you'd never be able to reach otherwise and offering you the chance to cultivate some new donors. It can also inspire people with a feeling of excitement about your group. I love fund-raising events and have been involved in many. But watch out: If you're doing the wrong type of event at the wrong time or for the wrong reason, you could end up squandering a lot of money and energy that could have better served your organization in another way.

>PROS: **Brings in new people, can raise awareness, probably has the chance of raising the most money of any of these choices.**
>
>CONS: **If you don't have the resources or audience for an event, you may end up putting in far more effort than the results warrant. For small, new groups whose members don't know a lot of people with the means to give, an event often drains money and energy that could have been used differently.**

Powerful Parties: Secrets to a Successful Fund-Raising Event

So at this point, if you've decided that a fund-raiser is the way to go for you—and who doesn't love a good party?—heed these tips and you'll be well on your way to planning a wonderful event!

Tip # 1: Know Your Target Audience

Who out there is going to buy tickets to this event, and how much are you likely to raise? This is probably the key question you have to ask yourselves, and if you don't like the answer, you may be better off not holding a fund-raising event at all.

After all, if you only know twenty people who might support your group, you'd be better off scheduling individual meetings and simply asking for a check. Or invite a few guests to a question-and-answer session at your home, serve some cocktails, and send everyone away with all the information and inspiration they need. Why go to any more trouble than that?

Now, don't get me wrong: Events serve a far larger purpose than simply raising money. They're also a way to boost awareness of your cause and to cultivate people who will be your loyal supporters over the long run. But you can achieve those goals without taking the time and trouble a major fund-raising event requires. *The only reason to hold a fund-raising event is if it will pull in significantly more people and significantly more money than you could do any other way.*

If you think your event will accomplish this goal, full speed ahead. But if not—and believe me, there are lots of times the answer will be no—save your energy for other tasks.

Tip # 2: Put Together a Good Committee: Volunteers Who Will Work Hard to Make Your Event a Success

This one is crucial. The people on your committee are the folks who will make or break your event, so if you can't put together a good committee, postpone your event until you can.

Here are just some of the jobs for which your committee members will be responsible: identifying your target audience; setting the correct price for the event based on the maximum the target audience will pay; bringing that audience in through personal invitations or by other means; soliciting free or reduced-cost contributions from local merchants, graphic artists, and others; creating and mailing invitations; getting publicity; finding a location; planning the entertainment; making arrangements for the food and drink . . . the list goes on and on and on.

I personally think that creating an event can be lots of fun and there are often side benefits: the local merchant who becomes inspired to get involved, the committee member who discovers an unsuspected talent. But without a strong committee, your event won't work—no ifs, ands, or buts about it—so make sure you have one before you commit to *anything* else.

Tip # 3: Find or Decide Upon the Best Location

The real estate people know what they're talking about when they say the three most important factors in buying property are location, location, and location. The same goes for event planning. The place you hold your event will play a huge role in how many people come and how they feel once they get there. And if you have to pay for a place, rather than getting it for free, your rental costs will likely be a huge portion of your budget.

Choosing whether to hold your fund-raiser in a fancy hotel downtown or at a lively community center in the neighborhood you're trying to serve isn't necessarily an easy decision: There may be pros and cons to each option. Make sure your committee takes all

the time it needs to weigh these factors and make the right decision—it will have a huge impact on your success.

Tip # 4: Don't Rush

I recommend allowing at least a month just to scout locations. Take
your time putting together a committee and figuring out your target audience, too. You can't hold a successful event unless you know
whom you're inviting, how much they'll pay, and what location
they're likely to prefer. One of the most common mistakes people
make in event planning is not giving themselves enough time.

Tip # 5: Budget, Budget, Budget

You must know from the very beginning how much money you have
to spend. The point of a fund-raiser is to make money, and you can
only know if this is possible if you know how much you have to
spend. Though we all hope to get as many things donated as possible
and that companies will provide a nonprofit with discounts, there will
always be a cost associated with planning an event, no matter how big
or small. You need to determine how much you have to spend early on
so that you can hire your resources based on this important number.

Bonus Tip: Fund-raisers Should Be Fun!

I've saved the most important secret for last: Make sure you put the
fun in your *fund-raiser*! Even if you're raising money for a disaster or
a sad cause, you want your guests to have a good time. It may seem
odd to party for a cause like cancer, suicide, or famine relief, but if
your guests don't enjoy themselves, they won't come to your next
event, and you'll have missed out on a tremendous opportunity to
build goodwill, inspire action, and cultivate your next group of major donors. There's nothing wrong with taking a solemn moment to
remember the victims of a hurricane or the horrors of AIDS, but the
vast majority of the evening should be a celebration. After all, you're
all getting together to make a difference. Isn't that cause for joy?

I'm proud to say that our TNBC Foundation events always offer
our guests a fabulous time. At that first cocktail party, Nancy was
very ill, and we all had plenty of reasons to be sorrowful, but people

had such a great time at that event that the next year, we brought in even more people. The sorrow is the reason to be there, but so is the joy, and if you're going to plan a successful event, you've got to remember to keep them in the right balance.

One other hint: Consider local celebrities who might add a little sparkle to your event. A TV newscaster or weatherperson, the host of a local morning show, or even the well-known owner of a local business can be a valuable asset in drawing attention—and attendees.

Gift Bags Galore

Sending your guests away with a gift bag is always a nice touch if you can produce them at a low cost. Looking for some inexpensive gift-bag items? Ask a local department store to load you up with sample cosmetics and perfumes, perhaps in exchange for putting a card with the store's name in each bag. See if local boutiques will give you "$10 off" gift certificates—which they know will bring in more business from a new clientele. Or check out these websites, which can help you find some lovely choices that can be decorated with a slogan or your group's logo: mugs, water bottles, baseball caps, pens and pencils, candles, T-shirts.

Branders.com	www.branders.com	877-272-6337
Memorable Gifts.com	www.memorablegifts.com	800-998-4830
The Stationery Studio	www.stationerystudio.com	847-541-5800

And for the bags themselves:

Bags and Bows	www.bagsandbows.com	800-523-8888
Paper Mart	www.papermart.com	800-745-8800

By the way, make sure to include a mission statement from your organization—a nicely designed one-page sheet from your home printer is fine—or, of course, pamphlets if you have them. You want your contact information in every gift bag, so your guests can follow up with further donations if they're so inclined.

Timing Is Everything

Now that you have some overall guidelines, it's time to get down to the nitty-gritty. As tip #4 suggests, the fastest way to derail your event is to not give yourself enough time. And remember, choose your date wisely: Make extra sure that there are no major conflicts, such as a religious holiday. If you're inviting parents, make sure you're not holding your event during a school holiday. Check your local newspapers, magazines, and websites to make sure that no other group is holding a similar event on the same day. If your newspaper has a social editor, find out whether he or she knows of any potential conflicts. And ask around—word of mouth can be your most effective weapon!

Suppose you decide in December that you're going to hold a fund-raising event sometime in September, just after everyone's home from vacation and the kids are back in school. Your event committee should be meeting every month, in person or by teleconference. And your schedule might look something like this:

January: 1. Hold your first committee meeting.
2. Divide up the tasks.
3. Choose a location.

February: 1. Solidify the date, time, and place of your event.
2. Finalize your decision on what type of event it will be.
3. Work on your guest list.
4. Make appointments to view potential spaces for your event.
5. Set a budget.

March: 1. Check the status of your guest list. If you need more names, make a plan for getting them.
2. Choose a space.
3. Write letters of invitation to anyone you're inviting to be honored or to speak.
4. If you're having an auction, write letters to potential donors.

April: 1. Once again, review your guest list. If you still need more names, make a plan for getting them.

2. Make a list of vendors that you'll need, such as caterer, florist, photographer, equipment rental, printer, audiovisual, valet parking.

3. Identify which local vendors will donate goods or services for free.

4. Get bids from at least three vendors in each category.

5. Ask your graphic designer to submit versions of an invitation for you to approve by the following month. (If you're trying to save money, consider an e-mail invitation—but ideally still a designed one.)

May: 1. Review the invitation, the response card, and the envelope, and work with your designer to finalize them.

2. Choose your vendors based on your April bids.

3. Contact your printer to find out when his or her deadline is.

4. Do a walk-through of the space with all vendors who need to see it.

5. Begin following up with your auction donors and try to obtain the items.

June: 1. Send out a "save the date" notice to your guest list. If you have decided not to print this, then do it by e-mail.

2. Meet with the house staff at the space to identify all of the elements that they will take care of, so you know what staff you need to bring in. During that meeting, find out what rentals and/or equipment they may let you use for free, which will reduce your costs.

July: 1. Begin addressing invitations by hand, sending them to a calligrapher, or putting them into a spreadsheet for labels.

2. Obtain all auction items and begin to prepare them for display.

3. Complete your confirmation of all honorees and speakers.

4. Order plaques and/or awards that will be given out.

5. Ask the honorees or speakers if they would like their remarks drafted for them. If so, prepare them in bullet points or speech form, based on their preference. If not, give them guidance as to what should be said and let them know their time allowance.

6. Send out your invitations, timed to arrive six to eight weeks before the date of the event.

August:

1. Begin following up on your guest list. This should be done via telephone. However, if you prefer to send an e-mail first, you should follow up with a phone call. I promise you, this is the most effective way to ensure success.

2. Do another walk-through of your space. Make any necessary changes with your vendors based on that visit.

3. Meet in person with your event committee to go over all last-minute details.

4. Find out and make note of how every vendor should be paid. Many vendors require a deposit but don't expect final payment until the event. For those requiring payment the day of the event, have checks or cash ready. For those who require payment after the event, solidify how that will be done: by bill, a charge to your credit card, or some other method.

5. Determine the amount needed for tips the night of the event and who will be responsible for having the cash on hand.

6. Make the final determination of who will speak and do public thank-yous at the event.

September: 1. Choose the date that all items will be delivered before the event, particularly rentals and equipment.

2. Determine what time the other items will be delivered the day of the event, particularly flowers and ice.

3. If you're having gift bags, choose a date a few days before the event to assemble them. If the space allows you, it is great to have a team go in a few days before, assemble the bags, and leave them there.

4. Write up your shot list and submit it to your photographer. Let the photographer know who will be working with him or her.

The Day of the Event... Tips, Tips, and More Tips!

• If you are serving cocktails, hors d'oeuvres, and/or food, make sure that you are ready to have your guests enjoy the goodies as soon as they arrive. They should not have to wait for something to eat or drink.

• Know where the restrooms are and make sure everyone working the event does as well. Make sure the restrooms are checked periodically to ensure they are stocked and clean at all times.

• If you have music, make sure that someone turns it down while your speakers are addressing the group. But have someone standing by so that the minute the speeches end, the music comes right back up—no dead air!

• If you're using video, set it up and play it all the way through before the event starts to make absolutely sure there are no technical problems. Then recue so it's ready to go.

• If you're using a microphone, make sure it works before the event starts.

• If you have a podium, check with your speakers to see if they want to carry their own notes or have them placed on the podium ahead of time. I personally always keep copies of everybody's speeches, which I ask to have submitted a few days before the event. That way, if a speaker forgets his or her notes, I can come to the rescue!

Avoid These Common Mistakes!

I'd like to steer you away from some of the most common mistakes people make when planning an event. Stay away from these pitfalls, and you'll save yourself a world of trouble!

Mistake # 1: Creating a Committee Whose Members Are Too Similar

Nothing is more frustrating than a committee where everyone is good at flower arranging and no one knows how to write a fund-raising letter, hire a band, scout out locations, or put together a silent auction. You want your committee to be comprised of members who have a wide range of talents, not to mention folks who know many different types of useful people: local business owners who can donate goods and services; graphic designers who can do a pro bono invitation; guests with enough money to make significant donations. Make sure you've got a diverse committee so that everyone brings something different to the table.

Mistake # 2: Not Planning the Event "Flow" Correctly

All too often, events get bogged down. Sometimes you put too many speakers on the program, allowing too many people to speak too long. Sometimes you let a speaker take too much time with the educational portion of the evening or allow the question-and-answer portion of the event to get out of hand. After all, even if people are there to learn something, they also want to have fun!

Here are my personal rules for good timing:

Keynote speaker: fifteen minutes
Other speakers: two minutes each—even if you're honoring them
with an award!

Video: three minutes max, unless you put it on a TV and loop it, so people can come and go as they like.

Mistake # 3: Skimping on Food and Drink

Yes, you're trying to save money—and you should. Cut corners everywhere you can. Get a cheap local band instead of a big head-line number; limit the number of floral arrangements; rely on a few inexpensive items for your gift bags; serve wine, sodas, and water instead of having a full bar. But never, *ever* cut corners on the food and drink, especially if your event is organized around a breakfast, lunch, or dinner, or if it's scheduled for a time when your guests would normally eat. If your event is planned for seven to nine P.M. and you serve only hors d'oeuvres and no dinner, what do you think is going to happen? As the evening wears on, more and more people will slip out of your event in search of a good meal. You can cook the food yourself, you can choose an inexpensive menu, you can save money in all sorts of ways. But *don't* skimp! It's one of the best il-lustrations I know of "penny-wise and pound-foolish," because you'll lose out on so many donations as soon as folks get hungry.

Also, you don't *have* to have a bar—just wine is plenty. But if you *do* have a bar, make sure it's a full bar with at least some version of the basics: scotch, bourbon, vodka, and gin, along with whatever so-das and juices you need to make up the basic drinks. No one will hold it against you if there is no bar. But if you have one, people will be seriously annoyed if they can't get the drinks they expect.

Mistake # 4: Misjudging the Price of Your Ticket

Too high, and you drive away potential donors. Too low, and you didn't raise all the money you might have. Getting the price right is tough but crucial, so make sure you and your committee spend enough time figuring it out.

Obviously, your ticket price should be based on the audience you expect. Are the folks coming to your event mainly college students? Middle-aged? Rich? Struggling? What would they normally spend for a night on the town? What would they spend for a special occasion?

Your price will also reflect what you're offering at the event, of course. You can't charge people $5,000 for a table and then feed them hors d'oeuvres—you've got to give them a full sit-down dinner or at least a huge buffet.

Finally, your price may reflect how urgent people feel your issue is. Right after Hurricane Katrina hit, lots of people who'd seen the storm on TV were eager to help. When Nancy died and we did our first Triple Negative event, her friends were looking for a meaningful way to respond. On the other hand, if you're trying to raise awareness for a cause most people don't know about yet, you might have to set your sights a little lower.

By the way, our TNBC Foundation events are a great example of how to vary your price to suit your audience. We charged people $10,000 to $35,000 to attend our first cocktail party as sponsors, which is high for just drinks and hors d'oeuvres—usually, for that price, you have to have a full meal. But we served our hors d'oeuvres buffet-style and we had a ton of them, plus live music. The whole event was so beautifully done that people felt very much as though they'd gotten what they paid for.

Those figures tell you what an affluent crowd we were targeting, which made sense, because Nancy was part of a group of women in Bergen County who knew lots of well-off people. But we wanted to reach a broader audience as well, as we also hold a $125 tea and shopping event at Saks Fifth Avenue at Riverside Square Mall in Hackensack, New Jersey. Our guests get tea and light refreshments; a fifteen-minute Q&A with a doctor and patient moderated by Lori Stokes, a local ABC News anchor; and the opportunity to shop till they drop. We get the $125 entry fee and, thanks to Saks Fifth Avenue's generosity, a percentage of all the sales. Two very different price points for two very different crowds, adding up to two very successful fund-raisers.

Mistake # 5: Failing to Seek Pro Bono Services and Discounts with Local Retailers

My motto for fund-raising events is always "Don't pay for what you don't have to." That sounds obvious, but too many people believe that you've got to pay top dollar for everything or you're not going to produce a nice event. After years of organizing shopping days, cocktail parties, fashion shows, and banquets, I'm here to tell you that no event is so fancy that you can't cut corners *somewhere*, and often a lot of places. See the rest of this chapter for ideas on how you can scrounge, beg, and borrow to put on a beautiful event for far less money than you might think. And remember: Every dollar you *don't* spend is a dollar you have to donate to your cause.

Mistake # 6: Choosing Music or Entertainment That Doesn't Reflect Your Guest List

Okay, maybe you can't go disastrously wrong with this one, but without the right music and/or entertainment, you run the risk that your guests won't have quite as good a time. You don't want to blast your older audience out of their seats with hip-hop or bore a younger crowd with "oldies but goodies." If your crowd is a mixed bag, make sure your music program is, too, with a little something for everyone.

Mistake # 7: Letting a Vendor Drop Off Items Too Close to Your Start Time

You don't want to be rushed—and you want plenty of time in case something goes wrong. So whether vendors are delivering liquor, flowers, tables, chairs, linens, or some other key item, consider having the delivery arrive the day before or, at the very least, as early as possible on the day itself. I would always insist on, say, the seven-to-ten A.M. window rather than then ten-to-two P.M. window if an event is scheduled for that evening. Ideally, I'd have everything delivered the day before so I could leisurely go over my supplies and confirm that all is in order.

Lots of people don't realize that if you're renting linens, they'll arrive folded up in their little packages—i.e., *wrinkled.* So you need to build in some ironing time, too! You certainly don't want to be doing *that* the day of your party, so figure on some time the night before. And what if you get a cracked chair, a broken piece of kitchen equipment, or a popcorn maker that just won't pop? Even the best rental company can bring you a few bad items, but if you look over everything and test it the day before, you've got time to make things right.

And if everything arrives in perfect order? You still want time to set up. If you're holding an indoor event, my advice is to set up the entire thing the day before, if you can. If you're using a rented location that restricts you to the day of, ask, "What is the earliest time that my rentals can be dropped off? What is the earliest time I can come in and set up?" Push as hard as you can for the earliest possible time—you'll be glad you did!

Mistake # 8: Not Having Enough Staff or Volunteers Working Your Event

This is one of those things you want to really think through. By yourself or, ideally, with a few trusted committee members, talk through every facet of the event, from the moment your guests arrive (Do they need someone to help them with their coats?) through the entertainment (Who's going to introduce the speaker? Does she need someone to escort her to the stage?) to the time your guests leave (Will someone need to call taxis for elderly guests? Do you have someone handing out the gift bags?).

I'm always astonished by how much work it takes to keep an event running smoothly and by how many people need to contribute their efforts from beginning to end. A little pre-planning ahead of time can save you lots of headaches on the actual day. You should also designate one person as overall coordinator or troubleshooter and one person to be the coordinator's "runner" or assistant. That way, if a problem comes up—a broken microphone, not enough liquor—you've got someone who can dash out to a local store, make a few phone calls, or otherwise pitch in to save the day.

Mistake # 9: Not Designating a Job for Every Volunteer

Nothing is worse than showing up to help out at some event and realizing that you've got nothing to do. If the event is so well-organized that they don't need you, maybe that's a good thing. But if everyone is running around frantically and yet you can't seem to pitch in, that spells trouble. Make sure your volunteers all know what they're supposed to do and when they're supposed to do it. They'll enjoy the event more, everything will go more smoothly, and you'll have a much easier time asking them to volunteer again.

Mistake # 10: Failing to Follow Up Afterward

This is probably the most common mistake people make, believe it or not, and it's probably the saddest, because it's such a waste of a good event. If you've held a successful breakfast, shopping day, or cocktail party and taken in lots of money, terrific! But you should also have built a solid donor list for future solicitations and events so that your fund-raising efforts have a future.

Do You Need to Start a Nonprofit Organization?

Though we felt the best option for us was to officially apply for nonprofit status for the Triple Negative foundation, that isn't necessarily a requirement. Many people assume their first step in getting a group together is turning it into a formal nonprofit organization, but gaining and maintaining nonprofit status can be a huge hassle, and if your group is small and informal, you may not need to go there, especially not at first.

True, if you are a nonprofit tax-exempt organization, people can make tax-deductible contributions to you. Besides *nonprofit* status, you also need *tax-exempt* status for people to be able to deduct their gifts. But there are two ways around this problem:

1. Just raise money and donate it to the group of your choice. Or you can choose a tax-exempt group to donate to and have people write checks to it. You can then give the checks directly to the charity.

2. Find a *fiscal sponsor*—an existing nonprofit group that already has tax-exempt status. A local religious group, school, or charity might be willing to accept donations on your behalf and then channel them back to your cause. Often, groups charge a fee— sometimes as high as 8 percent—for the bookkeeping involved in

this arrangement, but that cost might be preferable to the legal fees that frequently come up in the process for obtaining nonprofit status.

If you are still committed to becoming a tax-exempt nonprofit group, read on! I'll talk you through it, step by step.

How to Start a Nonprofit Organization*

Step 1: *Identify a need* that should be addressed: a worthy cause, a pressing issue, or a group of people who need help. You should feel passionate about the idea and eager to put in the hard yet rewarding work that it takes to start a new nonprofit. Your motivation needs to be that you care deeply about helping others and not about the money.

Step 2: *Identify your mission and write a short, concise mission statement* that fully describes what your organization will offer as well as your target audience.

Step 3: *Choose a name* that best fits your mission.

Step 4: *Build a board* slowly. You want to create a board full of members with diverse skills, connections, and resources. They should all be people who are willing to work and who feel deeply committed to your cause, so take your time and invite just the right people. Make sure to check out the laws of your state; you're often required to have a certain number of board members when you incorporate.

Step 5: *Draft bylaws* and get board approval. Bylaws specify how your organization will be run and how the board will operate.

Step 6: *Incorporate your business* in the state where you live. For more specific information on how to incorporate, visit the Internal Revenue Service's website (www.irs.gov) and check under your state's requirements for charities and nonprofits. To use the IRS site, click on the "Charities & Non-Profits" tab

---

*These eleven steps were compiled with help from Quick Easy Guides' *How to Start a Non Profit* and the Foundation Center at www.foundationcenter.org.

at the top. Then click on the "Exempt Organizations FAQ" link and then "FAQs About Operating as an Exempt Organization." If you Google your state government's website, you can find instructions for registering with your state.

Step 7: *Open a bank account.* You'll want a business account in the name of your new group. Depending on your bylaws, you may want an account that requires more than one signature to withdraw money.

Step 8: *Apply for federal and state tax-exempt status.* Incorporating as a nonprofit organization is only the first step. If you want to be excused from paying taxes, you have to get tax-exempt status as well.

Step 9: *Contact your state attorney general's office* to determine whether your state has laws governing charitable solicitations.

Step 10: *Consider hiring a lawyer* to help you incorporate, apply for tax-exempt status, and trademark your group's name.

Step 11: *Develop a concise fund-raising plan.*

Celebration and Sorrow

Because triple negative was so poorly understood, Nancy was at first misdiagnosed and given the wrong type of treatment. By the time the doctors understood her condition, the disease had metastasized. It was now too late for the correct treatment to work, and she was told to expect only a few more months to live.

When Nancy died, she went peacefully, surrounded by friends and family, and with the knowledge that she had moved her friends to action. She had the satisfaction of knowing that a foundation had been established in her honor and that we had already raised enough money to launch a website that was already being used by thousands of women diagnosed with triple negative breast cancer. What truly warms my heart is that one day Nancy's daughter will know what an amazing mother she had, a woman who left this earth thinking of her family, her friends, and what she could do for any other woman diagnosed with this disease. What a beautiful legacy.

As for us, her friends, we took our memories of Nancy, our sorrow at her loss, and our joy in her friendship and channeled our energy into the Triple Negative Breast Cancer Foundation, the first organization to raise money solely for funding research to help develop a targeted drug and a cure. So I guess we're part of Nancy's legacy, too. As I said, sometimes a cause just comes and finds you.

I also think our story illustrates the power of a new group of stay-at-home moms, women who once had top jobs on Wall Street or in other professions and who are now raising children full-time. As a result, they've got the time and energy to channel some of their professional savvy into volunteer work, drawing on a wealth of expertise in advertising, magazine work, law, and the like, including my own background in public relations.

If there's one final thought I'd like to leave you with, it's this: Find as many creative ways as you can to get people to contribute—and then find equally creative ways to thank them for doing so! Use your consumer power to support the businesses and people who give back to their communities, and don't be afraid to keep asking for more support as you need it.

In fact, you need to remember that when you ask someone to contribute, you're doing that person a favor. People love to be part of a good cause, and at the end of the day, there's no greater joy than giving back. I keep thinking of the quote with which I began this chapter: *To the world, you may be one person—but to one person, you may be the world.* Who doesn't want to feel like "the world," even to one other person? When you draw people into your service work, that's the opportunity you provide.

MY JOURNEY: VOLUNTEER ANNIE HAUSMANN

Annie Hausmann is a full-time volunteer living in Bergen County, New Jersey, where she resides with her husband and two children. We became friends because we were both friends of Nancy's and both got involved in the Triple Negative Breast Cancer Foundation. We soon realized that we were kindred spirits in a lot of ways, sharing the same philosophy: *From those to whom much is given, much is required.*

We also both believe that it is our motherly duty to pass that kind of attitude on to our children. You read an interview with Annie's son, Jack, in chapter 3—he's the boy who decided to ask his friends to donate to Journey for Change instead of giving him birthday presents. Clearly, Annie is raising children who are as giving and committed as she is.

Annie has been a mainstay of the TNBC Foundation. She single-handedly runs the auctions as well as doing a tremendous amount of fund-raising. She's probably been the person who has brought on more new people to support this cause than any other woman involved, including myself.

Annie has a fascinating background that reminds me a bit of my husband, Chris: She grew up in a poor neighborhood but ended up making a lot of money—in her case, on Wall Street. She's never forgotten where she came from, though, and she's never stopped giving back.

Q. I know you grew up in the Bronx. What was your neighborhood like and what can you tell us about your childhood?
A. I was born in the South Bronx, New York, in the Morris Avenue Houses, a.k.a. the projects. When I was nine we moved to a nicer housing project on Staten Island. Though my neighborhoods were not the best, I have wonderful memories of walking in and out of my friends' apartments and being a part of their families, and they were also a part of mine. I remember listening to my friends' mothers as if they were my own. I still have a hard time believing that we were poor because I did not feel that way. I remember my oldest brother (there are seven of us and I am the youngest) ordering me to stay out of a certain area of the playground, and I have a vague memory of needles being on the ground there. However, I had no clue what they were.

Q. How did your childhood shape your current commitment to service?

A. My mom is a beautiful human being. There were five of us in six years; looking back I don't know how she did it. We often had people living with us and eating with us. One Christmas my oldest brother, Dennis, brought home a few kids from a residential facility he was working at to ensure that every child had a place to go. I had to give up a gift. I was not happy as there were not many. My mom used to dress as Santa every year at work. I was so embarrassed by this but now I love the memory. She also worked at the rectory in our parish and was very involved with our church and the fundraisers and parties they held. I loved the white elephant sales at the church. Maybe that is where my knack for coordinating charity auctions comes from.

Q. Does anyone else in your family serve, and if so, how does it influence you?
A. I think all of us serve in whatever capacity we can. My three oldest siblings work or have worked with residential facilities for children, mental health centers, in public school districts, and/or rehabilitating nonviolent criminals. All three of their careers are community oriented. My parents taught us by power of example that you help your fellow man. My sister Carol literally saved my life. There was a time in my life where I really had no direction and was making really bad choices, and she literally kidnapped me to live with her and her husband, Jim, in Trenton, New Jersey. Carol is extremely involved in their community and I watched in awe how she and her husband communicated and worked together on what I deemed "silly things" at the time. I witnessed their deep level of respect for each other. I had never before experienced a healthy relationship. That experience helped to shape who I am today and how I conduct my relationships with others.

Q. When did you begin to volunteer and what was your first volunteer experience?
A. I was a Fresh Air Fund kid, one of many kids from New York City who go to a nonprofit summer camp outside of the city. We got on a train at Grand Central Station to get out of the city for a few weeks

each summer. Grand Central Station is still breathtaking to me. This was my first experience of receiving the rewards of someone's hard work on behalf of others. As a child, we had a lemonade stand every year to raise money for cancer. My first real volunteer job as an adult was for Covenant House, an agency that helps runaway teenagers. I was working on Wall Street at the time but barely paying the rent. I answered phones twice a week. Though we had loads of pranks, there were some very serious calls regarding domestic violence, drug abuse, and sexual assault. I felt so helpless, and since there was a no-trace policy, I had no idea what happened to these young girls and boys. It really affected me.

Q. Your professional background is on Wall Street. What was this career path like for you and how did it give you insight into working in the nonprofit world?
A. I have worked since I was ten or eleven. My sisters and I had a paper route. I have had some strange jobs—a supply girl at an army base, for one. I ended up on the floor of the American Stock Exchange by mistake. It was a summer job that I kept for fourteen years. It entailed multitasking, something I am pretty good at. I loved it there. The rush, the excitement, the adrenaline was all a part of the busy time in the eighties. Many of the people I worked for did charity work and I always helped. When I was about nineteen, my friend's dad gave me some raffle tickets to sell for the Police Athletic League for $100 per ticket (a very hefty price at the time). I sold about $4,000 to $5,000 worth of tickets. He was very impressed. What I learned back then is a basic tenet of mine to this day: Ask nicely, take no for an answer with grace, and don't count other people's money. It is that simple, I swear.

Q. How do you choose which causes and organizations to support?
A. Such a tough question . . . I used to jump on board every time I was asked. But this is just not possible anymore. My heart lies with . . . inner-city struggles, especially involving children. I am a product of an inner-city upbringing and I know how difficult it is to make your way out. Education is subpar, resources are almost non-

existent, and the pull of peer pressure is great. I am a great believer in the idea that it takes a village to raise our children. I also am drawn to women's issues, especially regarding health and equality.

Q. What lessons about service and giving have you taught your children?

A. David and I are working to teach our children about their responsibility to society. It can be quite difficult where we live. My kids go from one activity to another. I have overextended American children and part of me loves that they can have all these opportunities, but I do have to do some work on the material part. It is a real struggle for me. I do not want to shove anything down their throats about my childhood because it was not really worse, it was just different. The most amazing part of the Journey for Change trip is that my children are very involved now, going to Bushwick and washing cars with the kids there for fund-raising. . . . My children are seeing how kids in their own backyard are living. When I asked my son what he wanted for his birthday in October, he replied, "Mom, I have everything I want. Can I ask my friends to donate money to the Journey for Change?" I swear it is a true story. It was the greatest gift I have received as a parent. I mean, come on . . . how lucky am I?

Q. What is your favorite part of volunteering?

A. The absolute best thing for me is walking around an event I have planned and getting that feeling of satisfaction that is indescribable. It is about being responsible for creating an event that has something worthy attached to it. And of course, all those months of planning, disagreements, threats to quit, laughter, crisis, and pure fun fly out the window on the night, and it is so worth it. The sense of accomplishment is exhilarating, and I love that feeling.

Q. What advice do you have for volunteers who are just starting to serve?

A. I would say to start small, be open to learning, and get involved in something that motivates and moves you deeply. Gandhi said it best: "You must be the change you wish to see in the world." Things will happen.

Q. Do you have any specific advice for stay-at-home moms?
A. Family first, and find the right balance (David will get a chuckle out of the balance part). I initially got involved with my children's school because I wanted to see them there. There are all types of jobs in parent organizations in schools, ones that are creative and administrative. Find what is for you and jump in. It is the only way to find out what works.

Q. Do you have a last thought that I did not ask about?
A. I had a very bumpy road getting where I am today. I am truly a work in progress. I was brought up very religious, but I never embraced organized religion. It is just not for me. I am a deeply spiritual person today. When I sweep away prejudice, think honestly, and self-examine diligently . . . then . . . I am at peace. For me that is love, that is God.

Chapter 5

When Catastrophe Strikes:
Finding Strength and Confronting Challenges

■

You have within you the strength, the patience, and the
passion to reach for the stars and change the world.
—HARRIET TUBMAN

When you hear about a disaster on TV or read about it in the paper, how *do* you find the strength, patience, and passion to respond? Whether it's a hurricane in the gulf, a tsunami in the Indian Ocean, the genocide in Darfur, or any one of the dozens of earthquakes, tornadoes, cyclones, famines, epidemic outbreaks, floods, fires, wars, and massacres that seem to plague our planet with increasing frequency, disasters are a traumatic event for all of us, and never more so than in these days of twenty-four-hour news cycles. Maybe a generation ago, you would read a tiny newspaper article about a Mexican earthquake or a Caribbean storm. Now you'll be barraged with seemingly endless live footage of frightened children, ruined homes, and devastated lives. I'm glad that our planet feels smaller and our human family comes home to us so frequently—but it can be a lot to cope with.

The week Hurricane Katrina hit New Orleans, I remember watching the TV like everybody else in the world and being absolutely horrified at the devastation. But I was even more horrified at the government's neglect and its all-around failure to coordinate a rescue plan for the people. It was one thing to misjudge the hurricane—we'd all seen that happen before. But it was a whole other thing for local, state, and national governments to be completely unable to coordinate an effective evacuation plan once the storm hit.

Watching that particular natural and man-made disaster on TV was probably one of the most painful experiences I've ever had. I remember feeling absolutely helpless. Immediately, within a day, I did what a lot of people did: I wrote a check to the Red Cross. But it was one of the first times I had donated when I honestly did not feel that I could reach the people I wanted to help—the ones I was watching at the Superdome. I gave money because I had to do something, but I did not feel the usual satisfaction of doing my part.

But how could I? Even as I signed the check, I was still looking at the horrible conditions that the people of New Orleans were enduring. The situation of people who were able to leave was almost as bad, as they were forced onto planes and shipped off to parts unknown.

Although I cared about every human being who was devastated by the storm in all the gulf states, I will readily admit that when former U.S. senator Trent Lott of Mississippi was on the news whining about losing his vacation home and being in the same boat as everybody else, I had no sympathy for this wealthy and powerful politician. Instead, I wanted to help those still stranded in New Orleans as they struggled to cope with subhuman conditions. For the sake of these mostly poor and working-class African-American families from the lower Ninth Ward, the mostly Caucasian blue-collar residents of St. Bernard Parish (the only area in the United States to be 100 percent devastated by a natural disaster), and the elderly people who did not have the money or the transportation necessary to evacuate, I wrote on my check in big block letters, *FOR NEW ORLEANS ONLY.*

Of course, to most people of any color and background, it became readily apparent that there was a racial and class element to the tragedy: A huge population of poor, mostly African-American people had simply been deserted. They were deserted by everybody, including Mayor Ray Nagin, despite the fact that he, too, happened to be African-American. So as I watched the news, I, like a lot of people, was still struggling with my anger and my pain, along with a growing determination to do *something* that could really make a difference.

"This is not enough," I said to Chris, who was watching the devastation with me. "I don't know what the answers are, but this is not enough."

Finding a Way to Help

As things turned out, we were both blessed, because events soon came together to give Chris and me the chance to help. When Katrina struck, *The Oprah Winfrey Show* was on hiatus, but like all of us in America, Oprah was watching the Superdome in horror and disbelief. Then she made the decision to come back on the air and offer concrete, immediate help. Oprah and her team called upon her well-known friends to not only report on the storm but to do the hard work, too. They were brilliant in the way they used celebrities to bring awareness to the masses and joy to the hurricane victims as well as promoting ways that we could all get involved and help. Luckily for us, Chris was one of the people she asked to participate.

By the time Oprah was involved, the authorities had begun busing people to the Houston Astrodome, so the show sent Chris to Houston. The Red Cross was in charge of that particular operation and I remember Chris calling me and saying that he felt the organization was doing an exceptional job. The Red Cross has had its fair share of bad press due to mismanagement, disagreements among board members, and frequent turnover. And though to this day I do not think they did their job in New Orleans at all, I was grateful and relieved that Chris gave them high marks in Houston, where he said the Astrodome wonderfully organized, clean, and equipped with every necessary service.

It was a massive undertaking, for sure. Volunteers from everywhere had poured in, eager to help, and the Red Cross was coordinating them all. People needed all the usual kinds of help after a catastrophe—food, clothing, shelter, money, new IDs, and of course, all sorts of necessary items for their babies and kids: diapers, medicine, pacifiers, cribs, and toys.

The displaced people were also getting support in the form of yoga, acupuncture, and massage, which I'd like to think helped them cope with the horrific trauma and stressful aftermath of what they'd just been through. It was also an awesome way for these particular specialists to contribute. Computer programmers also came in handy, doing intake, ensuring that each person in the Astrodome was accounted for, and making records available to the government of Houston, which would soon realize that it had many new residents who could not go home to New Orleans. To my mind, Katrina was a national disgrace, as far as our government went, but seeing how many ordinary people were committed to helping out made me feel proud of my fellow citizens.

Besides the Astrodome, Chris also went to report on—and serve meals at—a food pantry that was helping to feed the hungry. He also went to an extraordinary facility called Bonita House of Hope. When he got back home, he gave me the card of the man who ran it and said, "You should call this guy."

So without knowing much more than that, I did. "Hello," said the message I left on his answering machine. "This is Malaak Compton-Rock. My husband was just at your facility, and he asked me to give you a call. He said that what you're doing is exceptional and that maybe there's something we can do to help."

The man, Tyrone Evans, called me back the following day from his car. "Thanks for calling," he told me. "We need everything."

I'd heard lots of urgent pleas for help but I needed him to be specific. "What do you mean, everything?" I asked. "Can you tell me exactly what you need and for how many people?"

"We need everything you could imagine," Tyrone repeated patiently. "Every imaginable item, we need."

"Tell me what you're doing exactly," I said. And then I listened to his story with amazement—and pride.

Basically, Tyrone had started Bonita in 1995 as a transitional facility for men. A recovering drug addict himself, though one who'd been clean for many years, Tyrone understood how much support people need to restart their lives. Men could come to Bonita and live in a structured environment while they were getting treatment until they were ready to move on.

After ten years of running Bonita, Tyrone was about to close the facility because he'd successfully raised the funds to open a brand-new treatment center for women, where mothers could actually live with their children while seeking treatment. I loved the idea that female addicts wouldn't have to abandon their kids while they got help, and I also liked hearing about the facility's apartment-living format, supported by a nursery school, cafeteria, and educational program. The new center was just a phenomenal facility, but to complete payment and then have the budget to run it, Tyrone needed to sell the first center.

He had actually received an offer the week before Katrina hit and was ready to make the sale. Then the storm swept through the gulf, and Tyrone learned that the authorities were busing survivors to Houston by the thousands, although there wasn't really anyplace to put that many people for a long period of time. The Astrodome could never be more than just a temporary refuge—where would people go after that?

Tyrone decided right then and there to let them live at Bonita. After all, the facility still had four walls and a roof. With such dire need, how could he do otherwise? Once he put the word out, the city immediately began to send families to the facility.

But if Bonita House of Hope had walls and a roof, that was pretty much all it had. When Tyrone closed the facility in order to sell it, he had emptied it of pretty much anything that made it livable. There were no beds, no sheets, no towels, no furniture or dishes. And of course, there were no disposable supplies either: no toilet paper, toothpaste, diapers, or soap. So when Tyrone said he needed everything, he meant it.

If there was ever a time that speed was of the essence, this was it. So I did something I had never done in this particular way—I relied on my husband's famous name and let him do the talking.

Now, everyone who knows my husband and me knows that I do all the talking in the relationship! The only place he talks more than me and better than me is onstage. So you *know* this was some kind of emergency. "Honey," I said to Chris, "we need to call retailers, and we need to get the highest person quick and fast and in a hurry. So when I make those calls, I'm going to say, 'Hello, may I speak to the president or the CEO, please? I have Chris Rock on the line.'"

We were fortunate to get an enormous amount of donations right away. We called Babies "R" Us, which donated every baby item you can imagine—cribs, car seats, blankets, crib mattresses, walkers—plus all the supplies a parent needs: diapers, wipes, bibs, bottles, baby shampoo, baby lotion. They not only gave us what we needed, they shipped it all down there immediately. We called Babystyle, a clothing store and online retailer with items for children from infancy through age three, and they also immediately shipped clothing down to Houston from their warehouse in L.A. We called Bed Bath and Beyond, which gave us all the bedding, towels, pillows, and blankets that we needed, plus every kitchen and bathroom supply you could ever think of. We called Crate and Barrel's national headquarters, and they in turn called their outlet in Houston and told them to give us enough furniture for every family.

Meanwhile, I was on the phone with a trucking company, which agreed to deliver everything for us. My cousin's resourceful husband found a warehouse company that allowed us to store some of the extra stuff until we gave it away, which we did once some of the families moved into empty apartments. We knew that with all of the Ninth Ward devastated and the rest of New Orleans's infrastructure in a shambles, many New Orleans folks would be staying in Houston for a good long time, maybe permanently. We could not give them the items from Bonita House of Hope when they successfully moved into permanent housing, because the second one family moved out another family moved in. So these donations were crucial.

I didn't forget the children. While my daughters went to their rooms and chose things of their own to give away, I got on the phone with Scholastic and got them to donate some children's books. I wanted to do something to make the children feel as though their lives hadn't stopped entirely, as though there was still pleasure and fun in the world. Children's books might not have been much, but at least the kids could dream of faraway places while their family members held them in their laps and read to them.

I was fascinated to discover the generosity of companies that I knew well as a consumer. Knowing these stores in another context, I was delighted to find that they were not only good companies but also good citizens.

The fact that companies like Bed Bath and Beyond, Babies "R" Us, Babystyle, and Crate and Barrel responded so quickly, so generously, and without the need for any public recognition was just phenomenal. Of course, I have told many people about their generosity, and now I'm telling you, along with my heartfelt hope that you, too, will frequent these retailers when you have the chance. Sure, all these companies have lots of competitors, but why not exercise your consumer power and shop at the places that value human beings and rise to the occasion when catastrophe strikes?

Passion, Strength, and Patience at the House of Hope

Soon after we sent Bonita House of Hope the donations we'd garnered, Chris and I made a second visit to Houston, just to cheer people up. I wanted to let these people know we were thinking about them. And, quite honestly, I wanted to bring some press attention to the situation as well. At this point, I still felt like the government was not doing its part. So many private citizens were, along with companies and nonprofit agencies—but where was the government?

Three months after the disaster, the people staying at Bonita House of Hope had still not been able to access their promised checks from the Federal Emergency Management Agency (FEMA). Tyrone Evans was not getting any money from the government, either, even though he was now paying for electricity and water again to keep his facility open, not to mention keeping a full-time staff on the payroll. I wanted the press to know the heroic measures he was taking and to help get the word out about how badly the government was failing him. Chris's publicist, Leslie Sloane, helped to promote our trip, and she did a fabulous job. We were fortunate that

People magazine ran a photo of Chris surrounded by residents, the Associated Press showed up, and both of us did a live remote with Anderson Cooper for CNN's *Anderson Cooper 360°*.

One of the first things I saw at Bonita moved me almost to tears. I walked into one of the apartments and there was this little girl holding a stuffed pig that Lola had sent down. She held that pig so tightly, you would have thought it was her last hope of comfort in this world. I was so proud of my daughter, who had given up one of her own favorite toys to cheer a little girl she had never even met. I couldn't wait to go home and tell her what a difference her gift had made.

Chris and I spent the day at Bonita, basically just hanging out. Although life was still pretty tough for everyone in the facility, I'd like to think we brought them at least a little joy, and I know for a fact they brought joy to *our* lives. I was very glad to let them know that we had not forgotten them. No one actually thought that Chris would ever come back—but there he was.

While we were there, I said, "Tyrone, what is the next step?"

"Money," he said succinctly.

So I started to fund-raise. I began calling up people I knew who wanted to do something and asked each of them to adopt a family. Tyrone helped me come up with a monthly budget—what exactly it cost him to house each group of people—and that's what I asked my friends to contribute.

The wonderful thing about coming up with this budget is that when people ached to help after learning of his work on *The Oprah Winfrey Show* and from the other press coverage and Tyrone was called by someone willing to give, he was able to give them a budget for his needs right away. I especially loved hearing about the small Massachusetts town that pooled its resources to sponsor a family. Eventually, the townsfolk even rented a bus and came down to meet the family personally. Several of my friends adopted families as well—but Tyrone still didn't have everything he needed.

Each Bonita apartment was a one-bedroom that had been built to accommodate at most five people. But as you probably know, many of the Katrina survivors had been separated from their family as they left New Orleans. As the people reunited, more and more family members packed into the Bonita units, sometimes as many as fourteen or fifteen.

I knew we needed to bring more attention to the people who were displaced, so I wanted to do some more public relations work. I tried to work the story without ever using the word *refugee*, which in this context I did not like. You are not a refugee inside your own country! Maybe your country has failed you, as I believe ours did, and so you had to evacuate—but you aren't a refugee. You are a citizen.

I also wanted to help with the next step, which was to help people go back to New Orleans if they could, or else move into permanent housing in Houston. Either way, people had to access their money from FEMA and find jobs with living wages, and I wanted to help with that, too. We'd need more funding, more support—and more publicity. I rolled up my sleeves and got to work.

Moving On

I cannot claim to have done even one-tenth of the work that Tyrone and his staff did for the residents. But what I did do was stay involved and lend an ear and some expertise to Bonita House of Hope whenever they needed it. Tyrone and I stayed in constant contact, talking or e-mailing at least every other day. Eventually, we started to put a plan together to help people move out of Bonita and into apartments and houses.

This second wave of housing activity was almost as difficult a problem as housing the displaced people in the first place. FEMA checks had finally started to arrive, but they weren't nearly large enough for what it actually cost to house people, and besides, just a check wasn't a sufficient response to the problem. How are you supposed to find housing and jobs in a city you've never been to before, when you've got your kids and maybe your aged parents and none of your own possessions with you?

Tyrone stepped up to fill in the gap, at least for the people at Bonita. He and his staff found places for people to go and helped to move them out, one family at a time. He literally checked out each apartment himself, making sure that the families had enough money for a couple of months of rent, that there were adequate schools close by for their children, and that they could afford the rent once they were working.

I really wanted the children to get the best schooling possible. I knew an education was more important than ever before and I did *not* want those children bused all across a city that they weren't even familiar with! How much more displacement did they have to go through?

There was yet another issue to consider. When people did find new housing, what were they supposed to do about furniture? So here is where our stored furniture came in handy. We were able to supply some families with furniture, and people who had adopted families stepped up for the rest. We then came up with several budgets based on people's ability to give. We planned for large amounts to cover rent, a used car (Houston is one of those cities where you have to drive or you will be on three buses to get to work), furniture, and incidentals. I stayed closely involved in the whole process, supporting Tyrone in his effort to find affordable apartments and making sure we helped to furnish them, because we knew that FEMA funds were not going to last forever.

Tyrone and his staff did a simply phenomenal job, and Chris and I couldn't have been more pleased. Every other year or so, we spend Christmas in St. Martin, but that year, we postponed our trip for a few days so we could spend Christmas with the Bonita residents. We went down there as quietly as we could—no press, no public relations this time—but we did bring presents. Tyrone put together a list of all the children, organized by age and sex, and we managed to purchase three presents for each child, including one gift card from Old Navy or the Gap so their parents could buy them clothes.

We also put on a spectacular Christmas party. Chris was supposed to dress up as Santa, but he just refused when he saw the suit I bought him—though at least he put on the Santa hat and took lots of pictures! We held a traditional Christmas dinner. And I had the pleasure of holding all the babies! So many times, on my service-related trips, having a child in my lap is my biggest reward. After all, what more could you ask for?

Getting the Word Out

Though we'd kept the Christmas trip quiet, I knew that if we didn't get the word out about these families, they wouldn't get the rest of the help they needed, especially since the media were now saying that "Katrina fatigue" had started to set in, unfathomable as that was to me. So I asked my friend Stacy Morrison, the editor in chief of *Redbook,* what she might be able to do.

Stacy is a tremendous supporter of everything I've ever done—not that she says yes to everything! After all, she is a talented editor and knows her magazine audience, but she always listens, and for that I am so grateful. When I told her about Bonita House of Hope, she loved the story and committed to doing a piece. Chris and I had found and funded a beautiful home for a family and helped to move them personally, but of course, the house wasn't furnished. "Will you do a story on this?" I asked Stacy. "Help us to get this house furnished—and other houses as well."

Stacy said yes but wanted an additional angle. So I turned to one of my best girlfriends, the actress and humanitarian Holly Robinson Peete, another one of my friends who has the need to give back like I do. With some friends you talk about husbands and babies; with others you talk about handbags and shoes; but with some friends you talk about politics and current events. Holly is the friend whom I can stay on the phone with for hours talking about our charitable endeavors, whom I can throw ideas around with, and who is always there when I need her. And it goes both ways. I try to support all of her wonderful endeavors and talk them up whenever I have the chance. HollyRod Foundation, anyone (www.hollyrod.org)?

Stacy loved Holly for the *Redbook* story, since her celebrity and her work for the people of New Orleans made it a natural fit. Holly met the family, helped me put up the finishing touches on the house, and took pictures for the *Redbook* story. She and I both did press organized by *Redbook*, and Holly did a wonderful story with CNN from the house. The feature story in *Redbook*, meanwhile, ended up being about three families who had moved out of Bonita House and featured beautiful photos of the professionally decorated house that Chris and I had funded. What was wonderful is that through the sponsors *Redbook* brought in and the interior designer, the family was able to choose the items they wanted for their home and have it decorated to suit their desires. The article also appealed to readers to donate funds to Bonita House of Hope so that all the other families who weren't able to receive these makeovers or didn't have sponsors could be helped.

Meanwhile, another type of New Orleans connection was brewing. Remember, although I'd been working with displaced people from that battered city, I hadn't yet been there myself since the hurricane. So I was happy to get a call from my friend Shannon Rotenberg, who used to work in the foundation department of the Hollywood agency CAA and is the current executive director of Matthew McConaughey's foundation j.k. livin. Shannon's husband is a partner at 3 Arts Entertainment, which used to be Chris's management firm, but Shannon and I had our own connection because we had similar backgrounds in service and just plain liked each other.

Shannon called to tell me that the Children's Defense Fund (CDF) was putting together a group of well-known or well-connected women. Our assignment was to go to New Orleans and view the devastation of the Ninth Ward—and then to raise a ruckus! Oh, and by the way, she said, *People* magazine would be coming along to do a feature on us. Did I want to be part of this project?

I wanted to be part of it so much that I actually flew to Los Angeles so I could travel with them. I wasn't content just to meet them in New Orleans. As soon as I could manage it, I wanted to join with this group of extraordinary women who were as outraged as I was about how we had failed so many people and who wanted to raise awareness about what had happened.

So I joined the likes of Cicely Tyson; Jennifer Garner; Reese Witherspoon; LaTanya Richardson Jackson (Samuel L. Jackson's wife and an actress in her own right); Jurnee Smollet, a phenomenal young actress and activist; Ruth-Ann Huvane (whose brother Kevin does Jennifer Aniston's publicity); Katie McGrath, a politically active woman married to TV producer J. J. Abrams; Michelle Kydd Lee, director of the CAA Foundation and an absolute dynamo who makes sure that the people who are so blessed in Hollywood give back; my dear girlfriend Holly Robinson Peete; and Marian Wright Edelman herself, among many others. The trip was really coordinated by Ruth-Ann, Michelle, and Katie, and after a lot of hard work, they found someone who agreed to donate a charter jet, so we flew out of L.A. at some crazy time—I think it was four in the morning—just so we could arrive in New Orleans by eight.

Now remember, the hurricane hit New Orleans on August 29, 2005. We landed in the city on May 8, 2006, and we couldn't believe our eyes. It was as though the storm had just hit town the previous week. We couldn't believe that so little had been done.

Our group went to a FEMA trailer park and we met with the families who were living there. Many of them had owned homes in the Ninth Ward that were now absolutely devastated. The fact that so much destruction took place in the Ninth Ward is especially sad because it is a neighborhood that is so rich in tradition. Families owned homes there and passed them down from generation to generation—and now that community was gone.

A lot of people don't realize that something like 60 percent of Ninth Ward residences were privately owned homes, while those who rented in that neighborhood had often been in the same place for fifteen years or more. People in that neighborhood kept up their homes. They just did not have flood insurance. Most people in the city hadn't thought to get flood insurance. Before Katrina, they didn't expect the levees to break.

In many ways, that was an excruciating visit. At this point, the folks had been living in these FEMA trailer parks for a very long time. We encountered a lot of depression, and I realized for the first time the extent of the mental anguish with which people were struggling. Not only were they not allowed to move back home, the government wasn't even helping them deal with the mental problems and the stress that threatened the most vulnerable among them. You could read the result in the statistics: the abnormally high rates of suicide, crime, drug abuse—everything that happens when your psyche is damaged.

I had a woman cry in my arms and tell me how depressed she was. She told me she went every day to look at her old house—a house she could walk to from the FEMA trailer park but couldn't move back into, because she didn't have the money to repair it and no one cared. I went to the temporary hospital set up in a Lord and Taylor department store, and it was the eeriest feeling, seeing the shoe department labeled "Triage." There was no electricity, no escalators; the whole facility was run by generators. Minirooms had been created out of army tents set up along the large floors.

Upstairs, where the critical-care facilities were, a makeshift waiting room had been set up in another department. Because all of us had flown in from L.A., we kept thinking that we had walked onto a movie set.

I was just so disturbed. I could not wrap my brain around the fact that this was a hospital. I didn't snap out of it until a woman who was waiting to be seen saw the look of disbelief on my face and snapped, "And whatcha gonna do about it?"

"What?" I said, barely able to focus on the woman who had spoken.

"You came and looked at us. All right. Whatcha gonna do about it?"

When Disaster Strikes . . .

"Whatcha gonna do about it?" is probably the question all of us ask ourselves when we first hear that disaster has struck somewhere else. Well, the first thing you can do is to write a check. Material support may be easy for you to give or it may represent a sizable portion of your budget. Either way, when disaster strikes, you can be sure that the need is great—and that any donation you make, of whatever size, will be vastly appreciated. To my mind, the Red Cross is the number one agency to consider. This is the disaster-relief organization that is always on the ground and moving immediately whenever anything happens. Often, the organization gets news of an impending disaster, such as a hurricane, tsunami, or series of fires, and mobilizes to be ready as soon as humanly possible.

After thirty-six hours, other organizations may have caught up, and you can donate to them if you like. Of course, not every group will be active in every disaster; for example, if there's a hurricane in Texas, UNICEF isn't going to be helping with that because it doesn't operate its disaster-relief work in the United States. So the Red Cross is really your best stop on the road to giving. Even though the organization has had some management issues, it is one of the oldest and best first responders in the nation. Just be sure to specify the exact disaster that you want your money to go to, since otherwise it can be put into general resources and might cover something else.

Use the News

Looking for organizations other than the Red Cross to donate to when disaster strikes? One good place to find names of other groups that are active in an area is on the websites of top news organizations. If you go to any of the following websites while a story is breaking, you'll find a list of disaster-relief groups to which you can donate:

CNN, www.cnn.com
MSNBC, www.msnbc.com
National Public Radio, www.npr.com
Huffington Post, www.huffingtonpost.com

If you see organizations you recognize as legitimate, feel free to simply donate. If you want to find out more about any of the groups you see, follow the research suggestions I offer in chapter 1.

What Else Can You Do?

When disaster strikes, it's easy to feel helpless. But that's a feeling we all need to resist, because in fact, there's quite a bit we can do. As we've just seen, you can always write a check for disaster relief to one of the many organizations that specialize in providing immediate help. But there are also other actions you can take. Here are a few suggestions.

1. Educate Yourself

If you want to do anything to help in a disaster-torn region, you need to really understand the needs on the ground. So the first thing you should do is pay attention to the news and read as much as possible about what's going on.

Being well-informed is generally a good idea, but it's doubly important if you intend to take action of any kind. Often, in a crisis situation especially, we can make the mistake of providing not what is truly needed, but what *we* think is needed. It's so meaningful and fulfilling to help—but for that help to mean something to the people it's intended for, it must be based on the proper research and understanding.

Most people don't realize that whenever an organization receives something that it doesn't really need, it actually costs money to store, redistribute, or simply dispose of the unneeded items. So if you want to do more than just send money, educate yourself through websites, newspapers, and the media outlets I previously mentioned.

2. Organize a Drive

If the catastrophe is a local one that has wiped out people's homes, one of the most urgent needs is simply basic necessities: food, clothing, emergency supplies, and medicine. A fantastic way to help is to organize some sort of drive among your friends, neighbors, and coworkers, or at your religious group, union, community center, or other organization. Just make sure you're collecting goods that people actually need.

Once you've figured out what kinds of goods people need, find a place where everyone can drop off their contributions. Maybe you can volunteer your home or garage, or perhaps you can find a central location in a religious building, union hall, or community center. Use your local media to publicize this location and the hours that donations are accepted. See if you can find creative ways to let people know what you're doing and how they can help.

Your next step is to find a way to get the goods to where they're needed. Shipping can be expensive, so you might need to raise some money to send your donations. But you may be able to find a cheaper way. If you're collecting things for another country, check with the local consulate or immigrant association to find out whether trucks, ships, or planes are already headed to the disaster area and might perhaps be able to take a few extra boxes.

Sometimes, too, such shipping companies as FedEx and United Parcel Service (UPS) will take goods into areas where they're already sending planes. You can check on those companies' websites and with international relief organizations to find out, or make a phone call and see if you can talk them into helping. Sometimes local trucking companies are already doing runs, and with a little research, you may be able to locate them.

I know that after Hurricane Katrina hit, many of my friends were collecting clothes, food, and medicine in New York and then finding trucks that were already going down to New Orleans and were willing to add some extra weight to their load. In New York, one friend made cold calls and found four trucking companies that agreed to carry extra goods free of charge. It was a beautiful example of how when disaster strikes, people are eagerly seeking a way to help. Don't be shy about picking up the phone and calling local trucking companies for help.

If you are sending goods to a disaster area, make sure you have an agency that's prepared to accept delivery or a location where goods can be picked up in a timely way. The Red Cross and some local organizations are logical candidates. Be sure that whoever you're sending the goods to can actually use what you're donating and has the facilities to distribute or store them. Otherwise, again, you could do more harm than good.

3. Collect Money

Often, the simplest way to help is also the most effective: cold, hard cash. That way, disaster-relief agencies can use their own judgment about what they need and they've got the flexibility to respond moment to moment.

You can get creative about how to raise money: "parties with a purpose"; bake sales; phone calls to friends; speeches at churches, synagogues, or mosques. You can also involve your children, who might collect money from their friends, make things to sell, start a lemonade stand, or find some other way to pitch in. (See chapters 2, 3, and 4 for more ideas on how to raise money, with or without your kids' help.)

4. Help the First Responders

When disaster strikes in the United States, the first people on the ground are known as first responders. These may be people from private organizations or from government agencies, such as the fire department. Either way, the first responders are out there twenty-four hours a day, and they need food and other kinds of support to make them comfortable.

I remember how helpless I felt in the first hours after 9/11 because I could not find a way to really help that made me feel like I was a part of the event. Like most people in the area, I couldn't get down to Ground Zero, but I could go to the places where first responders went to rest and recuperate: a convention center in midtown New York, areas set up within reach of the disaster area, sites where the Red Cross was operating. My friend Lauren Pemberton and I would make sandwiches on the weekend and take them down, knowing that volunteers would be distributing them to rescue workers. Watching the news, I discovered that people needed socks and support pads to ease their bleeding feet, so we took up a collection to buy some of both and then dropped them off. It wasn't much, but it felt good to be doing something.

5. Volunteer

In many cases, you can actually go to a disaster area and pitch in—always with the reminder that you should check with an agency and make sure it needs the kind of help you're able to offer; never just show up!

Once again, the American Red Cross will likely be your first call, as they coordinate volunteers. In fact, most of their force is volunteers. They usually have shifts you can sign up for, anywhere from a week to a month. Let them know what skills you have or that you're willing to do anything that's needed (if you are).

Finally, if you're looking to volunteer in a disaster area abroad, you might try to contact local immigrant groups from that area. Those kinds of "self-help" societies are the first place immigrants contact after a disaster, seeking to find out what happened to their family and friends back home, and they may well be able to steer you to people in a disaster-struck country who would welcome your help. Check the Yellow Pages, search online, or look for a local church, synagogue, or mosque with an immigrant-based congregation.

Now, again, I don't want you just running down to a disaster area at the first alarming news story. Do your homework first. Otherwise, you might be putting yourself in danger and you could definitely get in the way. As good as it feels to offer your help, people on the ground might very well prefer your money or donations to your labor. If you want to be effective, take the time to find out how. You'll be glad you did—and more important, the people you're trying to help will be glad, too.

Volunteers (Still) Needed in New Orleans!

It's been several years since Hurricane Katrina hit, but volunteers are still needed to rebuild after the devastation throughout the gulf coast. If you'd like to help out, here are a few groups you might consider donating labor or money to. While a family vacation to a construction site may be a bit unusual, it's a terrific way to introduce your kids to the joys of service.

St. Bernard Project, www.stbernardproject.org
Founded by volunteers Liz McCartney and Zack Rosenberg, this is an organization helping to rebuild one of the most devastated communities in New Orleans. After Hurricane Katrina, according to the St. Bernard Project website, 100 percent of the homes in low-lying

St. Bernard Parish were rendered uninhabitable. When Liz and Zack came down after the 2005 storm, they intended to help out for a few weeks at most. Instead, they ended up founding an organization that they're still deeply involved with—and that you, too, can become part of, even for a few days.

Habitat for Humanity, www.habitat.org

This nationwide organization, founded by Nobel Prize–winner President Jimmy Carter, builds houses for low-income people who need homes, so it's natural that they've become active in the gulf coast area after Katrina and the other devastating storms of the past few years. You can pretty much count on them to be anywhere that people need housing, but if you're especially interested in helping out in Louisiana, Mississippi, or Texas, give them a call or check out their website.

Relief Spark, www.reliefspark.org

Relief Spark provides a unique way to enjoy the sights and sounds of New Orleans through "voluntourism." They provide posts to rebuild homes, serve/deliver meals, or rescue animals. At night, they offer city tours, events, and dinners for visiting volunteers. What a great way to see the city!

Taking a Stand

When that woman in the New Orleans hospital asked me, "Whatcha gonna do about it?" I didn't know how to answer her aloud. But inside, I was saying to myself, "I'm gonna scream, I'm gonna raise bloody hell, I'm gonna go back and tell everyone I know. . . ." But mainly I thought, "I am going to do something that will make a big difference here."

A seed was planted for me when I was in New Orleans with the CDF group and learned that a Freedom School was to be established in the Ninth Ward but that the project had stalled for lack of funds.

Freedom Schools are a project of the Children's Defense Fund. They've been operating since 1992 as havens for poor children.

In the summer, they're open all day long; during the school year, they stay open after school. Their goals include helping children experience what they call the "five essential components: high quality academic enrichment; parent and family involvement; civic engagement and social action; intergenerational leadership development; and nutrition, health and mental health."

I think the schools operate on an absolutely tremendous model. The staff are all trained Freedom School workers—known as Ella Barker trainees, after the civil rights activist. Each day when the children arrive, before homework, tutoring, meals, reading, or counseling, they participate in Harambe, which in Swahili means "working together in unity." At the Freedom Schools, Harambe is a wonderful upbeat call-and-response sing-along that is filled with phrases to inspire confidence and pride. As part of the schools' health component, kids have access to doctors and dentists through mobile vans, while parents are supported through mental health services.

I believe so wholeheartedly in the Freedom School program that I'd like to share with you the core beliefs of the schools and of all CDF youth programs:

- All children are capable of learning and achieving at high standards.
- Culture and community conditions influence child learning.
- Appreciation and knowledge of one's culture engenders self worth and the ability to live in community with others.
- Education, teachers, and mentors are transformative agents.
- Literacy is essential to personal empowerment and civic responsibility.
- Effective teaching requires planning, creativity, and implementation, with reflection and processing.
- Learning communities that offer a sense of safety, love, caring, and personal power are needed for transformative education.
- Classroom discipline and management are integral parts of instructional practice.

- Parents are crucial partners in children's learning and need support to become better parents.
- As citizens, children and adults have the power to make a difference in their communities and be advocates for themselves.

CDF had acquired a storefront in the Ninth Ward that would make a lovely school, and we even had a ribbon-cutting ceremony to celebrate its acquisition, but the resources were not there to begin the program for these children who were so devastated by the storm. Meanwhile, our group had the chance to be part of a tremendous question-and-answer session with children and their parents who had come back to the city, or who had never left, and were still suffering tremendously. I heard stories so horrible that they froze my blood. Some people had gone without their heart medication or their diabetes medication because their doctors had left the city and they could not refill their prescriptions. Even more disturbing were the parents whose children had chronic illnesses, such as cancer, but whose doctors had left the city and who no longer had ATM cards even if the pharmacies had been open to sell them the medications their children needed. It was just a complete breakdown on every level—and ten months after the storm, it seemed almost as bad as ever. Something had to be done.

Reaching for the Stars

Our group had flown out from Los Angeles in a kind of celebratory mood. After all, we were a group of blessed women embarking together in a passionate desire to make a difference.

Our flight back was an entirely different matter. We were all quiet, and when we did talk it was about what we had seen and what we could do to help. All of us who went on that trip have done something since then, and I have to admit, I'm proud of us for that.

Reese Witherspoon and Jurnee Smollet, for example, joined the board of the Children's Defense Fund. Other people sent checks. Holly Robinson Peete, LaTanya Richardson Jackson, and I were all saying that we have a special responsibility, not just as women and as mothers, but as African-American women. We are so fortunate because of the way our lives have gone—and we needed to do something about New Orleans.

So I called up Dr. Jean Middleton-Hairston, national director of the CDF Freedom Schools program, whose friends all call her Doc. "Okay, Doc," I said to her. "What do you need to get the Ninth Ward Freedom School really open and running?"

Doc sent me over a budget showing what it would cost to open the school and keep it running for a year: $180,000. I thought, "That's all? Really? That's all? We can raise that and we will raise that."

So LaTanya, Holly, and I sat on Holly's floor one day in L.A. and wrote letters to all of our friends, asking each of them to give $10,000. Of course, each of us kicked in $10,000 as well. We strategically chose African-American women like us who had substantial resources because of the grace of God and because they or someone in their family had had great financial success. We also wanted the Children's Defense Fund to be able to use us as an example of how African-American women were pitching in to help the children of New Orleans.

Our group had the same who's-who quality as the initial delegation of CDF women, and I was proud to be a part of it. Among those who contributed were

- the amazing pianist Pauletta Washington, whose husband is Denzel Washington
- Erica Reid, a phenomenal mother and concerned citizen, whose husband is the legendary record executive L.A. Reid—and who is one of my best friends
- philanthropist Juanita Jordan
- Grammy-nominated gospel singer DeLeon Sheffield, whose husband, Gary, played professional baseball
- Tonya Lewis Lee, a lawyer, author, and activist whose husband is Spike Lee

- expert art collector Kathryn Chenault, who is also a noted philanthropist and whose husband, Kenneth Chenault, is president of American Express
- lawyer and philanthropist Carol Sutton-Lewis, whose husband, William M. Lewis Jr., is cochairman of investment banking for Lazard Ltd.
- successful TV show creator and producer Yvette Lee Bowser
- motivational speaker Pat Smith, a beautiful mother whose husband is the legendary football player Emmitt Smith

The next time I talked to Doc, our conversation was simple. I said, "Okay, I have the $180,000 you needed. Holly, LaTanya, and I kept our promise and worked to get it together for you. I am FedExing it to you from L.A.—what's your address?"

There was a brief silence at the other end of the line. I could tell that Doc was simply overwhelmed—and overjoyed. The Ninth Ward Freedom School continues to this day and all of us who donated are so proud of this fact. As African-American mothers, we are beyond grateful to God that he gave us the wisdom and the resources to help the children of the storm the way that we did.

I have continued to help New Orleans recover in any way that I am asked to. I have partnered with the Essence Music Festival on two occasions to raise awareness and funds, and I continue to visit New Orleans on behalf of the Children's Defense Fund and recently took the Journey for Change kids to rebuild houses with the St. Bernard Project in St. Bernard Parish. And you know what? I will be there until they do not need us anymore. And as we approach the five-year anniversary of the disaster, I am here to tell you, they need us. Join me!

MY JOURNEY: JOURNALIST SOLEDAD O'BRIEN

Another person who realizes that Hurricane Katrina not only wreaked havoc on the city of New Orleans the day of the storm but continues to cause pain to the residents is CNN Worldwide anchor and special correspondent Soledad O'Brien. Her reporting during the storm and her coverage since the storm have won her legions of fans who are thankful for her in-depth coverage. I am proud to call her a friend and am appreciative that she agreed to chat with me recently when we were in New Orleans together for the 2009 Essence Music Festival.

Q. When did you first arrive in New Orleans to report on Hurricane Katrina?
A. I arrived five days after the storm hit. I felt like I was in a totally abandoned city. I live in New York and on Saturdays the financial district feels eerily quiet. New Orleans, a normally vibrant city, felt like that too.

Q. What exactly did you see?
A. I always say it was like a war zone, but I have never been in a war zone, so I am not quite sure I can say that. But for me, it felt as close to a war zone as anything I could imagine. There were trees down everywhere, rubble in the streets, military patrolling, and injured and dead people everywhere. It was just so bizarre to walk through the empty streets when normally they are teeming with people.

Q. Were the residents who were abandoned in their homes still at the convention center when you arrived in New Orleans?
A. No, after all of the coverage of seeing poor, elderly, and largely African-American people living in such squalor at the convention center, the buses had finally come to evacuate them to other cities. There were some people still there, but by and large they were people who had serious mental issues and injuries. But what I do remember when I was walking around the convention center was a dead body in front of gate C covered in a blood-splattered blanket. And when I went back two days later, the body was still there.

Q. Who do you think is to blame for the many lives lost because of the terrible or nonexistent evacuation plan?

A. Clearly the response was terrible. There was a lack of understanding of the population and the number of people who had no money to leave. History should have made the officials aware that people would stay as well. The fact that Mayor Ray Nagin told people to "grab an ax" if they stayed instead of putting together a plan to get them out was ridiculous to me. There was a failure on the national level as well. We had a FEMA director, Michael "Brownie" Brown, who was so out of touch it was mind-boggling. I remember Paula Zahn interviewing him about what was happening in New Orleans and he was completely unaware. Ten hours later, there was still no response. This has really stuck with me.

Q. As a reporter, what were you trying to get across to your viewers when you first arrived?
A. To me a story is about people and only about people. It was important for me to find people who wanted to share their stories with the world. If you do not get at the heart of the matter by actually talking to those affected, you might as well just have a wide shot. And I am telling you, that would not have been effective. So I set out to tell stories through the voices of the actual people harmed by the storm.

Q. Tell me more about your coverage.
A. I was one of the first reporters to go into St. Bernard Parish. The parish had been 100 percent devastated. The parish was literally wiped off the face of the earth. This is something that normally only a tornado could do. The fact that water was the source is just so unimaginable. I was introduced to the sheriff of St. Bernard Parish by the sheriff of Jefferson Parish. I took a helicopter with him to reach the parish because you could not enter it any other way. Mind you, normally it would be a ten-minute drive from the lower Ninth Ward. It was just so chilling to be there and I am proud of my ability to report from this very isolated area. Because you could get to the lower Ninth Ward and report from the convention center, that was primarily what you saw on the news, but there were many parishes that we could not get to in order to show the world that some of these residents were abandoned too.

Q. Do you think that the response was racially motivated?
A. Yes and no. As I already said before, the people who were largely at that convention center, who were treated so badly for so many days, were black. But the residents of St. Bernard Parish are and were mostly white people. And many of them did not evacuate and were struggling after the storm. You could not get to the parish. Logistically it was impossible. Things might have been seen in a different light if we could have reported their stories right away.

Q. Why did you stay in New Orleans so long and why have you continued to tell stories related to Hurricane Katrina?
A. Like I said, a story is about the people. And when I hear compelling stories, which I still do based on the storm, I will try and tell them. My initiative Children of the Storm and documentary *One Crime at a Time* demonstrate my continued commitment to covering stories out of New Orleans.

Q. Are you proud of your reporting?
A. Yes, I am. I was initially in New Orleans for two weeks. People know this. Now when I walk through airports, people come up to me and thank me for the coverage. I am proud, sad, and emotional all at the same time. People trust you with their stories and it is a huge responsibility. People kept coming up to me and continue to come up to me wanting me to tell their story. The moment felt momentous. I knew I was a part of something really big and life-altering. I felt like as a reporter, I went to a new level because I was doing something incredibly important. People still scribble me notes of thanks and tell me not to quit and keep up the great work. It is a tremendous compliment but comes with a lot of pressure. I have to report with honesty, integrity, and with the knowledge that the people of Katrina are watching me.

Chapter 6

Citizens of the World

■

Be the change you want to see in the world.
—MAHATMA GANDHI

I'm always struck by how strongly people feel about where they want to serve—and where they don't. Often people ask me, "Why do you help internationally when we have so many problems here at home?" But then there are those who wonder why I focus my attention on issues in the United States when there are so many more pressing problems abroad.

I personally think very globally, and because I live by the philosophy that "it takes a village," I feel it's my personal duty to help *wherever* there's a need. I *do* work a lot abroad, but I also work within this country—often within an hour or less of where I live.

So I don't have a problem with people saying either one of those things. There are severe problems at home and severe problems abroad, and at the end of the day, it's not a contest. Work in one area or the other or in some combination of both, but whatever you do, don't feel guilty! If you're serving in some way, you have the right to feel good about yourself. And if you're able to discover the mode of service that speaks to the truest part of yourself, then you'll know the joy of giving—and you'll be far more likely to stay in it for the long haul.

But I would like to share with you why I love serving in other countries and why I believe in it so deeply. I believe that if you care about people, you should care about *all* people. And if you really believe that we are all part of this human race, all global citizens, then it makes sense to care about all people and to help people anywhere in the world.

Certainly, the individuals who receive your time, money, and support appreciate it. But I also think each of us benefits when we serve internationally. There are the cultural benefits, such as learning more about another way of life and understanding other parts of the world in a more in-depth way. Even more important, I think we come to feel that the world is a warmer, friendlier place and that we are part of a human family that sustains us all.

Since I left the U.S. Fund for UNICEF, my main international focus has been South Africa, specifically the township of Soweto and especially Diepsloot, a shantytown in Johannesburg. So even though I'm working in another country, in a sense it's very local, hands-on work: sitting in the shanties of granny-led households and households led by orphans and vulnerable children, finding out what they need and figuring out how to get it to them. I don't know why I feel so deeply at home in those neighborhoods, but I do, and I know that sense of connection has helped to give my work whatever effectiveness it has had.

Certainly, we all need to feel that sense of connection, however briefly, in order to donate, serve, or volunteer at all. I was so struck, during the week after the 2004 tsunami, to see that, contrary to the popular myth, Americans cared very deeply about what was happening abroad. Our then-president, George W. Bush, started a commission to raise money for tsunami relief and asked former presidents George H. W. Bush and Bill Clinton to jointly head the commission, making public appeals for Americans to help the millions of families who were devastated by the tragedy. Their advocacy included a website that enabled Americans to send donations that would go directly to meet the needs of the people.

As I read about this union, I thought what a historic moment it was to have two former presidents, one Democrat and one Republican, come together to help people in a region halfway around the globe. I asked myself what had made so many Americans give so generously to people so far away, and I thought it might be at least partly a result of how the news media covered the catastrophe.

The media coverage extended past the extraordinary number of deaths to encompass the human side of the story, too: how many people had lost their livelihood and their home; how many villages and towns and even cities had been destroyed. Americans responded not only to the need for food and medicine but also to the import-ance of rebuilding the infrastructure of village and urban life.

Perhaps, too, because the world *has* grown smaller and because of the beauty of Thailand, many Americans were in south Asia dur-ing the tsunami, which took their lives along with those of local res-idents. As a result, many of us lost loved ones in the catastrophe, knew someone who did, or at least heard stories about the deaths of many Westerners. Nate Berkus, the talented interior designer who appears regularly on *The Oprah Winfrey Show* and was host of *Oprah's Big Give,* lost his longtime partner in the tsunami—and went on to promote the needs of the region's people on *Oprah.* Pe-tra Nemcova, the Victoria's Secret model, lost her fashion photogra-pher boyfriend. Many less well-known Americans were there, too, on business or for the winter holidays.

Numerous other Americans were firsthand witnesses to the tsunami, so they were able to come back and tell us about the har-rowing sights they had seen. These testimonies gave a personal di-mension to the catastrophe and maybe made it more "relatable" for many Americans.

Certainly, more Americans gave in response to the tsunami than to any other natural catastrophe in the history of this country, with many new donors who had never given before. If something good *can* come out of a tragedy like that, maybe it's that we joined to-gether as global citizens to cry and mourn for the people whose lives were devastated by the tsunami—but more important, to give in ways we never had before.

South Africa: My Second Home

Although today it seems inconceivable to me that there ever was a time I *hadn't* been to South Africa, I actually made my first trip there just a few years ago, in 2005. The trip was originally planned as a va-cation only, but as you've read, I loved working at the U.S. Fund for

UNICEF and I've remained very close to the organization. Whenever I travel, whether for work or pleasure, if there's a UNICEF-assisted project in the vicinity, I make sure to visit it if I possibly can. And it was the UNICEF portion of the trip that connected me to the country most deeply.

My family and I went to South Africa during Christmas vacation to visit Cape Town and Johannesburg, with safaris planned for the Madikwe Game Reserve and the Sabi Sands Game Reserve in Kruger National Park. I had always wanted to visit South Africa, but I must admit that the true catalyst for the trip was Oprah Winfrey, who had been visiting the country for many years and had also fallen in love with its beauty and history, but more important, its people. At the time, she was building the Oprah Winfrey Leadership Academy for Girls. Though Chris and I do not see Oprah a whole lot, it seemed that whenever we did, we would end up talking about South Africa and Nelson Mandela. I remember her telling us very pointedly one time that if we had the ability to meet this great man, then it was our duty to do so, and of course, I couldn't have agreed more.

I was inspired by the new nation that was being built after apartheid had been once and for all defeated. South Africa is a beautiful nation filled with a juxtaposition of gorgeous landscapes, wide savannas, tall skyscrapers, rolling countryside, sandy beaches, crowded markets, tin shantytowns, farmland, traditional homesteads, and monuments that detail the painful past of the country and pay tribute to the country's many strong and brave freedom fighters.

Of course during our visit we had hopes of meeting the former African National Congress (ANC) leader and first black South African president, Nelson Mandela. You cannot think of the country of South Africa without feeling awe for his service to his people as a freedom fighter and head of the ANC, or without admiring his courage and dignity while in jail.

After his release from Robben Island, Mr. Mandela became the first black president of his nation—the nation that kept him in prison for twenty-eight years. But to really understand Mr. Mandela is to pay respect to the crucial human rights work that he has been doing through the Nelson Mandela Foundation since his release from prison.

Both Chris and I admire Mr. Mandela beyond words. So we put in an official request to meet him. To our delight, the whole family was invited to spend a few hours having tea with him and his wonderful wife, Ms. Graça Machel, at Mr. Mandela's farm in his home province, Eastern Cape.

That day goes down as one of the best days of my life. Together, our family took the ninety-minute flight down from Johannesburg to the airport nearest the Mandela farm, which is located close to the place where Mr. Mandela was born and is where he stays when he is not in Johannesburg. Since it was Christmastime, he was spending the holidays in the country with his entire family, including his children and grandchildren. The kids happened to be big fans of Chris, so that was fun for all of us. Chris was amazed that they all wanted to take pictures with him when we were the ones in awe of being in Mr. Mandela's home, having such a good time with his family.

I was also so grateful to have tea and time to chat with Graça Machel, a beautiful and brilliant woman who works tirelessly on behalf of the people of her adopted country of South Africa and her home country of Mozambique, where she was once that country's first lady. I knew a lot about Ms. Machel's work because she is an avid supporter of UNICEF and while I worked there wrote one of UNICEF's most respected reports, "The Impact of Armed Conflict on Children," so we had a wonderful conversation about that.

Though our tea was scheduled to last only half an hour, we were thrilled to spend almost two hours with the family. And we had the extraordinary luck to be there when Mr. Mandela's official photographer was taking candid shots of the day. So as a memento, I have really great pictures that I will treasure always.

The story of those pictures is actually sort of funny. As you can imagine, I lectured my children the whole time we were flying to the countryside that they were visiting a hero, a former president, a Nobel Peace Prize winner, and one of the most respected men in the world. So they had to be on their best behavior and have impeccable manners, which I ended up calling "Nelson Mandela manners."

And now when I need them to have flawless manners, to this day I say, "I want Nelson Mandela manners, girls," and they know Mommy is not playing.

Of course, being the little children that they were—only two and four at the time—they did not have a clue as to who we were meeting. Other than having great fun adding sugar to their tea and mixing in the milk, they found the rest of it rather boring, except when I had to run after them when they decided they wanted to go "play" in Mr. Mandela's private office. But Mr. Mandela loves children and Lola loves attention, so Chris and I had an amazing time watching her hug the great man and sit on his lap while he played and chatted with her.

Two-year-old Zahra was another story. Whenever Mr. Mandela asked for a hug, she actually told him, "No." I kept thinking to myself, "One day you are going to regret this, child!" because for an entire hour, he tried to coax her into his arms to no avail. Of course, I was telling the photographer, "I cannot believe my child will not take a picture with Mr. Mandela. Can you imagine that I am going to miss this opportunity to have this keepsake for life?"

Finally, Zahra got into the fun and decided that she liked playing with Mr. Mandela. She would even scoot forward half an inch every time she was asked. So I have the most wonderful series of photos of Zahra inching toward Mr. Mandela, both with smiles on their faces, ending with Zahra finally on his lap! That photo is prominently and proudly displayed in my home.

Throughout most of the visit, Chris was for once in his life completely speechless. He was thinking, "What is a comedian from Brooklyn going to say to the most respected man in the world?" He likes to tease me that I was chatting away with Graça Machel about human rights while he was nervous and tongue-tied. But Mr. Mandela was as hospitable as you can imagine and did everything he could to put us at ease.

Finally our magical afternoon was over and we flew back to Johannesburg. I had called my old boss Chip Lyons, who at the time was the president of the U.S. Fund for UNICEF and asked him to set up an official visit for us to see the projects that UNICEF was running in Johannesburg. The way our schedule worked out, we made that visit as we returned from the Mandelas' farm, calling on a few different UNICEF-assisted programs.

I remember one of the first visits was to an orphanage, which I found to be so heartbreaking. South Africa, like many African nations, has a very strong family structure, and traditionally, a child who had any relatives at all could count on being taken care of. But the devastation that HIV/AIDS is wreaking on the continent has put an intolerable burden on African families. Hence, large numbers of children are filling up orphanages and group homes as never before. One thing that made the visit tolerable is that the children were being cared for in a lovely and clean setting by workers who clearly loved them and took amazing care of each child. Other children are able to stay with family when their grandmothers or great-grandmothers take them in or when they serve as heads of their own households. The official terms for these arrangements are "granny-led" and "orphan-led" households. We visited with families like these at our final stop of that day, Diepsloot, an illegal shantytown of two hundred thousand residents crammed into a small area a stone's throw away from where I was staying in a beautiful hotel. At the time, UNICEF was helping to run a project to support granny-led households and was also running programs for orphaned and vulnerable children.

As so often happens on UNICEF visits, and really all visits in Africa, the children created an amazing greeting, singing and welcoming us. Within minutes, my children were playing with the local kids, running up the steps of an old, rickety, and dangerous-looking slide in a community-center playground, shrieking with glee as they slid down together.

While the kids played, Chris and I heard from the grannies, who told us how they were struggling to raise their grandchildren after their own kids had died of AIDS. As far as I'm concerned, the grannies are the unsung heroes of the continent, for they selflessly care for their grandchildren and sometimes great-grandchildren after burying their own children. They manage to keep their families together, despite old age, exhaustion, illness, and lack of resources, including, most important, money. So many communities would fall completely apart if it weren't for the many grandmothers caring for their families with few resources but a lot of love. Half the world's population lives on two dollars a day, and that is certainly the case in Diepsloot, where two to four dollars a day is the average income.

I thought of those numbers as we spoke with the grannies, wondering where they found the strength to keep on. Of course, it was humbling, and after you have been exposed to these women's resilience, you feel really ridiculous when you complain about something you do not have in your own life. At least I do! I keep myself constantly in check because of my work with these families.

One of the four families we visited that day was the Skhosana family, and for some reason—I still don't know why—I felt one of those instant connections you sometimes feel with every one of the family members. As usual, I felt closest to the children, fifteen-year-old Trecious, eleven-year-old God Knows, and six-year-old Wendy. But I was also drawn to the grandmother, who was doing her best to make a good life for her grandchildren against incredible odds. Though Gogo (that is the name for grandmothers in South Africa) Skhosana does have two living children, she has lost three daughters to AIDS. She lives with her three grandchildren in a one-room shack and at the time when I met them, they did not have electricity, running water, or toilet facilities. Instead, they relied on a water pipe and a port-a-potty shared with hundreds of other families. They were lucky enough to have a couch and a chair, as well as one bed, and that is where we sat getting to know them and bonding to the point where I could not get them out of my head.

Gogo Skhosana, the grandmother, had only one working arm but was strong. In fact, she was a leader in the community, attending all of the support groups available to her. Trecious was smart and confident, but God Knows was shy and quiet. Despite a learning disability and a perennial lack of funds for school fees, he tried his best in school whenever he was able to go.

And then there was Wendy—sweet, sweet Wendy. Born infected with HIV and having lost her mother to AIDS, she remains gracious, polite, mellow, and so friendly. And through the grace of God and the help of UNICEF, the U.S. President's Emergency Plan for AIDS Relief (PEPFAR), and a local nonprofit on the ground, she is healthy because of access to the antiviral drugs that have made her disease undetectable at the moment.

That first visit passed quickly, but finally, it was time to leave. If I reached a turning point during that trip, it was as we left. When the field-workers were saying good-bye to me, one of them remarked, almost casually, "You know, we get a lot of visitors and we get a lot of high-profile visitors, but nobody really comes back. Nobody really contributes to this particular area." The rest of the workers nodded.

"No," I found myself thinking. "No. I feel like I would want to come back to this area."

Finding My Way in Diepsloot

Soon after our visit, Trecious got pregnant. Maybe she was even already pregnant but I did not know about the pregnancy until after the baby was born. Granny Skhosana wanted to show her appreciation for our visit, so when Trecious had her baby, she asked Trecious to name him Chris Rock. When I got an e-mail that there was a baby named Chris Rock, I was flabbergasted and asked for a photo.

That may have been my second turning point, because from then on, I really wanted to make a difference for this family and respond to their needs in a substantial and sustainable way. I also have to admit that I found it funny that there was a little boy named Chris Rock Skhosana in the middle of Johannesburg.

Soon after little Chris was born, the Skhosana shack burned down. This is sadly common in shantytowns: The flimsy wooden shacks catch fire easily, and the candles that are the main source of light and heat often spark a blaze. So in my first act of service toward Diepsloot, I offered the Skhosanas money to help rebuild their home and purchase necessary possessions. The NGO working directly with the family outlined a budget of their needs and I was able to wire the money immediately. I felt very fulfilled when they again had a roof over their heads, no matter how minimal.

So their most immediate needs were met, but I wondered how I could continue to offer my support most effectively.

First, I wanted to help out with the kids' schooling, because like most African nations, South Africa has no public education system. Not only does it cost money to go to school, you also have to purchase your own uniform, shoes, book bag, and supplies. So I agreed to pay all school-associated expenses for Trecious, God Knows, and Wendy, and committed to pay for Chris Rock's schooling when he was old enough.

Then, after educating myself and listening to the advice of the field-workers, I understood that just helping the kids attend school was not enough. If they were to do well with their studies, they needed to eat regularly, have enough light to do their homework, and possess a thousand other necessities. So I moved on to food and incidentals, making sure that the Skhosana family had a regular income that afforded them the luxury of having electricity in their shack. Electricity makes a huge difference in the life of a shanty dweller. It allows for better cooking options and the ability to keep refrigerated items.

The problem of electricity reaches further than people realize, by the way. It's not only a matter of convenience but also directly affects the diet that people can manage on a daily basis. Because most people in Diepsloot can't afford electricity, let alone a refrigerator, their daily meals often consist only of mealie-meal (a porridge-like substance), canned beans, and tea with sugar—a very unbalanced diet. How can children do well in school when they are hungry or malnourished?

I was glad to be helping the Skhosanas, but the idea of returning to Diepsloot continued to nag at me. First, it had just about broken my heart when I'd heard the field-worker say, so calmly and flatly, that nobody ever came back. I wanted to be the one who did. And second, I was drawn to that community, though I still didn't know why. I wanted to help not just the Skhosanas but as many people as I could reach.

I knew that to truly be of service, I would need to understand far more about the community. So in 2006 I returned for a longer visit, talking with people on the ground, just walking around Diepsloot, meeting families less formally than I had before, and sitting in on support group meetings. I remember attending a group meeting for women living with HIV that addressed both their health issues and the larger question of how they were going to improve their lives.

I also met a wonderful aid worker with the Olive Leaf Foundation, a woman named Margaret Xaba. To me, all field-workers are God's angels on the ground, but Margaret is one of the most special angels. She is so patient, calm, and dedicated, and she is so deeply determined to fight for the life of her community. She inspires me every time I think about her.

When I asked Margaret about Diepsloot and her work there, she told me, "Diepsloot is an informal place where most of the necessary services are not available; for example, the clinic closes at four P.M. and if there is an emergency after four P.M. we have to take patients to neighboring hospitals. The nearest is Coronation Hospital, which is sixty kilometers [about thirty-seven miles] away. There are times when you have to render medication to children who are terminally ill and you find that there is no food in the house for the child to eat. This is a big challenge because as you know you cannot give medication on a hungry stomach. There are times when you have to provide even from your own pocket, and this is difficult because we do not make a lot of money in the relief field. There are lots of problems and we deal with each one differently, according to the need."

I could see from speaking with Margaret that it wouldn't be easy for me to grasp the problems faced by the people of Diepsloot and that I'd have to be willing to give myself some time to learn what mattered to people and what *they* thought the solutions were. That gradual immersion into the neighborhood was very important to me. I know that most people don't have the same opportunity to visit a country and spend some meaningful time there, but I recommend trying to replicate this experience any way you can.

For example, a good nonprofit will have testimonials on its website from the people it helps, so you can hear directly from the individuals who benefit from your volunteer work and your donations. A good website will also tell you in great detail the areas where the agency is working, what it is doing, who benefits, and exactly how much money is going to its service work. To help effectively, you need to have your own sense of what the problems are, what the solutions might be, and how service work can make a difference. Otherwise, it becomes very difficult to judge whether you are being useful and to sustain your desire to help. In my opinion, you should never give large sums of money in ignorance or on blind faith; you need to be a knowledgeable donor.

What was most important to me was figuring out what the people in Diepsloot needed—not what I thought they needed, but what the people themselves said they needed. That's part of the reason I went by myself and not as part of an official delegation. UNICEF had created a phenomenal first experience for me that had allowed me to learn a great deal in a very short time, but now I wanted something different: just to walk around Diepsloot and see the community for myself, talking to people and soaking everything in.

Though I was, of course, saddened by the level of poverty I saw, I found myself very happy just to walk through the narrow dirt alleys, to visit with the grannies and play with the children. "Yes," I caught myself thinking a couple of times. "I was right. This place feels like home." It didn't look like any of the places I had ever lived, and it certainly didn't resemble the neighborhood I had grown up in. Somehow, though, I had a profound connection with Diepsloot that only grew with every passing day.

I find this question of home so interesting. Why do we feel at home in some places and not in others? Why did Diepsloot speak to me so deeply, more than any other area in Africa that I had visited? Why was it Diepsloot where I felt most at home? I kept asking myself this because I have visited and worked in many other parts of Africa where the need is equally great or sometimes even greater. And though my commitment to this one South African community has not stopped me from supporting other parts of the continent through donations to other NGOs, Diepsloot has a special pull.

So though I could not answer the question of why, I did honor the profound connection I felt. Madonna has a great response when people ask her why she is so involved in Malawi, doing such phenomenal work there and even adopting a beautiful son and daughter: "I didn't choose Malawi; Malawi chose me." I feel the same way about Diepsloot.

Meanwhile, I was starting to understand the full scope of just how difficult the challenges of that neighborhood were, particularly for the grandmothers who were raising multiple grandchildren on little or no money. What the grannies kept telling me was how much they wanted to work and to have some source of income, while the field-workers who cared for the orphans wondered why so many of these abandoned children weren't getting government grants, had so little access to schooling, and had so little support for their education.

I was also struck by just how vast the HIV/AIDS epidemic is in Africa. Working the phone lines for the Gay Men's Health Crisis (GMHC), for example, had taught me volumes about AIDS and HIV, but in the United States, our focus had been on gay men and American people of color, so I was shocked to learn what a deadly and equal-opportunity killer it is worldwide. The statistics themselves are frightening: According to UNAIDS (the Joint United Nations Programme on HIV/AIDS), "an estimated 1.9 million . . . people were newly infected with HIV in sub-Saharan Africa in 2007, bringing to 22 million . . . the number of people living with HIV. Two thirds (67%) of the global total of 32.9 million . . . people with HIV live in this region, and three quarters (75%) of all AIDS deaths in 2007 occurred there." In South Africa alone, according to the World Health Organization's "Epidemiological Fact Sheet on HIV and AIDS, 2008," some 5.7 million people are living with HIV.

The raw numbers are shocking enough. But the percentages are even more disturbing. For example, more than 18 percent of all South Africans aged fifteen to forty-nine are living with the virus. These were the devastating hard facts I had to confront. How could I begin working with grannies and orphans if I did not know the history of why these vulnerable old and young people headed so many African households?

Thanks to my time at styleWORKS, I had a strong feeling for the kinds of support women needed in order to get jobs, care for their children, and move on to economic independence. But understanding these issues in New York City was very different from understanding the needs in Diepsloot, where there was no public welfare system, no public education, and really no infra-structure to effectively help the poor.

What's been clear to me in all the communities I've worked in, from New York to Diepsloot, is that most people aren't looking for handouts. People really do want to make their lives better, to sup-port themselves and their families, to have the kinds of skills and savvy that enable them to get a job, inhabit a home, expect some se-curity. They may not know how to fulfill these desires or have access to programs that can help them, but by and large, everybody wants the same basic thing: a better life for themselves and their family. And what was it going to take to achieve that goal?

The grannies needed three things: They wanted to earn an in-come to support their grandchildren, especially when it came to providing them with an education; access to healthy food on a reg-ular basis; and to obtain some ordinary necessities such as electric-ity, cleaning supplies, and hygiene products. The orphans heading households wanted to go to school and to have someone to care for their younger siblings while they were at school. And of course, they needed nutritious food as well.

I went home knowing that I had somewhere to start.

Meanwhile, as luck would have it, my family was invited by Oprah Winfrey to attend the opening of the Oprah Winfrey Leader-ship Academy for Girls and we found ourselves in South Africa again. Among the hundreds of others also attending this momen-tous occasion was my close girlfriend Holly Robinson Peete, along with her husband Rodney Peete. As Chris and I so often did, the Peetes had brought their children with them.

Given the Peetes' commitment to humanitarian causes, it's not surprising that when Holly heard about our visits to South Africa and saw my pictures of Lola and Zahra playing with the kids in Diep-sloot, she wanted her children to have a similar experience. We had a beautiful time together with their oldest two kids, eight-year-olds Ryan and Rodney Jr., bringing letters with pictures attached from their classmates to give to the kids of Diepsloot. What is especially wonderful is that the visit had the effect on all of the Peete kids that Holly wanted it to: making them aware of this other culture—and this other degree of poverty—halfway around the world. Ryan in particular continues to be highly moved to act because of this visit.

Finally, about six months later I went back to Diepsloot. And that's when everyone was really, really, *really* shocked to see me again, field-workers and residents alike. I wanted people to understand that I cared for them—and I think, maybe, on that visit, that was the message they got.

They weren't the only ones who learned something about my commitment. That visit solidified my connection with Diepsloot, too. Finally, I realized I really was in this for the long haul.

It's a Small World After All

InterAction is the largest coalition of United States–based international NGOs focused on the world's poorest and most vulnerable people. Collectively, InterAction's 172 members work in every developing country. If you'd like to donate to the people of a particular country, visit www.interaction.org and choose an organization to support. Or if you'd like to learn more about international issues, check out www.globalonenessproject.org to view the online material created by the Global Oneness Project, which is "exploring how the radically simple notion of oneness can be lived in our increasingly complex world." I love the idea of "oneness," and I'm so glad there's a website where you can explore this idea further. Enjoy!

International Involvement: Ways to Serve Our Global Family

I'd like to help you think about some ways that you, too, can serve our global family. Here are four ideas:

1. Fun with a Purpose: Volunteer Vacations

A volunteer vacation offers you a chance to visit a foreign country, such as Jamaica, Senegal, or Honduras, where you spend most of each day doing some kind of volunteer work. You get the satisfaction of knowing you've contributed, but you also get the fun and fascination of working in a country as opposed to simply being a tourist. On your days off from serving, you can take in some sights—and this will be coordinated for you as well. There are travel agents who specialize entirely in volunteer vacations and will organize the whole adventure for you, including your flights, airport pickup, housing, daily service schedule, and someone to take you to and from the work site.

Your first step is to decide whether you want to go alone, with your family, or with an organized group. You should also know how long you are able to stay in a particular country. Different agencies specialize in different types of vacations—some, for example, help seniors and retired people find appropriate trips, while others are more geared to young people—so make sure you know what you're looking for.

Whatever your choice, definitely do your homework, since not all volunteer vacations are the same. Some volunteer vacations are geared toward giving you a completely "authentic" experience, meaning you will rough it and live like the locals do. Others are designed to let you contribute while still maintaining some of the comforts you're probably used to. Either is fantastic—you just need to know the kind of person you are and the kind of vacation you want to have. Only you know your level of stamina, how exotic you want the location to be, what level of comfort you need, if you are fine sharing a house or want a private room, and what type of service work you want to do. Do you want to try something new and different or do you want to serve doing something you already know how to do?

I know one family who went on a volunteer vacation in Cambodia and had a phenomenal time. But it was extremely hard living, to say the least, and they couldn't necessarily get away from the demanding conditions when they went back to their quarters for a few hours of sleep. That would not have been the right vacation for me! After I spend all day visiting my grannies and children in Diepsloot, at the end of the day I must admit I like to take a nice shower, sleep in a comfortable bed, and enjoy indoor plumbing! I don't feel guilty about it. When I am away, I also like access to the Internet so that I can work at night, but this is not always possible and I do go without it a lot.

If more comfortable quarters are your preference, too, find a volunteer vacation where you can have the basics that you are used to. After all, aren't we working for a world in which every human being has access to clean water, sanitary plumbing, and a bed to sleep in? This is what I wish for all of my grannies.

Now, if you are a roughing-it kind of person and you enjoy outdoor activities like camping with minimal items, hiking, or skiing in the U.S. wilderness, then working and living side by side with a third-world community might be perfect for you! And sometimes, for sure, the rewards that you get out of service far exceed the hardships of the living conditions. I have experienced this myself when I totally roughed it (by my standards!)—no toilet and bugs crawling on my body while I slept—to get up close and personal with one of Africa's oldest tribes in Tanzania. I would brave the same conditions again and again for that experience.

One criticism that I have heard about volunteer vacations is that not all of them provide a genuinely helpful volunteer experience. Tourists may end up helping with tasks that they're not qualified for, working on poorly organized projects, or feeling that their vacation money might have been better spent simply paying local people to do the work that they themselves are volunteering to do. If this is a potential concern for you, again, do your homework, because this is certainly not the case with the organizations that have been planning these types of trips for a long time. As you would do with any travel agent, get a list of references from the agency and contact people who have used the company before. Also, ask the agency how it addresses these and any other issues that concern you. As with all service, you'll get more out of it if you take some responsibility to find out whatever you need to know and think about how you see your volunteer vacation going.

That said, I think volunteer vacations are a terrific way to get to know the world as a citizen rather than as a tourist. My own work is always a kind of volunteer vacation, and I feel blessed to have had the chance not just to visit South Africa as a tourist but to learn, work, and make friends there. If you're looking for a similar experience, check out the respected agencies below.

GLOBAL VOLUNTEERS

Global Volunteers (www.globalvolunteers.org), which has been operating since 1984, was one of the first groups to develop the notion of volunteer vacations. They stress the "people-to-people" model of service, outside the bounds of government, political, or faith-based groups, working only at the invitation and under the direction of local leaders. The group looks for ongoing partnerships with the host communities so that volunteers will have a genuine opportunity to serve.

Service opportunities include teaching conversational English; caring for at-risk children; painting, building, and repairing buildings; providing health-care services; working with infants and toddlers; working with young children; working with teens and adults; and working with community elders.

GLOBAL SERVICE CORPS

Founded in 1993, Global Service Corps (www.globalservicecorps .org) works in Tanzania and Thailand, focusing on community-development programs. You can volunteer for as little as two weeks or for as long as one year. Either way, your time with the program begins with an extensive orientation led by local residents or long-time expatriates. Cultural immersion is very important to this group, so you stay with a host family and have lots of chances to join in the life of the community.

Service opportunities include working in the fields of community training, international health, HIV/AIDS education and prevention, sustainable agriculture and food security, community development, and orphanage care. You also have the opportunity to teach English.

GLOBAL CROSSROAD

Global Crossroad (www.globalcrossroad.com) operates in twenty developing countries throughout Asia, Africa, and Latin America with a focus on helping the rural poor, particularly needy children in orphanages and women. It specializes in grassroots projects and cultural immersion and offers volunteers a language program, cultural tours, and village visits as part of what it calls its "mini-adventure projects." Some 90 percent of all volunteers stay with a host family. Operating since 2003, the group has tripled in size in five years. Note that unlike some of the other groups on this list, Global Crossroad's programs are for single people and students; it does not organize programs for families.

Service opportunities include community development, education, environmental work, and social welfare.

GLOBE AWARE

Offering one-week "adventures in service," Globe Aware (www.globeaware.org) thinks of itself as a "mini Peace Corps" whose projects focus on cultural awareness and on teaching skills to those who need them. Besides service opportunities, the company also offers optional cultural excursions that specialize in giving you a kind of inside look at local culture. You might spend time cooking local cuisine, singing with schoolchildren, or working on community projects. The group has been arranging cultural missions for fifteen years and organizing volunteer missions since 2000. You can serve alone, with your family, or even with a corporate group.

CROSS-CULTURAL SOLUTIONS

Cross-Cultural Solutions (www.crossculturalsolutions.org) offers a wide range of projects to volunteer with, including more than 250 community initiatives operating in partnership with local grassroots organizations. They take their work very seriously. Besides volunteering, you can also benefit from language training, listening to guest speakers, and other cultural activities, and you begin each volunteer experience with an in-depth orientation. You're also given plenty of free time and opportunities to explore on your own. You can serve solo, with your family, or with a community or corporate group.

Service includes caring for infants and children, teaching children, teaching English, assisting teachers, assisting local health officials, working with people with HIV/AIDS, caring for the elderly, caring for people with disabilities, working toward women's empowerment, and sharing your professional skills/experience.

You can learn more about volunteer vacations at the International Volunteer Programs Association (www.volunteerinternational.org) and the Association of Voluntary Service Organizations (www .avso.org).

2. Volunteer with the Peace Corps

The Peace Corps was founded in 1961 thanks to the leadership of President John F. Kennedy. Kennedy challenged students at the University of Michigan to serve their country and to work for peace by volunteering in a developing country. The idea for the Peace Corps was born, and soon there was a federal agency whose mission was to create world peace and international friendship.

The Peace Corps has continued for nearly fifty years, with more than 190,000 volunteers serving in 139 host countries, where they have worked on such issues as clean water, education, HIV/AIDS, the environment, information technology, and business development. Today, some eight thousand volunteers work in sixty-eight postings serving seventy-four countries.

Peace Corps volunteers commit for twenty-seven months, which includes vacation time. They receive a stipend intended to allow them to live at a standard of living that matches that of the people among whom they serve, along with full medical and dental care.

When their term is over, they receive an allowance of $6,000 to help them make the transition back into "civilian" life.

Anyone over the age of eighteen is eligible to apply for the Peace Corps. Although there's a minimum age, there's no maximum. People apply to the Peace Corps at all different times in their lives, but most often just after high school or college graduation, during life transitions, and perhaps at or near retirement. Miss Lillian, President Jimmy Carter's mother, served in the Peace Corps in India when she was in her seventies!

In order to serve with the Peace Corps, you fill out an application explaining your background, educational level, and skills. Although you'll be asked if you speak any languages other than English, language proficiency isn't a requirement. There's no set deadline and no set time for response, but volunteers are encouraged to apply nine to twelve months before they'd like to serve. If you're accepted, you are assigned to the country where you're most needed, based on your background and skills. Married couples can request to be assigned together, if each spouse is accepted.

People who return from the Peace Corps speak glowingly about the experience, though they usually agree with the group's slogan: "It's the toughest job you'll ever love." You might well find yourself living in a developing country at a standard of living far below what most of us are used to—maybe even below what you've ever imagined. You're working on a project intended to help the area but you may need to rally support from a local community that is sometimes resistant to what you're doing. Living among strangers from a culture so different from yours, you might feel isolated, lonely, or even depressed, especially because many areas may not have Internet connections or even phone service.

On the other hand, you have the opportunity to get to know a culture and a community at a profound level, not as a tourist or a scholar but as a service worker, devoted each day to an endeavor that could potentially improve the lives of hundreds of people. You get to discover who you are and what your home culture means to you, as well as broadening your ideas of how people live and what matters most in life. I've never met a Peace Corps worker who wasn't profoundly glad that he or she had served, nor one who didn't tell me that the experience provided an invaluable basis for the work he or she went on to do. In fact, I recently met the new U.S. consul general to South Africa, Andy Passen—and guess what? He was a Peace Corps volunteer, which he told me with enthusiasm within five minutes of meeting me. And yes, the experience shaped his entire life. Joining the Peace Corps isn't for everyone—but you may well feel lucky if you realize that it's right for you.

3. Creating Hope for Pennies a Day: Microloans

I think microcredit is an absolutely brilliant idea, and apparently the Nobel Prize committee thinks so, too. In 2006, they awarded the Nobel Peace Prize to Dr. Muhammad Yunus, founder of the Grameen Bank and international pioneer of the concept of microcredit.

Basically, microcredit involves making extremely small loans to people who need as little as one hundred to maybe five hundred dollars to start their own self-sustaining business. A woman supporting a family might use the money to buy chickens to sell, as the Diepsloot grannies were hoping to do, or buy the products necessary to produce baskets or clothing. Or a group of farmers might use the money to purchase a piece of shared equipment to run their farming business more effectively, or a man might buy a used car to start a taxi business.

As you can see, the multitude of businesses that are started through microloans knows no bounds! Microcredit reaches people who would never qualify for regular loans, don't really need to borrow large sums of money, and have no collateral. It enables poor people to become self-sufficient and to lift themselves out of poverty. The most comprehensive programs include banking lessons, home loans once a person proves self-sufficient, mentoring, and additional loans to grow the business.

Microcredit also offers a fantastic way for people in developed nations to lend their support—literally—to women and men in developing regions. If you'd like to learn more, visit the websites of some major microcredit organizations:

GRAMEEN BANK, WWW.GRAMEEN-INFO.ORG

This is the bank founded by Dr. Yunus. Its website has an extensive discussion of what microcredit is and how it works.

FINCA, WWW.VILLAGEBANKING.ORG

FINCA International provides financial services to the world's lowest-income entrepreneurs so that they can create jobs, build assets, and improve their standard of living. The vision of FINCA International is to be a global microfinance network collectively serving more low-income entrepreneurs than any other microfinance institution while operating on commercial principles of performance and sustainability. FINCA today reaches 725,000 clients in twenty-one countries.

KIVA, WWW.KIVA.ORG

Kiva specializes in person-to-person microlending. You go to its website and read about an individual who needs a loan, perhaps as small as $25. You browse entrepreneurs' profiles, choose someone to lend to, and then receive information about your recipient's progress over the six to twelve months it takes for the loan to be repaid. When your money comes back to you, you can decide to lend it out again to somebody else!

4. Fair Trade, Fabulous Gifts

Do you need the perfect gift for someone special? Maybe a gorgeous handmade knitted item, an extravagant box of chocolates, a decadent container of fresh coffee, or an exquisitely crafted handbag? By buying fair-trade goods, you can give these items and many others while also ensuring that the artisans and farmers are being given fair wages for their incredible work. And you can feel your own connection to people halfway around the world whose lives you are touching as you enjoy the products that they made.

Fair trade is a term that refers to the conditions under which products are grown, made, and sold. The concept comes out of the concern that when developed countries buy raw materials or crafts from developing nations, the trade takes place on unfair terms, since companies in the developed nations are powerful enough to call all the shots. This often leads to low wages, poor working conditions, and an unjust system in which workers have few or no rights.

Fair trade, by contrast, suggests that wages are fair, workplaces are safe and healthy, and workers have rights. The term has also come to suggest that the enterprises in developing nations are receiving the financial and technical support they need and are sustainable in the local environment, while the workers' cultural identity is respected.

To me, fair trade is a crucial part of balancing our relationships with people in other parts of the world. You can support fair-trade by buying products from fair-trade companies. For some great ideas about fair-trade products, like coffee, chocolate, and crafts, see the resource section, but here's the story of one of my favorite organizations supporting fair trade.

The Art of Fair Trade: Original T-Bag Designs

Original T-Bag Designs is run by a group of South African women who make original art and lovely crafts from used tea bags. I know that doesn't *sound* very attractive, but the art is absolutely amazing. If you don't believe me, go to the U.S. website at www.originaltbagdesigns.com or to the South African website at www.tbagdesigns.co.za and see for yourself. This beautiful art is actually made from used tea bags on which the artisans paint.

The story of how this group came into existence is just as remarkable as the art. In the early 1990s, thirty-five-year-old Jill Heyes moved to South Africa from England, having recently suffered a brain aneurysm that should have killed her. Although she survived, she was forced to stop working while she gradually regained her strength.

Two years after Jill's brain aneurysm, her husband, Charlie, an engineer, was transferred to South Africa, to the small town of Hout Bay near Cape Town. Hout Bay is similar to many places in South Africa: an area of beauty and great wealth as well as a community full of shantytowns, home to the poor and desperate who have been unable to find work. The so-called "settlement" was known as Imazamo Yethu.

One day in 1996, a woman knocked on Jill's door, looking for work as a maid. Jill told the woman that she didn't need someone to work for her but would teach the woman a craft, so she could earn a living as an artist.

The would-be maid rounded up four other friends and together, they began an art program with Jill and five women. These adult students were starting completely from scratch. Unlike most Americans, who get at least some exposure to art in kindergarten and elementary school, Jill's students had no art skills whatsoever. They literally had to learn how to hold paintbrushes and how to manipulate pencils; these were absolutely foreign implements to them.

Jill taught her students a number of techniques—collage, papier-mâché, potato printing—but none of it sold. For two years they soldiered on, but nothing seemed to work. Jill was feeling quite desperate. Not only had she invested time and energy in her students, they had invested their faith and trust in her. Jill was determined to teach these women a skill that would enable them to make a living.

One day a friend was visiting Jill from England, so the two Englishwomen sat down for afternoon tea. Jill looked down and saw an old tea bag drying on the table, and suddenly she had her eureka moment. She would teach the women to paint designs that incorporated these tea bags.

In 2000, Original T-Bag Designs was born. Initially, the artists made only greeting cards, but they eventually expanded to the many different items that they make today. The company now employs fifteen permanent staff and several part-timers. In addition, ten people with disabilities work for the company sanding products. The workshop has become a tourist destination, where the women sell their products. They also sell T-Bag items at Cape Town's V&A Waterfront Market, in Europe, and in the United States.

But to understand how Jill's little workshop turned into an international business, we have to introduce another character into the story, Jodee Hetzer. Jodee's experience is a testament to how when we lose ourselves in service, we may truly find ourselves at last.

In 2003, Jodee, a U.S. citizen, had just gotten divorced. Feeling very sorry for herself and very lost, she decided to go to South Africa, because she'd always dreamed of seeing the animals there. Jodee didn't have enough money to go on safari—to hire a jeep and a driver to take her through South Africa's gorgeous national game reserves. She simply rented a car and started driving around South Africa.

Eventually, Jodee made her way to Cape Town. One day she was walking by the waterfront and came across a stall run by a woman named Donna—who, by the way, I've met at the same stall. Donna sells the crafts made by Original T-Bag Designs.

Jodee stopped to look at one of the T-Bag products, and Donna said, "Yes, you have seen what you think you've seen; they are dried tea bags."

Jodee was so amazed by the tea-bag art that she had to visit Hout Bay, where the work was made. She met the artisans and saw that they didn't even have a room to work in—the art was made in a simple garage.

Jodee chatted with the craftspeople, bought several gifts, and left. Two weeks later, she returned to the United States, feeling bleak at the ending of her vacation and anxious about her prospects. The divorce had taken what little money she had, her daughter was struggling with depression, and Jodee didn't even have health insurance. She did have a teaching certificate, so obviously, the sensible thing would have been to get a teaching job.

Instead, two weeks later, Jodee returned to South Africa. She just could not get those artisans out of her mind, perhaps because she'd gone to South Africa pitying herself and pitying her life, but now she felt she had met women who had the answers to life. Here they were living in a shantytown and yet they seemed so happy and had been so welcoming to her, treating her so beautifully. Something about their joy and love in the face of want changed Jodee's whole perspective on what mattered in life. "I have only a little money and no connections," she told the artists, "but what you do is lovely and I want to help you sell more of it."

And so began Jodee's role as promoter of Original T-Bag Designs. For the first few years, she would use her own money to buy products from them and then hoped to make back what she'd laid out by selling it to stores and galleries. Now, five years later, the workshop is doing well enough to ship Jodee their products without money up front—and they're selling T-Bag art in more places than ever before. The five workers Jodee first met have become twenty-four, who are in turn helping to support a community of a hundred and twenty-five. They've found a kind of security they've never known—and so has Jodee.

When I asked Jodee what moved her to spend so much of her time helping the company, she told me simply that to her, the South African women she had met had "all the answers." Though they had few material possessions, they had a sense of how life should be lived that, Jodee felt, shifted her focus and transformed her life. She was happy to serve the women who had helped her understand what mattered most.

Meanwhile, the company continues to change people's lives. Nomsa, one of the craftswomen, was recently able to move her family from a shack to a house. She says, "The most wonderful thing is hearing the rain on the roof and knowing my children are warm and dry."

I have continued to buy T-Bag art to enjoy myself and as gifts for the special people in my life. When Oprah Winfrey so graciously invited my family to the opening of the Oprah Winfrey Leadership Academy for Girls, outside of Johannesburg, I wanted to thank her by presenting her with a gift that had been made in South Africa.

Though I had visited the artists' small store on the V&A Waterfront in Cape Town and had purchased gifts online, I wanted something really special for this occasion, so I asked if I could commission something. The company and the artisans made an absolutely beautiful one-of-a-kind wall hanging. They also made tea-bag journals for each of the 150 girls who were to attend the school, which I presented along with a message from my family, congratulating the girls for being chosen for the inaugural year of the Leadership Academy.

I have to say, Oprah was overcome by both the beauty of the wall hanging and the stories of the women who had made it. Of course, the women found it an incredible experience to make something for Oprah Winfrey and to commemorate the opening of a school that will be so instrumental in the success of so many girls. Now the piece hangs at the Leadership Academy, a testament to the connections between the United States and South Africa that produced both the academy and the tea-bag art.

Speaking Out on Darfur: A Way to Not Be Silent

Sometimes an issue reaches out and grabs you even when you don't want it to, even when you don't have time for it, even when you can't make it your top priority. You have to find a way to do something about it anyway—sign a petition, write a letter to Congress, attend a rally. That's how it was with me and Darfur, one of the worst humanitarian crises and examples of ethnic cleansing in modern history.

Since rebels attacked Sudan's military sites three years ago, militias on horseback known as Janjaweed have brutally attacked civilians, killing people, burning villages, and raping women in calculated attacks that have been called genocidal. The Janjaweed are believed to be backed by the Sudanese government. Estimates of the number of people killed in Darfur over the past three years range from 180,000 to as high as 400,000. More than 220,000 Darfurians have sought refuge in the eastern part of neighboring Chad, and more than 2 million people have been internally displaced, many gathered into crowded camps with limited basic services.

If you, too, want to do something to help the people of Darfur, check out the resource section for more ideas about how you can get involved. History has shown us that when we remain silent, too many people die. Let's remember the Holocaust, Rwanda, and Kosovo and say "Never again" in Darfur.

From Grief to Action: Rescuing Child Slaves for Jantsen

In April 2009 I bought a book called *Jantsen's Gift,* which would come to have an impact on me. The book is written by Pam Cope, whose fifteen-year-old son Jantsen died suddenly of an undetected heart defect ten years ago. Needing to get away from everything that reminded her of the loss, she accepted a friend's invitation to travel to Vietnam. This pivotal trip was the beginning of a new life of service for Pam, as she decided to channel her pain into changing the world, one child at a time. Upon realizing that children in Vietnam suffer horrific human rights abuses in the form of slavery and trafficking, Pam and her husband, Randy, formed Touch A Life Foundation, without any previous nonprofit experience. She quickly expanded the foundation to include rescuing and protecting children in Cambodia and Ghana. I was particularly touched by the experience Pam describes of reading a *New York Times* cover story with a picture of a six-year-old boy named Mark who was fishing on Lake Volta after he was sold into slavery for approximately $20 per year. What she did next was miraculous. Pam actually flew to Ghana and rescued Mark! She rescued the very boy whom she saw on the cover of the newspaper! In addition to Mark, Touch A Life Foundation has rescued seventy more Ghanaian child slaves whom they house and educate in a loving environment. I finished *Jantsen's Gift* and did something I have never done before. I found Pam's contact information on the Internet and I called and left her a message. She called me back that very day, and we talked for over an hour, met two weeks later in my home, and are now fast friends. More important, we are now partners. I will visit her projects in Ghana in January 2010 and the Journey for Change kids are scheduled to visit and volunteer in March 2010. Following the trip, we will join Touch A Life Foundation to advocate in the United States to eradicate child slavery worldwide. For more information on Pam, visit the foundation's website at www.touchalifekids.org and/or purchase her book *Jantsen's Gift.* I know you will be as inspired by this citizen of the world as I was.

Grannies and Gardens

By the time I returned to Diepsloot for a fourth visit, I had given some serious thought as to how to help the grannies make money. Two things they'd said to me during a previous visit really stuck with me: first, that most of the ways they knew to make money hadn't worked. For example, they had thought about going to a nearby farm to buy chickens to raise, but without cell phones, they couldn't call ahead and make sure the farm had chickens for them. Instead, they spent money they didn't really have on bus fare and rode all the way out there—only to discover that the farm had no chickens and they had wasted money on an expensive trip. They had also tried to sell used clothes, but too many people were already doing that.

The second thing they told me was that they had wanted to set up community gardens, where they could grow food both for sale and for their own use. But the soil in that part of South Africa is unforgiving. You can't just throw seeds into it and expect them to grow. You need to dig a pretty deep trench and then keep watering your garden, which means you need strength, shovels, water, seeds, and fencing for security—none of which they had. Even though some of the grannies had pooled their money to buy seeds and a few shovels, without the other items, they could not possibly be successful.

So I had two issues: What could the grannies sell to make money? And how could they grow food in their gardens?

For the gardens, I realized, we needed a group that could take over the actual labor of digging and tending them. Some of the work could be done by the grannies, if they were taught what to do. But for some things—the heavy digging, locating a site with access to water, and the overall care of the site—outside help was needed.

I did a lot of work researching organizations that could create food gardens for the grannies. By the time I had received a few estimates, I realized that this was not an inexpensive venture at all. I also learned through a local nonprofit that there were many gardening groups in Johannesburg, often doing their work on school grounds. In South Africa, the government provides orphaned schoolchildren with one meal a day, but basically what the kids get is the white maize known as mealie-meal—no meat and certainly no vegetables. If there are gardens producing vegetables on school grounds, however, the school cooks those vegetables for the orphans for lunch and gives them the extra to take home for dinner for themselves and to share with their siblings.

I finally settled on a group called Food Gardens Foundation and came up with a plan for them to do gardens at eight Johannesburg schools located in Soweto. These gardens would grow carrots, tomatoes, spinach, collard greens, potatoes, lettuce, yams, and other vegetables, giving the children and their families access to fresh, healthy, delicious food on a regular basis. At the same time, I took the grannies' advice and decided to set up gardens in Diepsloot for the members of the granny support groups so that they could have food to sell at markets close by and also use some of the vegetables to feed their families. Additionally, members of the HIV/AIDS support group also voiced an interest in being a part of the project, so I welcomed them to join us.

Meanwhile, I came up with another way the grannies could make money: selling handbags. Liz Claiborne Inc. had been a major donor to styleworks, giving us beautiful handbags for our clients. I knew that the grannies needed something they could sell *outside* of Diepsloot, where they could reach the many prosperous working-class and middle-class people of Johannesburg. What if Liz Claiborne Inc. donated handbags for them to sell?

I discussed this idea with the women I'd met, and they were all enthusiastic. Now we needed an infrastructure for getting the bags to them, storing them, and helping them to market and distribute their products. We also needed to set these women up with bank accounts and other financial services, instead of having them store money in their mattresses, as they usually did, risking not only theft but the loss of all their savings if their shanty caught fire and burned down.

Liz Claiborne Inc. generously donated six thousand bags. Through an intricate series of negotiations, I found a way to ship them from New York to Johannesburg. The Diepsloot Standard Bank helped us set up accounts. And Mark Doyle, a Rotarian in

South Africa who was part of Rotarians for Fighting AIDS, turned to his large network of Rotarians to help us find a storage facility. He ended up finding us free storage at a place owned by the Rotary Club. We are working with the Olive Leaf Foundation and other companies and NGOs to teach the grannies about inventory, marketing, and selling, along with the banking and savings components, so that they know how to run a proper business. They will even have their own uniforms for this program, which now has the name GoGo Style Income Generating Project.

So basically, through GoGo Style, the grannies now had a beautiful product to sell—and they would get to keep 100 percent of the profit. There was no way they could not make money with *that* arrangement! And if the project is as successful as I know it will be, I can go back to Liz Claiborne Inc. or on to other corporations for more donations.

I was thrilled to have found solutions to the problems I'd learned about—and the grannies and field-workers I knew were thrilled, too. But as much as I loved my time in Diepsloot and felt that I was on track to make a real change in the lives of the people I loved, I knew in my heart that my journey for change wasn't over. For about two years now, I had been working with the Salvation Army Bushwick Community Center, helping the neighborhood center where Chris had gone as a boy and getting to know the children who went there now. I got it into my head that somehow I could find a way to bring those two worlds—Bushwick and Diepsloot—together.

MY JOURNEY: PEACE CORPS VOLUNTEER
JULIE BERNSTEIN

Julie Bernstein is director of international programs for Susan G. Komen for the Cure, one of the nation's leading funders of breast cancer research and education. I met her through a trip to Ghana she helped to organize for a group of breast-cancer advocates and educators—all of us named Susan G. Komen for the Cure Global

Ambassadors—to learn more about conditions there. One of our trip's main focuses was triple negative breast cancer and the fact that 70 percent of all women in Ghana who have breast cancer are not diagnosed until they have reached stage three or four. I was immediately impressed by Julie's passion, her organizational skills, and her friendliness, and I was intrigued to learn that Julie attributes much of her interest in international issues to her tour of duty in the Peace Corps, for which she served in Papua New Guinea (PNG) at age twenty-five with her twenty-six-year-old husband. Here are excerpts from an interview I conducted with her for this book.

Q. How did you hear about the Peace Corps as an avenue for you and your husband?

A. Peace Corps recruiters came to the University of Wisconsin–Madison during my senior year, 1992. They set up a table all week at the student union. I must have walked by that table a dozen times before I mustered up the courage to stop and ask a few questions. . . . I left the union that afternoon dreaming of being a Peace Corps volunteer but afraid to take that plunge alone. I knew my parents would be wary and think I was just putting off the inevitable— real life after college, real life filled with real responsibilities. So the application sat in my beat-up backpack for months until I cleaned it out after graduation.

By this time, I had accepted a job at a prestigious law firm in Washington, DC, where I'd work and study for the LSAT while I applied for law school that next year. Peace Corps remained a secret adventure I'd daydream about while date-stamping legal documents or pulling cases for a trial.

I met Roy a few weeks after I moved to DC. It might sound corny, but it was love at first sight. . . . I didn't last very long at the corporate law firm and found a rewarding job working for a women's nonprofit organization. Roy was teaching sixth-grade world studies to low-income middle schoolers.

Three years later, we both started to feel burned out at our jobs, like we wanted a change, and we were itching to travel. We started talking about Peace Corps again. Roy had gone a step farther than I did back in college—he actually completed a Peace Corps application but never sent it in. We met with a recruiter in DC and started the application process together. Fourteen months later, we were accepting an invitation to be rural community development volunteers in Papua New Guinea—scheduled to leave six weeks after our wedding!

Q. What made the two of you decide to enlist?
A. We wanted to help others and experience life in a different culture, in a different part of the world. We wanted to share our knowledge and skills . . . and in the process, learn from our host-country counterparts. The cultural exchange was very appealing, along with discovering a beautiful new country. We were also looking to change professions and saw a Peace Corps tour as a clean break and an opportunity to explore our strengths and weaknesses in hopes of figuring out what path to take once we returned home.

Q. How was the experience, and how did it compare to what you expected?
A. Being a Peace Corps volunteer in PNG was incredibly challenging. I was very idealistic going into the experience and I felt a bit naïve once we started training in-country and began living with our host family in the village. I didn't realize how hard it would be for me to follow the strict cultural rules that American women must follow when living in a village in rural PNG. From not making eye contact with men to never having physical contact with my husband, Roy, my feminist self faced an incredible challenge. I had just worked at a women's rights organization in Washington, DC, where we fought for social, political, and economic equality for women and girls, and here I was in a country where pigs had more value than a female human being. I was told to accept this and work within the system. It was drilled into us that if we broke these rules—and I held my husband's hand—it would literally put me in physical jeopardy. It took many months and a few reprimands from our Peace Corps trainers to convince me to change my mind-set and alter my behavior. . . . After all, we were still in the first year of our marriage!

Q. Describe what you did while you were there.

A. We were sent over as rural community development workers. We ended up teaching at a Catholic mission high school in Tari, in the Southern Highlands Province of PNG. I taught math, commerce, and drama to ninth- and tenth-graders. Roy taught tenth-grade English.

We quickly learned that HIV/AIDS was hitting PNG very hard and we wanted to do something to help while we were serving there [but] in the midnineties many developing . . . countries were still in a state of denial. We came to realize that many educators had little or no understanding of HIV and the AIDS virus.

We designed the first HIV/AIDS national education curriculum for teachers in the country. We held the first-ever teacher training seminar in Mount Hagen, the capital of Western Highlands Province in PNG, funded by the World Health Organization. We secured this funding and planned the entire training, including logistics for teachers participating in the training.

We also secretly taught basic sex education to our high school students. Discussing sexuality or sex ed was so taboo in PNG culture that ignorance was literally killing people there. Roy quickly discovered that his male students had no idea about STDs and that myths about how girls get pregnant were quite pervasive among the students. During study hour and nightly dorm duty, Roy would talk with the boys and even distributed condoms to those students who were sexually active and requested them. Of course we did this clandestinely since the American nuns running the school would have expelled us if they discovered we were teaching sex ed to the students. They strictly forbade any conversations related to sexuality.

Q. What was the most challenging aspect of your time in the Peace Corps?

A. I lost my independence while living, working, and serving in PNG. I was accustomed to going places on my own—from taking a run to going grocery shopping—and my actions and movements were very limited. I was tied to Roy's side—figuratively of course, as we could never touch in public. We had three guard dogs that went everywhere with us around the school that at once highlighted our vulnerability and our insecurity about . . . personal safety.

The isolation and lack of contact with the outside world, especially my family, was also a great challenge. There was no Internet or phones—we were dependent on snail mail, which came once every month or so. Sometimes the post office in Tari didn't open for weeks. We'd see mailbags stacked on the floor but the door was locked and no one showed up for work. We even offered to volunteer in the post office to sort mail for the entire town, knowing there were letters in there with our names on them, but we were turned away. We waited months for letters, and packages sometimes didn't make it to us. News from our families and friends was often outdated as soon as we read it.

Q. What was the most inspiring aspect of your time in the Peace Corps?
A. Connecting with my students, especially the girls I taught, was very inspiring. Their hopefulness and curiosity helped to keep me going through the lonely times. While teaching three subjects to nearly 150 students was very challenging and time-consuming (imagine all those tests I graded every week!), my students gave me the energy I needed to get up every day and go to work. Ultimately, their inspiration gave me hope that my work there was making a difference.

Q. How do you think you made a difference to the people you served?
A. Beyond the cultural challenges and isolation, the American nuns that ran the mission school were very difficult to work with. They had left the U.S. in the sixties and built themselves a fortress in PNG. They ran the school more like plantation owners than Catholic missionaries in a developing country there to help the disadvantaged. The students were terrified of them—they literally ruled with an iron fist, were verbally abusive and borderline physically abusive as well—and these nuns were the only Americans they had ever known. I believe one of our most valuable contributions was to

show our students that Americans can also be kind, gracious, and respectful of them as human beings. We were diplomats in the truest sense, doing our best to counter the image and attitudes conveyed by the schoolmistresses.

Q. How did the people you served make a difference to you?
A. I learned so much from my students. They had so little—from clothes to food to material possessions—yet they always had smiles on their faces. They worked hard to become the few that were chosen for high school and their entire village pooled resources to pay the school fees required to attend Tari High School.

I was without Western influence for two years. I read books, played Scrabble, and wrote in my journal. I learned to slow down, to put my competitiveness on hold and not let the little things bother me. Trust me, this was a learning process and not something I achieved easily or quickly. The culture, with all its challenges, ultimately changed me and made me a better person. During training we were often told to prepare to "just be" and to find peace in that. What I learned was that "just being" was code for just being bored sometimes and being okay with that.

Q. What would you say to other people who are thinking about enlisting or who are seeking some meaningful way to do international work?
A. I would be honest about my experience and all the challenges that I faced. I'd tell them the truth and not sugarcoat what it's like living and working in a place like PNG. But I'd also tell them to follow their heart and go for it. So much work needs to be done to help people around the world. If you're able to give of yourself and adapt to a new culture, and you want structure and support from the U.S. government, then the Peace Corps is for you. . . .

While I'm glad that I served, I'd never do it again. Being a Peace Corps volunteer is a once-in-a-lifetime job, *once* being the operative word here. It has definitely enriched my life and my career. I truly believe that it has opened doors for me and my husband in terms of job interviews and opportunities afforded to us in our careers.

Q. How did the experience change your life?
A. It changed how I looked at the world. It taught me to respect all human beings, our precious environment, and cultural differences. What might seem odd to one person is perfectly normal to another. I learned to adapt and be flexible. I trained myself to hold my tongue and keep my opinions to myself. This forced me to look deep inside myself, beyond the superficial, and ultimately changed my perspective on life and what is really important. Serving as a Peace Corps volunteer changed my life in a profound way. I incorporate the lessons and skills I learned working in PNG almost every day of my life.

Chapter 7

Spreading the Seeds:
The Power of the Media

■

I still believe that if your aim is to change the world,
journalism is a more immediate short-term weapon.
—TOM STOPPARD

From the moment I got my first taste at the Terrie Williams Agency, I have always loved public relations and special events. When you work hard pitching the media about a person, project, event, or product, you get a great thrill from receiving the attention you were seeking and from making people aware of your client through the media. Media work takes a lot of persistence, too. You need to be good at building relationships, you have to be creative, and sometimes you just have to get lucky.

Though I left the entertainment industry for the nonprofit world, still nothing makes me happier than to plan an event, promote a cause, or publicize something that can really help people or change lives for the better. I feel very blessed that I can use my media skills to help a large national organization, a small local nonprofit, a public-service announcement (PSA) campaign for change, or just a friend who is starting a new website or coming out with a book.

But throughout my entire career, I have almost always been the one doing the pitching—never the one in front of the camera or in the magazines. The exceptions came for two reasons and two reasons only: to promote a nonprofit cause or to support my husband in his career.

I have been asked to step over to the other side—to host a TV show or appear as a regular guest—but I've always said no, and not because I'm a TV snob. But as much as I like watching TV, the idea of appearing on it never seemed to be as fulfilling as what I do every day.

But you never know where life is going to take you or what is right around the corner. This is what makes life exciting, right? So when life offers you an unexpected path on your journey, you either take the safe road or you hold on tight and take the ride! Pretty much all my life, I've done the latter—and that is how I ended up as one of the judges on *Oprah's Big Give*.

A Call from Oprah

As I already mentioned, I've known the wonderful Oprah Winfrey for several years, partly because she has been so supportive of Chris's career beginning way back with his first appearance as Little Penny, one of the coolest characters in a Nike commerical. She continues to support him now, too, as he appears on her show often to promote his movies, TV shows, and HBO specials. I try to go with him whenever he's on because I am such a huge fan of that show. I absolutely love Oprah's studio audience, and it is always fun to see her and some of the producers, whom I have also known for years. My kids have fun too. Lola has been going to Chicago for the show since she was a baby, but it is my ham Zahra who truly loves being on set and seeing herself on TV.

Oprah has also been extremely supportive of me and all my non-profit work, beginning with a short segment about styleWORKS that was part of *The Oprah Winfrey Show*'s fabulous "Remembering Your Spirit" segment, which she used to do at end of each show for years. After my segment ran, I was contacted by an editor who wanted to do a profile on styleWORKS in *O, The Oprah Magazine*. Needless to say, her belief in what I was doing brought a lot of welcome attention to styleWORKS, creating credibility for my cause and rewarding my new and much-appreciated sponsors. Of course, anyone who works for a nonprofit organization that's been fortunate enough to be featured on Oprah's show knows that her attention can help you immediately and immensely.

Even after Oprah stopped doing the "Remembering Your Spirit" segment, she still gave out the Oprah's Angel Network grant to worthwhile local nonprofits as a part of a monthly special feature. I loved watching that segment, learning about what her organization did to effect change and watching her give that big old fat check that you knew was going to go so far for that particular group.

And, of course, Oprah blessed my family by inviting us to the opening of the Oprah Winfrey Leadership Academy for Girls in South Africa. Even though she and I may give at very different levels, she knows that we share a mutual love for the children and grannies of South Africa. Of course, Oprah doesn't judge people by how much they can give. She just continuously celebrates anyone who does something to effect positive change. I love that about her.

A couple of years ago, Chris happened to be promoting a movie, and for the first time, our entire family appeared on *The Oprah Winfrey Show* together. Every other time we'd gone to the show, Lola, Zahra, and I had sat in the audience, though sometimes Oprah had questioned us there. This year, because we had just returned from the opening of Oprah's school, we all sat onstage with Chris. He and I were able to express what being a part of the Oprah Winfrey Leadership Academy for Girls opening meant to us individually and as a family. And my girls had a ball. My little Zahra certainly hammed it up that day! Even now people tell her how cute she was.

Eventually the girls and I left the stage while Chris was interviewed solo about his movie. Oprah's talented makeup artist at the time, Reggie Wells, caught up with me backstage and suggested that I do television. I told him that television didn't really interest me— my nonprofit work was where my heart lay.

Somehow, this conversation got around to Harpo, Oprah's production company, which unbeknownst to me was developing *Oprah's Big Give.* The new show had a simple but brilliant premise: Several ordinary people from across the country would compete for a big prize in what is now the standard reality-show format. But instead of having contestants compete for money by doing things that would only benefit themselves, *Oprah's Big Give* would be a reality show the only way Oprah herself could do it: The contestants would compete each week to out-give one another—to be the biggest giver, the biggest life-changer. Every week, they would be allotted a certain amount of money and a person to help, always with the message "Give big or go home." On the opening episode, for example, contestants were given the name of a complete stranger and told that they had just three days to change his or her life. Each week, a panel of judges would evaluate these efforts and eliminate a person from the show.

And one night—I remember it was a Thursday—Oprah called me at home and asked me to be one of the judges. Now, this was an unusual phone call for me, because Oprah doesn't usually call me at home—or call me, period. After I picked myself up off the floor, I listened carefully while she explained the premise of the show, which, of course, I loved right away.

But when I learned the show was going to start shooting very soon, I had a lot of reservations. After all, didn't we already have one entertainer in the family? Even if I did want to do television, could I pull it off with my schedule as a mom and while coordinating my work around Chris's schedule? He and I are both very much committed to at least one parent being home with our children at all times, especially if the other parent is traveling any distance. Could I manage the *Oprah's Big Give* schedule and still make sure that our kids were okay?

After Oprah got off the line, I spoke with her producers. "I had a vacation planned," I told them. "Chris just finished a movie and he asked me to schedule a vacation. He never asks for a vacation. I am the travel horse in the family, so I can't cancel the vacation."

The producers laugh at me about it now. At the time, they tried to act like what I was saying made sense. "Um, can't you, like . . . *postpone* the vacation?" one of them said carefully.

In the end, it all worked out. Chris understood what a terrific opportunity this was and felt it was right up my alley. Since he had just finished a long period of work, he was able to stay with the children. And the night of the show's finale, I was on a plane to St. Martin, joining my family for that slightly postponed family vacation and feeling so blessed to have had the opportunity to be a part of the show. And, yes, the producers teased me about even thinking of not taking this amazing opportunity the entire time we shot the show.

On the Air with *Oprah's Big Give*

Once I got over my concerns about the schedule, I had one other issue to resolve: I was nervous! Although I'd been interviewed on television many times, I hadn't really had any TV experience of this kind. Oprah had signed up a great host, the wonderful designer Nate Berkus, who appeared on *Oprah* all the time. As my fellow judges, she'd chosen the charismatic and funny chef Jamie Oliver and the NFL star and—yes, I will say it!—heartthrob Tony Gonzalez, both of whom were far more used to being on television than I was.

So I was a little bit intimidated when we started shooting. All right, more than a little. In fact, to tell you the truth, I felt like I had no idea what I was doing! But I got some spirit-lifting words of encouragement from Gayle King, Oprah's best friend, editor at large for *O, The Oprah Magazine,* host of *The Gayle King Show* on Oprah Radio, and regular contributor on *The Oprah Winfrey Show.* Gayle is one of the kindest people I know, full of good advice, and her warm support never fails to lift me up.

I realized, too, that Oprah had chosen me because she did not want a superstar actress or a professional news person; she wanted me to be myself. And hadn't I spent my entire life thinking about how to serve people and how to evaluate my efforts to serve? In the end, how was this any different?

Once I settled into my skin, I began to enjoy myself. I liked the travel, which gave me a chance to visit some cities I'd never seen before. I enjoyed meeting the contestants. Even more, I enjoyed meeting the people whom the contestants helped.

I always asked everyone the questions I wanted to ask about my own efforts: Did the person who was giving listen—really listen—to the person who needed help? Did the giver choose a gift based on the recipient's needs or on his or her own? Did he or she let the recipient explain the situation or simply make assumptions? I think we need to be knowledgeable donors, guided by our hearts, yes, but also by our minds, and always, always put the needs of the recipients first. Part of the power of the show was seeing the contestants grow as they came to understand the beauty of giving. Although *Oprah's Big Give* was set up to be a competition, none of the contestants were ever told what they would win. On some level, they had to be doing it for the pleasure of being generous, of serving well. And indeed, as they continued to give, they responded deeply to the people whose lives they touched.

I remember a New York–based episode that required contestants to work together to fulfill a man's dying wish. This man was dying of cancer at a relatively early age, leaving behind three small children. He was worried about his mortgage, about his kids' college funds, about his old car breaking down, not to mention the emotional hell of coping with his disease.

This episode came near the end of the competition, and the contestants were very much in competitive mode. But they had to work together in order to give this family what they needed—and they did. They found a way to help with his mortgage and got someone to donate a brand-new truck and even some money for the kids' college funds. They also created a wonderful day in New York for the man and his whole family, complete with makeovers, a Broadway show, and shopping at Saks Fifth Avenue. Frustrated, tired, competitive, and even mad at one another, the contestants nevertheless went beyond their individual needs to win to devote themselves entirely to the needs of that family.

The contestants were a widely diverse lot. They included a young man who was already a millionaire in his early twenties and loved the power of business; a father of three girls who'd been involved with international giving and had shared this passion with his daughters; a medical student who'd been born and raised in Kenya; and even a fortysomething woman who admitted that she had never given before and had not been a particularly good friend, daughter, or sister. She had really just spent her life thinking about herself and doing things only for herself. In other words, we had people of all

ages, from all backgrounds and cultures, with widely different un-
derstandings of philanthropy.

I remember one man who didn't perform well at all in his first
challenge. But there was something in him that all of us judges liked,
and we all thought that he might ultimately have what it took to do
well. He had come to the United States without a lot of material
things and yet had achieved a lot in his life. That doesn't usually
happen without help from someone else. So I definitely thought he
could learn how to be the biggest giver.

He proved me right, though not until we had reached the middle of the competition. The contestants on the show were always
given minivans or SUVs when they reached a new city, so they'd
have some way to get around. As they neared the end of that week's
challenge, with maybe an hour left to go on their clocks, they received a text message from Oprah saying that they had to give away
that week's car—and make it count.

That week, contestants had had to seek out their own person
or group to help, and the man I'm thinking of had already visited a local hospital in a fairly poor neighborhood to see what they might
need. He'd been told that when mothers at that hospital gave birth,
they rarely had cars to get home. A new mother in that hospital had
to carry her baby in her arms on the bus—no ride, no car seat,
nothing.

As soon as he received Oprah's text, this contestant went back to
the hospital, car keys in hand. He said to the hospital administrator,
"If I give you this car, can you promise me that it will be used to give
a ride home to any mother who gives birth and doesn't have her own
ride?"

Talk about a gift that keeps on giving! That was definitely one of
my favorite moments!

The gift of the car may have been a highlight, but honestly, every
week was awesome and I always had fun—we all did. Oprah realized
that if she picked judges who enjoyed watching people learning how
to give big, the audience would enjoy watching the process, too.

The man who ultimately won *Oprah's Big Give* was a very strong
contestant from the beginning. He was very well-off, lived in a beau-

tiful part of the country, and had a wonderful close family. While we were on the road, even though we could not talk to the contestants much, I always heard him saying how much he missed his family. He had been giving all his life but, before the show, really only to international causes.

One of his most challenging weeks came when contestants had to go home and give in their own neighborhoods. This man lived in a very wealthy community, in a spectacular house among other homes that were equally spectacular. When the producers sent me to visit him, I quickly caught on that he was having a hard time because his giving had never before been concentrated around where he lived.

I could identify with his struggle because I, too, am blessed to live in a prosperous community, but my first thought was to tell him to look at all the people who work for him or work for his neighbors—the housekeepers, nannies, landscapers, gardeners, each of whom comes to work at an honest job every day. They can't live very far away—and *some* of them must need some assistance.

Of course, I couldn't share these thoughts with him, but he came up with his own wonderful solution: He discovered that his town had a boys' home. So he donated a TV, some sports equipment, and some other items as well as arranged to have their driveway paved. The whole experience was a big wake-up call for this man, because although he had spent time and money helping the poor in Africa and had even taught his children about them, he had never really grasped that he could help right in his own neighborhood. From then on, I knew, he'd look at his own life differently—and because of the kind of father he was, his children would look at their lives differently, too.

Small Gifts, Big Rewards

I loved that the contestants on *Oprah's Big Give* were able to give huge, fabulous gifts based on the week's challenge, gifts that were sometimes splashy and extraordinary. It was so satisfying to see someone—maybe someone who had never really given before—give in a way that transformed the life of a person, a family, a community, and ultimately, themselves.

But I also loved the little gifts on that show, and in some ways, they ended up meaning just as much to me. My very favorite moment involved one of our contestants in a situation where she had just a few more minutes to give away the rest of the money she'd been allotted and she didn't know what to do.

As she ran down the street, seeking answers, she passed a flower stand. Seized by inspiration, she bought up all the flowers and just started giving them away. She literally ran up to people's cars, saying, "Here, take this bouquet home to your wife." Or she'd jump on a bus and give everybody flowers. Everyone was so happy and so touched. It was such a small, simple act, but it brightened people's day like you wouldn't believe. To me, that moment sums up the whole show—and my own philosophy about a life in service. And some of the contestants have continued to do such wonderful acts of service. One man started the CAN-DO organization, which stands for Compassion into Action Network (www.can-do.org). He then started virtualvolunteer.tv, the first online real-time video website that allows viewers to watch as their contributions make it into the hands of those in need in the wake of a humanitarian effort or natural disaster. How cool is that?

What made *Oprah's Big Give* such a phenomenal experience, for me and for everyone who watched it, was understanding that *anybody* can be a big giver. You don't need a lot of money or even a lot of time. You just need to take a moment's thought, follow your instincts, and feel a willingness to serve. Your heart will do the rest.

Getting the Word Out

Working on *Oprah's Big Give,* I was struck all over again by the power of the media to reach people, raise awareness of issues, and promote causes. Imagine all the people who were turned on to the idea of philanthropy and service because they were intrigued by the competition among the contestants and found themselves thinking about how *they* might serve.

In fact, one of the questions I get asked most often is "How do I promote my cause?" In the rest of this chapter, I'll share with you my best public relations secrets. I'll talk you through the process of placing pro bono ads; writing press releases, media alerts, and "one-pagers"; and cultivating relationships with the media. I'll give you a step-by-step guide to promoting events, and I'll clue you in on some of the most common myths about the media.

My suggestions should be enough to get you started, and they may well be all you need. If you'd like a more in-depth look, check out the resource guide.

Promoting Good Causes with Pro Bono Ads

A pro bono ad is one whose time or space is donated for free (literally, "for good") by the newspaper, magazine, radio station, or TV station where it appears. Pro bono ads can be an extremely powerful element in your public relations campaign, since many media outlets are happy to offer their support to promote a good cause.

I had tremendous success with pro bono ads when I set out to promote Champions for Children, a group I started to help raise awareness about recognizing and responding to the ten signs of child abuse. Champions for Children includes many well-known individuals who have agreed to use their name and likeness in support of this important cause. As part of our campaign, I put together a list of the names of the people, including such celebrities as Kelly Ripa, Spike and Tonya Lee, Susan Sarandon, Iman, Star Jones, Al Roker and Deborah Roberts, Holly Robinson Peete and Rodney Peete, and of course, Chris and myself. With the support of my partners, we also created a radio PSA with some of the same people, for which Clear Channel provided free radio time. Altogether, we received over 27 million media impressions, with our ad appearing in magazines, elevators, billboards, and radio shows.

It's not only large national organizations that can benefit from pro bono advertising. Your small local nonprofit should also be able to establish a good relationship with local media, which are frequently willing to offer their support. When we began promoting the Triple Negative Breast Cancer Foundation, we were very successful in getting pro bono ads placed in local media outlets that wanted to support this local effort. A magazine in Bergen County gave us space for a free ad. We had the ad designed, again pro bono, by Richard Menage. This publicity was instrumental in drawing the attention of new attendees to our events, soliciting new donors, and getting our cause out there to be recognized by our constituency. It also helped create recognition for our logo.

Perfecting Your Press Releases

Writing a good press release can be quite a challenge, but the project is well worth your effort. There's nothing more effective than a well-written, hard-hitting press release for grabbing the attention of a local newspaper, radio show, or TV program. If you want to get the word out, you'll need to be able to put your message into a press release.

I've been able to inspire quite a bit of interest in causes I support through the press releases I've written for various groups. Here is a press release I wrote for styleWORKS that helped me get both local and national coverage.

FOR IMMEDIATE RELEASE

Contact:	Jane Jones	Mary Smith
	Clairol Retail	Clairol Professional
	(212) 000-0000	(212) 000-0000

Clairol Helps Women Put Their Best Foot . . . and Face . . . Forward with styleWORKS

October 19, 2000, New York, NY—Clairol is pleased to announce its association with styleWORKS, a unique nonprofit organization founded by Malaak Compton-Rock that provides free comprehensive makeovers to women who are transitioning from welfare into the workforce.

In celebration of this partnership, Clairol is sponsoring a fund-raising breakfast and accessory drive on Tuesday, October 24, at the Broadway Ballroom of the Marriott Marquis Hotel in New York City. Participating in the event are Malaak Compton-Rock, founder and executive director of style**WORKS**, and Mpule Kwelagobe, Miss Universe 1999 and Clairol Textures & Tones spokesperson, who will present U.S. secretary of labor Alexis M. Herman with the first annual Clairol/style**WORKS** Leaders for Change Award for her outstanding efforts in effecting welfare reform.

Secretary Herman is widely credited as an important leader in the effort to move people from welfare to work. She believes in a prepared workforce, a secure workforce and a quality workplace. The implementation of the welfare reform system has resulted in a 56% decline in the number of people on welfare, from 14.1 million to 6.3 million. Secretary Herman's commitment to manage the transition for people from welfare to work with dignity entails knowing that these people have gone into real, long-term jobs that will help them get on the road to independence.

Supporting this effort is style**WORKS**, which, with its dedicated core of volunteers and hair care products donated by Clairol Herbal Essences and Textures & Tones, provides women who are moving from welfare to work with free comprehensive makeovers that include hair color and styling, makeup application, skin-care analysis/facials/waxing, clothing, accessories, and image consulting. style**WORKS** clients are referred from 10 participating New York City–based job-training agencies. "When a woman feels her best, she can reach her full potential, and then everyone around her benefits," notes Malaak. The ultimate goal is to give these women the confidence and help they need to maintain a positive attitude towards their work.

Additionally, Clairol is excited to announce the launch of the Clairol/style**WORKS** Mentoring Program. This program supports women who have recently entered the workforce and specifically offers guidance on job-retention skills. Many of Clairol's female employees have volunteered to serve as mentors, sharing their expertise with style**WORKS** clients and serving as a safe resource to which a mentee can turn when she has questions, needs advice, or just wants to talk. It is documented that the first three months of employment are the most critical time in a new employee's life, and it is the company's hope that this new mentoring program will help make the transition into the workforce as smooth as possible.

Extra, Extra: Some Suggestions for Your Next Press Release

• Put the most important information in the first paragraph. Each additional paragraph should have less-important information. That way, if someone stops reading, he or she will be more likely to know the information you're most concerned about.

• A snappy title can make the difference between catching an editor's attention and being passed over. Don't get too cute, though. The editor should be able to know what the story is about as soon as he or she reads the headline.

• Your press release should almost always run one or at most two pages. You need a *really* good reason to make it longer. Write it as though you were writing an article that is going directly into a newspaper. A TV or radio program will use your press release to decide whether to send a reporter, but some newspapers and local magazines will actually print the release itself.

Alert the Media with Media Alerts

A press release should go out about two weeks in advance for short-lead newspapers and magazines (weeklies and dailies) and five or six months for long-lead press (monthlies or for items that do not have a deadline), but there is a much quicker way to alert the media, known as a *media alert.*

A media alert is a one-page document giving only pertinent details about an event. You send it out no more than one week before the event. Based on the response you receive, you can decide to resend it a few days before the event and then one day before as well. I very much recommend resending your alert the day before the event because a lot of assignment desks do not assign writers and crews until the day of an event.

This document is very much "just the facts, ma'am." In fact, you often organize media alerts in a basic "who, what, when, where, why" format. Here's a media alert we used for a Triple Negative Breast Cancer Foundation event.

MEDIA ALERT

FOR IMMEDIATE RELEASE: **January 30, 2008**

The Triple Negative Breast Cancer Foundation Hosts Its Second Fundraising Event: The First Annual Tea and Talk for Awareness Shopping Benefit

WHO: The Triple Negative Breast Cancer (TNBC) Foundation Holds the First Annual Tea and Talk for Awareness Shopping Benefit

Host: Saks Fifth Avenue
Celebrity Q&A Moderator: Lori Stokes, WABC News Anchor
Q&A Guests: Karen Neely, Lawyer and TNBC Survivor, Dr. Deborah Toppmeyer, Director of the New Jersey Comprehensive Breast Care Center

Special Invited Guests: Malaak Compton-Rock, Lenora Klein, Deleon Sheffield, Melissa Silver, and Andi Wolfer

WHAT: The TNBC Foundation will raise funds and awareness by holding an exciting shopping event, featuring the latest in Spring Designer Accessories and Fashion, and a Q&A segment that will both inspire and allow the organization to continue its work towards finding a cure.

WHEN: Wednesday, February 6, 2008
11:30AM until 2:00PM

WHERE: Saks Fifth Avenue
The Shops at Riverside
Hackensack, New Jersey
Second Floor

WHY: This benefit will support the mission of the TNBC Foundation, which is to raise awareness of triple negative breast cancer and to support scientists and researchers in their effort to determine the definitive causes of triple negative breast cancer, so that effective detection, diagnosis, prevention and treatment can be pursued and achieved.

SPECIAL EVENT INFORMATION:

EVENT MEDIA CONTACT: Mary Smith at 646-000-0000 or Mary@groupname.org

LORI STOKES MEDIA CONTACT: Jane Jones at 201-000-0000 or jane@othername.com

MEDIA SPONSOR: (201) Magazine

DOOR PRIZE SPONSORS: Judith Ripka Inc. and Love, Peace, and Hope

CATERING SPONSORS: Food for Thought Catered Events and Party Rental Ltd.

For more information, please visit www.tnbcfoundation.org.

The media contact information at the end of this document is necessary. The rest about the sponsors is not. We made the personal choice to add this information based only on the fact that our sponsors were giving us pro bono or reduced-rate products and services.

Getting into the Media Mind-Set

The first step in connecting to the media is to remember how important your cause is and how it can make a difference in someone's life. That sincerity and commitment will help you articulate your message and convince the media that they should promote your cause.

My best advice to you is to think locally. This advice holds true even if you live in a major city with national media, and it's even more true if you live in a smaller city or town. National news media are often flooded with requests for coverage, whereas local news organizations are more likely to be looking for material to fill pages or airtime and focus on local stories.

And if you do get local coverage, you may find that your story is suddenly picked up by the national media. Check out any copy of *People* magazine and notice all the local stories they cover. Human-interest and feel-good stories often come from small-town newspapers and suburban magazines that the big-city folks routinely scan in search of new ideas.

You can't control your story getting picked up nationally, though, so concentrate on local TV stations, news radio stations, morning TV shows, and newspapers, as well as those free neighborhood or community newspapers that can be found in so many areas. For all of these media outlets, you're looking for either an assignment editor or a story editor, whose name and contact information you can usually find with a single phone call or online search. You may also be able to find that information on the masthead or elsewhere in the publication.

Once you've found the contact information, you can use it to e-mail, fax, or snail-mail your press release or media alert. Be sure to find out their lead time, too—the time they need to be able to assign a story.

Once you've sent your release or alert to a media outlet, don't be afraid to follow up. It's very rare that anyone will call you; it's up to you to call them. Many people become discouraged or shy, or start to lose confidence in their cause. These feelings are natural—but you must resist them! Even at this point in my career, I have to pitch stories like anyone else. I still get far more nos than yeses but I've learned to be persistent and never to take anything personally.

You also need to distinguish between two different kinds of seemingly negative responses. If you're told, "This isn't the sort of thing we cover," that's a definite no, and you should simply accept it. If you can, ask, "Can you help me understand what you do cover, so I can approach you with something more appropriate the next time?" Then make a note of what they tell you and go on to the next call. Remember, they're saying no not because your idea is bad but because they can't figure out how it applies to their particular audience. When you understand their audience better, maybe you can figure out a better way to reach it.

However, if you're told "We're not sure" or "This is so interesting, but we don't have time for it this week," then you've gotten a very different message. "We're not sure" means you should keep checking back every so often. "We don't have time for it this week" means you should send them a press release the next time you do an event—and start the whole process over again.

Photo Opportunities: Seeing the Big Picture by Using a Photo Alert

One trick for getting publicity is to provide photographs of your event to a local or national magazine. Often a magazine will even tell you, "We don't have enough staff to cover your event, but if you send photos, we will consider putting them in." So it's worth finding a professional or volunteer photographer who will take pictures for free or a reduced rate. Make sure you—and your photographer—know what the technical requirements for the magazine are: color or black and white. Also find out how they want to receive the pictures: via e-mail or through a disk that you mail to them. If by e-mail, what format should the pictures be in?

Don't be afraid to send your pictures to local magazines and local newspapers across the country if your event has a national scope. You might be surprised at how many local newspapers are looking for content and will run your photographs. Always remember to follow up so you can have a record of all of your placements.

Send your pictures in the form of a photo alert: Choose the best shots, attach a short paragraph about the event, and name from left to right the people in the photographs along with their affiliations. Always include information on how to contact you or your press person, in case the publication has questions or wants to do a more extensive story. And don't forget to give your photographer credit!

For example, if the picture was of me, my friend Holly Robinson Peete, Marian Wright Edelman, Colin Cowie, and my mother at an event I hosted, the photo alert might read as follows:

PHOTO ALERT

The Angelrock Project hosted a small cocktail party on March 2, 2010, to raise awareness for the HollyRod Foundation. The event, held at the home of its host, Malaak Compton-Rock, was attended by leaders in the world of business, entertainment, and philanthropy, invited to understand the critical work being done by the HollyRod Foundation, whose mission is to help those suffering from Parkinson's disease and autism.

(Pictured from left to right) Malaak Compton-Rock, founder and director, the Angelrock Project; Holly Robinson Peete, actress and cofounder of the HollyRod Foundation; Colin Cowie, event planner and president of Colin Cowie Lifestyle; Marian Wright Edelman, founder and president of the Children's Defense Fund; Gayle Fleming, activist.

For more information, call Jane Doe at 000-000-0000
Photo Credit: John Smith

Once you have your photographer lined up, prepare a *shot list:* a list of photographs you want to be sure to get. Here are some snapshots you might want on your shot list: your group's president with celebrities or other important guests; your guests enjoying themselves; your board members, if applicable; any honorees accepting their awards; and the awards, flowers, and decor. You might also assign a volunteer to work with the photographer throughout the event, taking note of anything that needs to be recorded along the way.

Do-It-Yourself Promotion

*U*seful as the media can be in promoting your cause, you don't have to rely on them. You can also create pamphlets or leaflets and leave them in key places around town: nail and hair salons, coffeehouses, local retailers. We do this with the Triple Negative Breast Cancer Foundation, and I have the pleasure of seeing our pamphlets in the salon when I go in to get my nails done. I can attest from personal experience that this kind of do-it-yourself promotion really works: I've taken my kids to two fund-raisers from groups I've never heard of simply because I found their leaflets at my gym.

And of course, using a social media website like Facebook is a perfect way to promote your event and/or cause yourself. I love the fact that you can invite all of your cyber friends to an event or ask them to join your cause. And even if they cannot come to your event, the exposure is awesome. I used Facebook to invite people to the Journey for Change car wash, and I have a Journey for Change cause page too!

Keeping in Touch: Cultivating Ongoing Relationships with the Media

I can't end this chapter without reminding you to stay connected to the media people you've succeeded in reaching, whether they've come to your event or not. Developing relationships with reporters, editors, and producers can be so helpful to your organization over the long term. Send periodic updates, pitch more stories, and write thank-you notes for any coverage you get. Ask them what they're interested in covering, and get them to help you tool your pitches to their needs.

If you're supporting more than one cause, your ongoing relationships will pay off, because you can return to reporters or producers whom you already know in another context rather than having to make cold calls. You might also invite reporters or producers to social events, if that feels appropriate, as a way of thanking them and to keep cultivating the relationship.

MY JOURNEY: EDITOR IN CHIEF OF *ESSENCE* MAGAZINE ANGELA BURT-MURRAY

Essence magazine is the leading fashion and beauty magazine geared toward African-American women. I remember seeing it around even before I was old enough to read it, and when I did start reading it, it resonated with me immediately.

Susan L. Taylor, the original editor in chief, led the magazine for most of its life. She now runs a phenomenal mentoring organization called the National CARES Mentoring Movement. She happens to be the best friend of my first boss, Terrie M. Williams, and her organization received a $1 million grant from Oprah Winfrey!

A few years ago, Susan Taylor passed the editorial baton to Angela Burt-Murray, who has given the magazine a fresh and innovative new face. Angela is a friend, a colleague, and someone I've served on a board with, so I know her well and admire her greatly. She shares my belief that we can incorporate service into all walks of life, and so as editor in chief of *Essence,* she has always been receptive to ideas that I have brought to her. As a savvy editor, she is certainly not going to say yes to everything, but she's always willing to listen and to give great advice. I've learned a great deal from the articles published under her leadership, and I am also grateful to her for running a story on Journey for Change's trip to South Africa in the magazine's August 2009 issue. Here's an interview I conducted with Angela Burt-Murray for this book.

Q. What is *Essence*'s mission? Why do you think that mission is important?
A. *Essence* is the definitive voice of today's dynamic African-American woman. *Essence* is the premier lifestyle, fashion, and beauty magazine

that celebrates, inspires, entertains, informs, and empowers black women. While most magazines are either described as a window or a mirror, *Essence* is both: a reflection of our best selves and a window into the possibilities of living a fuller life. Designed to be an advocate for a reader that often feels marginalized in a racist and sexist society, *Essence* speaks directly to a black woman's spirit, her heart, and her unique concerns.

This magazine speaks to a woman with myriad responsibilities— she's overscheduled, overworked, and underappreciated. *Essence* connects with this reader by putting her *first*. Putting black women *first* is the organizing editorial principle. This magazine functions as a sacred support system that encourages and teaches readers that by living with a sense of genuine purpose, they will be able to extend their whole selves to their family, friends, and larger community. . . . *Essence* doesn't have a readership—it is a community. When readers bring a copy of *Essence* home they feel like their best girlfriend has come for a visit to talk, laugh, gossip, maybe even cry, but most certainly heal.

Q. What are some examples of service, volunteerism, advocacy, and/or nonprofit stories that you have run over the years? Please tell us about the people or organizations in these features.
A. *Essence* has a history of speaking truth to power, of breaking provocative features, of telling the stories of ordinary women facing and overcoming extraordinary obstacles. This is very important to our audience because often when African-American stories play out in the mainstream media they present us as victims or perpetrators, our perspectives are misrepresented, or the story simply provides little context for the larger societal issues of rampant racial and gender discrimination. But not in *Essence*!

Q. What qualities/elements do you look for in a story about service and/or advocacy?
A. *Essence* looks to highlight people or organizations that are having an impact on the grassroots level and finding creative solutions to help deal with core issues of concern for African-American women and by extension the black community.

Q. If people want to approach you for coverage, what steps should they follow?

A. Anyone interested in pitching a story to *Essence* should first familiarize themselves with the magazine and the types of stories we do. Interested parties can successfully pitch story ideas to an editor by identifying the ways in which their idea effectively speaks to our audience's areas of concern and how this pitch offers a unique and compelling perspective.

Q. What difference do you think it makes to your readers to learn about people who dedicate their lives to helping others?

A. Our 8.5 million readers are inspired by stories of ordinary women and men who are doing the extraordinary and try to find ways to implement the solutions and tips that they find in our magazine. I personally receive hundreds of letters and e-mails from readers who are grateful to *Essence* for sharing accounts of altruism and starting a dialogue that served to motivate them to either join a volunteer organization, donate to a charity, or reunite with friends in need.

Q. What difference do you think it makes to an organization or person in the nonprofit field to be publicized in *Essence*?

A. *Essence* offers a powerful way to reach African-American women and by extension black America, as we are one of the most respected brands in the community. Our voice is authentic and authoritative, and our relationship with the audience is intimate. Our relationship is like that of a girlfriend who always has the reader's best interest at heart and is always advocating on her behalf and giving her the critical information to live the life she deserves. As a result, coverage in *Essence* serves as a launching pad for many organizations looking to expand their membership or augment their fund-raising efforts.

Chapter 8

If It Takes a Village, Build One

■

If you want to go fast, go alone. If you want to go far, go together
—SOURCE UNKNOWN

I was sitting with Gogo Skhosana in her Diepsloot shack, enjoying the rare free hour I had to spend with her one sunny afternoon. Her home was a typical Diepsloot shanty, perhaps a little nicer than most, made of corrugated metal like all the others but with a linoleum floor rather than the bare dirt or scrap wood of so many of the other shacks. Because hers was one of the families I had been helping for a while, she was also one of the few people in the area who had electricity, by way of a single wire running close to the shack, like a clothesline.

Gogo lived in the shack with her five grandchildren, the children of her two daughters, who had passed away from AIDS. Her son and grandson lived there with her as well, so at that time there were seven people in that one-room shack. The shack would have been small even for one person, let alone six or seven, but Gogo had made the most of every inch. She had a couch, a little table, and a hot plate in the back corner, next to the little refrigerator that the electricity had made possible. She had draped a brightly colored blanket over the back of the couch and put some photos and a poem up on her walls. Her place was way down the back of a dirt alleyway, and all the kids from that part of the neighborhood played right outside her door.

I was sitting on Gogo's couch and suddenly this strange kind of electric feeling just came over me. I don't remember something like that ever happening, before or since, but with the feeling came a thought: that I needed to bring my Bushwick kids over to South Africa.

The Bushwick kids were the young people I had met in Brooklyn while I had been looking for ways to support the Salvation Army Bushwick Community Center in Brooklyn. My husband had attended that center throughout his childhood, and I had made it one of the main focal points of my work. I had come to know and love the children who came through its doors—to play basketball, learn computer skills, use the library, or take advantage of the many other programs offered by the center.

Now, as I sat in Gogo Skhosana's shack, I found myself thinking about those Bushwick children. Without even knowing I was going to, I started telling Gogo about it. "I want to bring some kids from Brooklyn who I work with to come visit you here," I told her. "I want them to experience travel, to experience giving back and serving, and for them to see how so many people in this world live. But I also want them to see the joy and the pride and the work ethic and the sense of family that the people I work with here have. I want them to understand that you can have just a little bit of material wealth but still have so much happiness inside of you."

I'm still not completely sure where the idea came from. But I think maybe it was because the two places in the world I felt most at home, besides my own house and neighborhood, were Diepsloot and Bushwick, so maybe there was a way to bring these two second homes together.

As it turned out, there was—but it was going to be an enormously challenging endeavor, requiring me to draw on everything I knew about partnerships, corporate sponsorships, and mobilizing a widely diverse group of donors to support a common goal. If there ever was a case where going far meant going together, Journey for Change: Empowering Youth Through Global Service was it.

Getting Acquainted with Bushwick

I'd always had a warm relationship with the Salvation Army Bush-wick Community Center because of my husband's work with the kids there throughout the years. Chris is a silent giver, a person who is extraordinarily generous but does his giving anonymously and without any fanfare. For years I watched him from afar taking hun-dreds of kids on fun and exciting outings to places like Toys "R" Us, the Radio City Christmas Spectacular, and, of course, baseball games. This was something that Chris did on his own with an assis-tant and I would usually find out about it only when I looked at his weekly schedule. I never went because it was his thing, but I was al-ways proud that he was so committed and that he personally went on all of the outings with the kids.

In August 2007, though, I came up with an idea. I asked him if we could bring the cast of *Everybody Hates Chris,* the TV show he had created, to Brooklyn for a holiday party with the kids at the community center. After all, even though the show was filmed on a Hollywood soundstage, it was based on Chris's life in Brooklyn. I just knew the kids would get the biggest kick out of meeting "their" characters in real life. Chris said, "Sure," but added that I would need to call Dawn Ostroff, the president of the CW network, and get her approval.

To my delight, Dawn thought it was a great idea and one that her team could use to promote the upcoming Christmas episode by screening it for the kids. I found out during our conversation that Dawn was born and raised in Brooklyn, too!

Once I had spoken with Dawn, I knew I had several elements set. The studio would ask the cast to participate and would fly them to New York. They would also help bring in the local CW network to promote the day, and they would provide us with two episodes to screen, giving DVDs of the show to all of the kids. Now, what else did I need in order to give two hundred kids a truly spectacular day? Clearly, I needed more sponsors.

Since this was a Brooklyn celebration, I thought that screening the episodes at the Brooklyn Academy of Music (BAM) would be perfect. BAM has a beautiful facility located in downtown Brooklyn with multiple screening rooms and space for a party. So I put in some preliminary calls, found out about costs, and reserved a screening room while I worked on the rest of the event.

As this was a Christmas event, I wanted the kids to have gifts, of course, so I needed to think of a great retailer that had stores in Brooklyn and that might be interested in partnering with us as a sponsor. Thinking of Target was very natural, because the store is one of my favorite retailers in the world. I buy everything under the sun from them. I love asking someone who visits my house, "Look in this room and tell me what came from Target!" And no one can tell me if it is the vase, the picture frame, the candle holder, or whatever else I have purchased.

But why I really like Target is because of that big sign that you see at the checkout counter that says they donate 5 percent of their profits, equaling $3 million per week. I love the fact that I shop at a retailer that gives away money to the community where I shop and to those areas around the world in which their products are made. I love even more that they allow their employees to have a say in what they support.

I knew that Target would have all of the hot toys and items for the kids and that they would also have things that the children might need, such as clothing and school supplies. Still, despite all my admiration for Target, I had never worked with them before, so I just had to simply ask and hope for the best. I quickly sent a few e-mails and made some phone calls. Once I had a bit of interest, I wrote a proposal and sent it to Target's social responsibility department.

If you're making this kind of ask, you need to let your potential partner know what you can bring to the table. I told them I could bring the cast of *Everybody Hates Chris,* who would go shopping with the kids. Obviously, we would have press there, which seemed like great publicity for Target.

Luckily, Target loved the idea, and wouldn't you know it, there is a great store right across the street from BAM. So with Target on board as our major sponsor, we were able to throw a phenomenal shopping spree in which every child received a $250 gift card. Target also sponsored a beautiful breakfast at BAM in a room that was decorated like a winter wonderland.

The kids had fun shopping with the cast, and they enjoyed viewing two episodes of *Everybody Hates Chris,* which was followed by a Q&A with the cast. After a wonderful day, the kids left with Target gift bags and amazing smiles. But what was really fantastic and added synergy to this project is that Target was already a huge supporter of the Salvation Army on a national level and had long been a supporter of BAM. So for them it was a very nice way to expand their support for organizations that they already cared about.

For me, the absolute best part of the day was the $100,000 check that Target presented to the Salvation Army Bushwick Community Center to renovate their facility, along with an additional $5,000 from the local New York CW affiliate. This is where my connection with the community center really took off. The people there weren't exactly sure how they wanted to use the money, but they knew they wanted me to be involved somehow.

As I'd done in Diepsloot, I started spending a lot of time at the center, getting to know the people and learning about their programs. I realized that although the center had a computer lab, it was quite old, which limited what they could offer the kids. The lab was only open for three hours after school—another limitation.

A second space that needed improvement was the library. It didn't have many books and quite honestly, it just didn't feel like a nice space for learning. I could imagine that with a more welcoming, comfortable environment, kids would be reading more and spending more time on their homework. So I suggested that we use the money for the computer lab and the library. The staff loved the idea, but they were also concerned that the center had no place to do any kind of visual arts. They showed me an empty room that wasn't being used and suggested that it be turned into an art room.

Now that we knew what we wanted to do, we needed more help. True, we already had the corporate sponsorship of Target, and this was major, but we did not want to waste a cent. We had not yet involved a designer or architect, and we needed this expertise.

With this mandate, one of our first "angels" was Dwight Johnson, the first tenured African-American professor at Pratt Institute, a respected art school located in Brooklyn. Though Dwight was now president of Dwight Johnson Design, a full-service special events firm, he was also president of Pratt's Black Alumni Association, which meant that he could introduce me to someone who might help us.

That person was Rodney Leon, a Harvard and Pratt graduate and the architect who had designed the memorial at New York City's African Burial Ground. Rodney had grown up in Brooklyn, too, in a family of modest means. He understood very well what life was like for the Bushwick kids, and so he agreed to design the computer lab and library space pro bono. As an architect who owns his own firm, AARRIS Architects Ltd., he was a very busy man—but a great man who wanted to give back.

Dwight also arranged for us to partner with the Pratt Institute, a partnership that is continuing to pay off for the Bushwick kids. After the library officially opened on November 12, 2008, for example, we created a program where Pratt students come over and teach graphic design and other types of computer-based design to the young people. When the art room opens, more students will teach there as well.

Our corporate sponsor Target continued its generosity, donating all of the furniture for the space once Rodney and his partner, a recent Pratt graduate named Darius Somers, had handed in their phenomenal designs. (PRODUCT) RED was also very generous. This amazing company, run by rock star and humanitarian Bono and politician and activist Bobby Shriver, raises money to eradicate HIV/AIDS in Africa through innovative partnerships with companies that sell (RED) items and donate a percentage of sales to the Global Fund. (RED) helped arrange the donation of eighteen (RED) Dell desktops for the library. I am proud to say that this initiative planted the seeds for Target to donate an additional $1 million to the Salvation Army for the sole purpose of erecting additional libraries in Salvation Army community centers across America. Chris and I were proud to make this announcement and even prouder to ensure that some of the funding would go to the center that now stands in his home neighborhood of Bedford-Stuyvesant.

All that time hanging out in Bushwick had allowed me to get to know the kids—and it had enabled the kids to get to know me. If they saw me at the center they'd run up for a hug and a kiss. They even called me "Auntie," showing both their respect and their feeling that I was part of their family.

Seeing how many individuals and corporations were needed to support the center, I realized all over again that it takes a village to raise a child. I'd been fortunate to grow up in a middle-class home in a house full of books and politics. Despite those advantages, I understood very well how difficult it is to dream of a better life when you've never known anything other than your own at-risk neighborhood. The Salvation Army Bushwick Community Center offered the children the warmth of a strong community, but the actual neighborhood was also struggling under the burdens of drug addiction, poverty, unemployment, and crime.

I'd always been one to get exasperated with people who didn't understand inner-city or rural kids and their lack of aspirations. "How can you aspire to something that you have never heard of and never seen?" I'd ask. "If we want these kids to dream big, we have to give them something to dream *about*."

Well, if I believed so deeply in the important of service—and travel—why couldn't I help expose the Bushwick kids to those experiences? I truly believed that all of them could become world citizens and ambassadors for change: people who helped to make the world a better place. Maybe I could help show them what they could become. And thus, the idea of Journey for Change: Empowering Youth Through Global Service was born.

The Journey Begins

So there I was, as I described in the introduction to this book, standing in front of the kids in the Bushwick Community Center, taking the first step on this journey for change and wondering which of these young people were going to take it with me. We had invited kids from all of the different programs the center offers, including the after-school program, and the ones who came for tutoring, computer classes, or to use the library. I especially wanted to make sure I reached the boys who came to the center to play basketball, the kids who came to the center just to get a meal, the ones just looking to get off the streets for a while. I wanted to reach *all* the children who came to the center—not just the motivated ones or the academically oriented ones. Probably the student who stood out most at that orientation was Jeremy Baker, a fifteen-year-old kid who came to the center for the rec program. Jeremy had shown up with a group of his basketball buddies—just the kind of kid I wanted to reach. He was a skinny, gangly kid with the brightest, sweetest smile you ever saw. At that first orientation meeting, though, he was dead serious. I had invited the children and their parents to ask any and all questions, and of course, the parents had a lot to ask, but many of the children were shy.

Except Jeremy. He was full of questions—good questions, about which people we were going to help and what they needed and what we were going to do about it. But what struck me more than what he asked was the *way* he asked: Each time he had a question, he stood up, very formal and proper, but you could see that he was bubbling with excitement each time. In that whole room, he was the only child who stood up to ask his questions.

I was especially pleased that Jeremy was there because of his connection to the recreational program. At the end of my talk, when I asked everyone who wanted to go to South Africa to raise his or her hand, I was sure Jeremy's hand would be the first one in the air.

But it wasn't. Several other hands went up, but Jeremy just sat there, quiet and still.

I couldn't let go of this bright, inquisitive youngster, so I went up to him afterward as everyone milled around, still talking about the trip. "Hey," I asked him, "why didn't you raise your hand back there?"

He gave me that sweet, brilliant smile. " 'Cause I don't wanna go."

"Are you sure? You had so many questions, you stood up to ask them, I love your confidence—are you sure you don't want to go?"

"Yes, ma'am. I'm sure. I don't need to go to South Africa. I'm happy to stay right here."

Well, I must admit, I was disappointed. Not only was Jeremy refusing to go, despite all his wonderful questions, but none of the other rec center boys had raised their hand either. I was thrilled with the interest shown by all the other children, and I was very happy to have spoken with so many parents and guardians, many of whom had told me how grateful they were that their children were even being considered for such a trip—just knowing that the Bushwick children were being given such a wonderful opportunity meant the world to them. Those responses made me feel great. But I could not accept that none of the basketball boys were applying for this trip.

Now, I believe wholeheartedly in recreational programs. They are absolutely needed, and I think they should be given even more support and funding than they are. But I believe just as deeply that every boy who comes to a community center to play basketball should be given the opportunity to get involved in something else. It scares me that so many youths want to be basketball players and that they have no one in their life to instill in them that they need to have a backup plan. Only through exposure to new possibilities can they start thinking outside the box; it's up to us to give them that exposure.

So I was very disappointed that I hadn't been able to reach any of the recreational center boys. And I decided to do something about it.

I asked the man who ran the center, Captain Travis Lock, to set up another orientation meeting. Unlike the first, which had been for everyone, I asked if this one could be just for the rec program boys. And unlike the first meeting, which had been voluntary, I asked him to make this one mandatory.

I didn't think I was the best person to speak to those boys in a way they would understand, so I asked my dear friend Kevin Powell to do it for me. Kevin is a prolific writer, an effective politician, and a very popular inspirational speaker. He's from Brooklyn himself, where he still lives and where he was raised by a single mother. He got himself to college, built a very successful career, and has remained deeply dedicated to all issues having to do with poverty. He's particularly interested in reaching fatherless young boys to help them grow into good and responsible men. Generously, he agreed to speak to the Bushwick boys about going to South Africa with Journey for Change.

Kevin gave just the most wonderful speech—better even than I could have imagined. He asked the boys to share their ideas about hip-hop and somehow he brought that idea around to the notion that in order to be a real aficionado of hip-hop, you have to be a lover of art, culture, travel, and all kinds of new experiences. He told them that he grew up in Brooklyn and still lived just five minutes away from his old neighborhood. But he had also been all the way around the world. He told them that they, too, could travel across the ocean to South Africa and still be part of their old world, so they shouldn't miss this opportunity.

Kevin spoke with those kids for an hour, and their attention was absolutely rapt. And when at the end of his talk he asked, "How many of you want to go to South Africa with Journey for Change?" half the hands in that room went up.

But still not Jeremy's. He had listened with the others, rapt like the rest, but he still hadn't expressed any interest in the trip.

This time when I went up to Jeremy, he happened to be standing with his best friend, fourteen-year-old Jonathan Severe, who is probably one of the shiest, quietest boys I have ever met. Jonathan is also an extremely talented basketball player who wants to go to the NBA.

But that day, they were just two teenage boys, a bit tongue-tied in my presence, especially when I asked them why they didn't want to come to South Africa.

"You were both so involved in the discussion," I said to them. "Why don't you want to go?"

They shrugged, the way boys do. "We just don't want to," they told me.

I had made up my mind before that first orientation meeting that I was only going to take on this trip the kids who really wanted to go. They were going to have to demonstrate some commitment, too: fill out an application, write a couple of essays, collect recommendations from people who weren't family members. So by rights, I should have left Jeremy and Jonathan to their own devices and moved on to the kids whose hands had gone up.

But there was something about these two young men that I just didn't want to give up on. So I found myself making a deal with them. "I want you guys to go on this trip," I told them, "so let's do this. You go on and fill out an application. And then, if you're chosen and you *still* don't want to go, I won't say another word."

Lucky for all of us, they agreed. They filled out the application, they were accepted—and in the end, they went. And let me tell you, they blossomed the second they got off the plane. They threw themselves into service in South Africa, and they've remained equally committed in Brooklyn. When I think of Journey for Change, I think of Jonathan and Jeremy and how much that trip meant to them.

But I'm getting ahead of myself. Before Journey for Change could go anywhere or do anything, we had to raise the money for the trip. And for that, we were going to need a lot of help.

Finding Our Partners

First, I obviously had to make sure that the people at the Bushwick center were on board with the idea and that they were up for all the work it would involve. I knew I would need them to relay information to the kids and their parents, help me to organize numerous orientation sessions, send at least four employees to travel with the group to South Africa, and assist with lots of other tasks that certainly would pop up.

I would also need help from the Salvation Army Greater New York Division to get approvals to take children out of the country, insurance, and the like. And I'd need the Salvation Army in South Africa to arrange visits to some of their projects over there. Since our children were so involved with the Bushwick Salvation Army, I thought it would be good for them to see some South African sites run by the organization that was already so important in their lives. It was the kind of global connection that I hoped the whole trip would help them make, enabling them to feel like world citizens both there and here.

With the Salvation Army on board, I started looking for other partners. One of the first came through the Salvation Army in South Africa, a great illustration of how networking pays off and how one good deed often leads to another. The South African Salvation Army used a South African public relations agency, Quo Vadis Communications, which generously offered their pro bono services to publicize our trip while we were there. I knew that we'd need that kind of media exposure to build future donor support.

More central to our trip's purpose was my partnership with the Olive Leaf Foundation, the South Africa–based NGO whose fieldworkers and manager I had met in Diepsloot and Soweto. My liaison with that group was a wonderful man named Cornelius Themba Xulu who's very involved in the nonprofit community in Johannesburg. I had a very distinct idea of what I wanted the children to see, based on my knowledge of the area, but I needed the Olive Leaf Foundation's help—and Cornelius's—in coordinating those visits in advance.

I wanted the Bushwick kids to visit the shantytowns and community centers of Diepsloot and Soweto. I wanted them to serve orphans and grannies and visit schoolchildren of all ages, to spend time in orphanages and clinics, and to pitch in by digging trenches for vegetable gardens and cleaning and painting buildings. But I also wanted them to see the beauty of the country and to learn something about its history. I wanted them to go on safari, to visit the Apartheid Museum and the Hector Pieterson Museum, which commemorates the antiapartheid activism of schoolchildren in Soweto. I wanted to take the Brooklyn kids to an African restaurant, so they could taste the best of South African food, and bring them to the Lesedi Cultural Village, so they could learn something about the many tribes and cultures of this huge and diverse nation.

For that aspect of the trip, I needed a different type of partner: South African Tourism. I reached out to the agency's New York office, which is headed by a wonderful woman named Sthu Zungu who has since become a good friend.

At the time, though, I hadn't met Sthu. While I was waiting to hear back from her, I happened to be in Los Angeles for something that had nothing to do with South Africa or Bushwick and I ended up going for drinks at the Hotel Bel-Air with my dear friend Colin Cowie, the esteemed event planner, author, and president of Colin Cowie Lifestyle, along with his business partner Stuart Brownstein.

Among other things, Colin is the mastermind behind most of Oprah Winfrey's events, including the opening of the Oprah Winfrey Leadership Academy for Girls. In addition, he has a fabulous home collection that he sells on the Home Shopping Network. Colin is also proudly South African and a humanitarian, which is why I had told him and Stuart about my plans. Lo and behold, when we met for drinks, he brought another friend he thought I'd like to meet—none other than Sthu Zungu!

"I can't believe this," I said to her. "I've been trying to get in touch with you in New York."

"Oh, I didn't get your letter," she explained. "I spend more time traveling than sitting in my office."

Luckily, she loved the idea of Journey for Change. With her help, and an introduction and lunch in South Africa with her boss, Moeketsi Mosola, the CEO of South African Tourism at the time, the agency came through for us in an extraordinary way, helping to provide us with many, many cultural and recreational activities as well as hosting an amazing bon voyage party for the kids at the South African consulate in New York City.

The partnerships kept coming, each more generous than the last. Signatures Network donated our gear: hoodies, sweatshirts, T-shirts, hats, backpacks, all featuring the Journey for Change logo. The logo, of course, was designed pro bono by Richard Menage. The Palazzo Montecasino Hotel, where I stay often on business and also with my family, offered us two rooms for free and discounted rates on the others. Champion Security, the firm I always use for driving and security in Johannesburg, offered us a 30 percent discount. LJR Airport Concierge Services, a company you can hire to help you negotiate airport lines and luggage, offered their services pro bono and came through for us like champions, creating special lines just for us, helping our first-time travelers with their passports and luggage, and showing the kids how to go through a security line. AlphaGraphics, a New York City firm, provided us with pro bono printing. Vision Integrated provided pro bono and reduced-rate photography services in South Africa. The Ford Foundation gave us a substantial grant. The HeronBridge Retreat, where the children stayed, provided us with reduced-cost lodging and meals. And of course, South African Airways was extremely generous with their group rates on our airline tickets.

These were all donations that I had in some way solicited. But I also received gifts that I never even asked for. I had approached It's Easy Passport and Visa Services, a company that walks you through the passport process and does most of the application work for you. I'd used them when Chris and I had to take our children abroad and needed to obtain passports for them in a hurry. I thought they'd be helpful with our Bushwick kids—but they weren't just helpful, they were crucial. It seemed many of our children had some special passport problem: incorrect birth certificate, absent father whose signature was needed on the passport application, names that didn't match their guardians' names—the list went on and on. It's Easy came through with every single passport for every single child—*and they did it completely gratis.*

That's right. They didn't charge us a cent. They even paid the government passport fees for us, which I never even asked for. But when Leslie Shapiro, the company's owner, learned who was going on our trip and why, she wanted to help. It can truly bring me to tears when I think about their contribution. As you know, without passports we were not going anywhere. And Leslie and all her staff, particularly Niema, were so kind and patient with our special cases.

These are only some of the partners who joined with us to help our Bushwick kids get to South Africa. The way I see it, we needed every single one of our partners, because each of them helped make it possible for us to go. There wasn't one partnership that was less valuable than any other. Every one of them was needed. Truly, we travel farthest when we travel together.

Asking for What You Want

Once I'd determined the pro bono donations and discounts I could expect, I looked at my budget and figured out what else I needed. Now it was time to write a fund-raising letter.

The first batch of letters that I sent out were somewhat personal, to friends and people who had previously supported my causes, such as the New Orleans Freedom School, the Triple Negative Breast Cancer Foundation, and Champions for Children. I then called on some of my donors and asked them if they could help me expand my list by suggesting other people who might be interested in supporting Journey for Change: Empowering Youth Through Global Service. A second batch of letters went out to these donors. Here's the letter I sent soliciting donations for Journey for Change. It's long—but I was asking for a lot. Sometimes you need to give a lot of information to make the project come alive.

JOURNEY for CHANGE®
Empowering Youth Through Global Service

March 27, 2008

Ms. Jane Doe
1234 Universe Place
New York, NY 11111

Dear Jane,

I am thrilled and excited to introduce you to a very unique and life-changing opportunity for youth from Bushwick, Brooklyn. The Angelrock Project, an online organization that I founded to promote my humanitarian endeavors, but more importantly to offer pertinent information on leading a life of service, is partnering with the Salvation Army Bushwick

Community Center and the Olive Leaf Foundation on Journey for Change: Empowering Youth Through Global Service, an extraordinary opportunity to take 30 at-risk children from Bushwick, Brooklyn, to volunteer in South Africa in August 2008. Our mission is to empower the children through global travel and community service. I am writing in hopes that you will consider sponsoring a child for this incredible opportunity.

Journey for Change: Empowering Youth Through Global Service Background

The Salvation Army Bushwick Community Center is a haven for youth of all ages, the elderly, the hungry, the homeless, and the mentally challenged, located in Bushwick, a neighborhood in Brooklyn struggling with drug trafficking, a high incidence of child neglect, a rising crime rate, and single-parent families. The Center serves as a place for youth and others to escape the streets for a nourishing meal, after-school tutoring, recreation, spiritual guidance, and mentoring. Just a sampling of their life-saving work provided in 2006 includes providing 1,586 items of clothing, 54,643 meals and snacks, physical education sessions to 4,140, 10,682 days of care to children, 5,694 hours of after-school instruction, and 5,291 holiday gifts. My husband, Chris, attended the after-school program and the summer camp program as a child and we have been supporting the Center in many, many ways for over 10 years.

Before I go any further, however, it is paramount to explain the three main goals of Journey for Change:

• To introduce travel to children who have not had the opportunity to do so, many of whom have never left New York City

• To introduce volunteerism and service to children who have been on the receiving end of aid, but not on the giving side of service

• To reinforce in the children, who feel as if they are disadvantaged, that they have so many more inherent opportunities by living in the U.S. than their counterparts in South Africa Due to the startling fact that education is not free in South Africa and there are few government social services offered to the poor, it is our greatest hope that the children will return to the U.S. with a renewed sense of gratitude for our social and governmental systems.

Furthermore, we want them to take full advantage of their ability to attend school, receive free books and resources, live in proper housing, and have access to food and other necessities of life. Ultimately, we want them to return to the U.S. encompassing a greater sense of understanding for their blessings, to dream big, and to challenge themselves to become the best young people that they can be.

In 2006, I was introduced to the life-saving work of the Olive Leaf Foundation, while on an official UNICEF visit in South Africa. I was so impressed with their work in the shanty-town of Diepsloot, Johannesburg, and in Soweto, that I have supported their work ever since then. This past February, I traveled to South Africa for the third time to expand our educational support for orphaned children and to start a community garden and micro-credit initiative. The Olive Leaf Foundation offers sustainable, high-impact, community-based services to the poor and needy on every inhabited continent, serving more than one million people annually.

Hence, I am so proud that together with my partners at the Salvation Army Bushwick Community Center, the Salvation Army of Greater New York, the Salvation Army South Africa, and the Olive Leaf Foundation, we are able to organize Journey for Change: Empowering Youth Through Global Service, a two-week volunteer-based travel program, to 30 at-risk youth from Bushwick, Brooklyn.

Moreover, I am thrilled with the diverse nature of all of the partners, each one bringing a particular expertise to the project that will make for a fruitful and multi-faceted program.

Journey for Change: Empowering Youth Through Global
Service Components

The children chosen will be between the ages of 12 and 15 (the age where they are typically lost to the streets) after completing a thorough process that will include completing an application, an interview with the child and the parent/guardian, a teacher and personal recommendation, and a written essay. We are currently in the selection process.

The 30 children from Brooklyn will then be paired with 30 young college students who will act as chaperones and mentors. We will conduct a two-day orientation in New York prior to the children leaving in order to establish the mentoring relationship, lead some team-building activities, as well as mentally prepare them for the 18-hour flight and for the type of poverty that they will encounter in South Africa.

Once they arrive in Johannesburg, they will have an additional orientation led by the Salvation Army South Africa before they begin their service experience. Following the orientation, for 10 days the children will volunteer on age-appropriate projects in Diepsloot, Johannesburg, and in Soweto, including but not limited to visiting an orphan-led household each day offering assistance, helping to re-build shanty-town shacks, painting schools or other sites, working in community gardens that feed the orphan and granny-led population, working with grannies on their income-generating projects, and working in the offices of the organizations in the field.

Coupled with volunteering, and also very important, will be educational, team-building and recreational activities. We will provide the volunteers with the opportunity of visiting historical sites such as the Apartheid Museum, the Hector Pieterson Museum, and Nelson Mandela's home in Soweto, as well as recreational activities such as a ½ day safari, a visit to Sun City, and lessons in African dance and the Zulu language. In addition, each evening the college-aged mentors will lead team-building and self-esteem workshops, as well as lead a discussion where the youths will be able to reflect and talk about their day of volunteering with a focus on how they were able to change lives through service.

With the help of the Olive Leaf Foundation staff who have extensive experience with global volunteer trips, we have determined the cost of the trip per child/young adult.

For a two-week volunteer experience, it will cost approximately $3,500.00 per child. This includes, but is not limited to:

- Airfare
- Lodging
- Transportation
- Food
- Recreational Activities
- Site Visit Costs

Sponsor Opportunities

As you can imagine, the children who we are taking to South Africa cannot afford the trip, so we are asking individuals to consider sponsoring a child and we hope that we can count on you. Your donation will not only change the life of the child you sponsor, but also the lives of the orphans and grannies that they will serve in South Africa. I have enclosed a separate sheet which details various sponsor levels, and I must say in advance that we will be grateful for any amount and that your contribution will be a truly monumental act of kindness.

Just for your information, I am personally sponsoring three children, plus making an additional donation to cover staffing costs, and our team is seeking corporate and foundation grants to cover other associated expenses. We are also seeking a media sponsor to promote the children's experiences. Our goal is to produce a classroom curriculum that will include a DVD of the trip in order to have an impact on other U.S. children who will not have an opportunity to travel.

Finally, prior to our departure in August, I am thrilled to announce that I will host a summer Bon Voyage party at my home where all of the children, chaperones, staffers, and volunteers will join our individual, media, and corporate sponsors prior to leaving. It will be a joyous occasion where the sponsors can meet the children in person and everyone can celebrate together as we embark on this life-changing volunteer mission.

Jane, I invite you to join me in this endeavor. Your contribution can be made payable to the Salvation Army Bushwick Community Center, which is a 501(c)(3) nonprofit organization.

Please see the enclosed sponsorship form, fact sheets on the Salvation Army Bushwick Community Center and of Greater New York, as well as information on the Olive Leaf Foundation. For information on The Angelrock Project, please visit www.angelrockproject.com.

I look forward to following up with you soon. Should you have any questions in the meantime, please feel free to contact me at xxx-xxx-xxxx or xxx-xxx-xxxx or e-mail me at Malaak@---------.com.

Thank you so much for your consideration.

Peace and many blessings,

Malaak Compton-Rock
Founder and Director
The Angelrock Project

It seems the Journey for Change letter was very effective, because with its help, we raised $270,000 in four months.

Never Underestimate the Generosity of Others

When you go out looking for your own partners and corporate sponsors, there's one thing I want you to remember above all: *People are eager and happy to help, way beyond what you'd ever think!*

Too many words? I can boil it down to two: *Just ask.* You'll be surprised at how much people want to help. Many people want to donate, volunteer, or contribute services, but they don't know how or simply don't realize that what they do for a living—graphic design, passport services, manufacturing sweatshirts—can actually be used for good. It may be up to you to let them know. And once you do, you may be astonished at how quickly they come through.

In fact, here's a great example of how even a tiny local business can come through for your cause. Because South African Airways could only fly so many of us out of New York City, half of our group had to take a bus down to Washington, DC, so we could fly out of there. I managed to get a bus to take us from Brooklyn to DC, but at the last minute I realized that we'd need food for the bus ride down.

I called my friend Annie, who was going on the trip as a chaperone. I remembered she had told me about Ronnie's Bagels, a little deli in Norwood, New Jersey, that had the best sandwiches ever.

"Can you get them to cater us some sandwiches and drinks and chips? And, Annie, we're at the absolute end of our budget—do you think they might donate us food for free?"

Annie made the ask in her irresistible way, and sure enough, Ronnie's Bagels came through. We didn't have to take extra time out of our trip, we didn't have to give the kids junk food, and we saved some money that we sorely needed. It just goes to show you what a small, local company can do—if only you ask them.

Expecting the Unexpected: Keeping a Contingency Fund

*I*n an uncertain world full of surprises there is one thing you can always count on: Your project is going to cost more than you thought it would. It never fails; that budget you labored over for hours or even days is just not going to include everything. At some point, you're going to have to come up with some extra cash.

In South Africa, for example, we realized about halfway through the trip that we were going to have to pay for the kids' laundry. We had thought we'd have laundry facilities where the kids were staying, but something went wrong and we had to have their dirty clothes done at my hotel. That was hardly the cheapest option, but at that point, we didn't have a choice. What we did have, luckily, was a contingency fund. I strongly suggest you have one, too!

Five Ways to Make the Most of Your Partnerships and Corporate Sponsorships

1. Get clear about what you're doing. In order to raise funds, you need to have a clear idea of what you're doing and why it's important. Communicating a clear message about your mission is key to convincing people to support your project.

2. Come up with a list of everything that's absolutely necessary. If you know what's crucial to your project, you'll be able to ask for donations or support with the urgency that fits the situation. Knowing what you need is the key to asking for it.

3. Look at the list and see if there's anything on it that you can get pro bono. Why pay for something if you can get it donated for free?

4. Come up with companies or people. Get creative: Who might have access to the goods and services you need?

5. Draft a letter. If you don't ask, you won't get. A simple letter explaining what your project is and why it's important can do wonders. If you like, use one of the solicitation letters in this chapter for your inspiration.

Raising Money on the Web

If you've got someone who can start a website for your cause pro bono, I urge you to do it. But if you don't have the resources to start off at such a high level, no worries. Join one of the social networking sites and put a page there. You might want to use one of those sites anyway.

Even though I have my own website, I also have a Facebook page for Journey for Change, so I can reach people on that site who might not come over to mine. You, too, might want to check out such social sites as MySpace, Facebook, LinkedIn, and Twitter to promote an event or publicize a cause. Nonprofits and celebrities are now using these sites in amazing ways to raise awareness and funding for their causes. Ashton Kutcher had a Twitter contest against CNN to raise money for bed nets to reduce malaria in Africa, and my good friends Lee and Bob Woodruff raised money through Twitter for their non-profit ReMIND.org, which supports injured troops, for Memorial Day 2009. And on Facebook, you can easily set up a cause page for something you care about and send out invitations for people to join. This is a great advocacy and fund-raising tool. Just be aware that each site has its own rules for what you can put up and what you're allowed to promote.

If you want to collect credit card donations online, you can use a PayPal account, but only if you have nonprofit status. This is a great way for a small, new nonprofit to bring in money, though big, es-tablished nonprofits use PayPal too. Go to www.paypal.com to find out how the service works.

Surf the Net: Online Social Action, Giving, and News Websites

Cyber Giving
Online giving provides a simple, easy, and secure way to donate money to charities worldwide.

• **Donors Choose:** An online charity connecting you to U.S. class-rooms in need. www.donorschoose.org

• **Global Giving:** Connects donors with community-based proj-ects that need support worldwide. www.globalgiving.com

• **Jolkona Foundation:** Believes that people, especially young people, can change the world . . . one small donation at a time. www.jolkona.org

• **Network for Good:** Online giving to charity made safe, easy, and convenient. www.networkforgood.org

- **Oprah's For All Women's Registry:** Support a mom, help a rape victim, save a slave, teach a girl, microloans. www.oprah.com
- **Razoo:** Philanthropy is not just for the rich and famous. Razoo exists to help every person experience the joy of giving. www.razoo .com
- **Vittana:** Investing in education, one loan at a time. Vittana brings student loans to developing countries through person-to-person microlending. www.vittana.org

Social Action Portals

- **Cause Cast:** Is a place to explore issues while helping you connect with a community of people wanting to make a difference. www .causecast.org
- **Take Part:** Is a cause-related site designed to help you explore today's issues and get involved. They believe that with the right information and tools for action, individuals can and will make a difference. www.takepart.org

Social Impact News

- **Huffington Post Impact:** A social impact blog with daily information on service, volunteering, philanthropy, homelessness, sustainability, activism, and civil rights. www.huffingtonpost.com/impact
- **Zoosa:** A single location for all social impact information and opportunities, including actions, ideas, news, blogs, jobs, and volunteering. www.zoosa.org

Social Network Fund-Raising

- **Facebook Causes:** Facebook is a social utility that connects people with friends and others. Causes provides the tools so that any Facebook user can leverage their network to raise awareness and funds for any U.S. registered 501(c)(3) nonprofit or Canadian registered charity. http://apps.facebook.com/causes/about
- **TwitCause:** Helps nonprofits get discovered on Twitter and enables passionate people to support the causes they care about. http://TwitCause.com

Staying Connected: Maintaining Good Relationships with Your Sponsors and Partners

Staying connected to your sponsors and partners is crucial if you want to go back to them for further support. Here are some of the ways we stayed connected for Journey for Change.

• We sent photos of the children taken while we were there. (RED) donated (CONVERSE) RED shoes to all the kids, so we sent them pictures of the children wearing their sneakers. They also arranged for Dell to donate (PRODUCT) RED Dell laptops to each Journey for Change participant—thirty of them in all—to keep forever! So we e-mailed photos of the children blogging on their laptops.

• (RED) also gave us Hallmark cards, so we had the children use the cards to write thank-you notes to our supporters: "Thank you for my Journey for Change clothing," or "shoes," "laptop," "logo," whatever. The letters meant a great deal to our sponsors, and I think it was good for the children to realize that their appreciation mattered, too.

• I personally sent thank-you letters to every single donor. I actually sent two letters: an acknowledgment upon receipt of the check and a longer letter after the trip, describing how well it had gone and laying out what we had planned next.

• I make a point of keeping major donors up-to-date with periodic e-mails, letting them know about program developments and new donations, and I invite them to the Journey for Change graduation.

Showing your appreciation for any and all support is vital. Here's the thank-you letter we sent to one of our sponsors, South African Tourism. The detail I include is intended to show how crucial the sponsorship was and what a huge difference it made in the lives of the children on the trip. Letting your sponsors know the effect their generosity has had is a terrific way to keep them involved over the long haul.

JOURNEY for CHANGE®
Empowering Youth Through Global Service

August 28, 2008

Ms. Sthu Zungu
President
South African Tourism USA
123 Any Name Avenue
Any City, NY 00000

Dear Sthu,

The Journey for Change: Empowering Youth Through Global Service participants are back from South Africa! Thank you so very much for your wonderful contribution by underwriting and coordinating the cultural and recreational activities for the group and for hosting our Bon Voyage reception.

I cannot tell you what an amazing experience it was for the children from Bushwick, Brooklyn, to travel to South Africa for two weeks of global service. As a matter of fact, every dream that I had for these children since the inception of the program came true on Day 3 as we volunteered in Soweto at granny-led and orphan-led households. This was the first day of our trip that the children were subject to extreme poverty, and though they were eager and excited to make the visits and meet the families of Soweto, the evening after the visit was very difficult for the children. There were lots of tears and feelings of guilt and disbelief. However, the children did a phenomenal job identifying the needs of the families by asking questions and observing their living conditions.

The next day was a happy and thrilling day as we shopped for the grannies and orphans and went back to their houses to deliver the goods. Instead of tears, there were smiles, hugs, feelings of pride, and joy at the opportunity to serve. Journey for Change continued with additional visits to families in Diepsloot and Soweto, school visits, quality time with small children at orphanages, building and cleaning projects at schools, and working at gardens that produce food for the orphan population.

As you can imagine, our partnership allowed our participants to have an even more incredible time in South Africa. They loved each and every experience that South African Tourism afforded them and have not stopped talking about Wandies, Lesedi Village, the Apartheid Museum, safari in Sun City, and Moyo at Zoo Lake. Boy did they love the ambience and food at Moyo! They truly enjoyed the beauty and history of the country and I cannot thank you and South African Tourism enough for the wonderful gift of our partnership.

Another part of the program is that the children had daily briefings in the evenings with our staff members so that they could share their feelings about the day's events. These meetings proved crucial to help our children digest and understand the level of poverty they were witnessing. They also wrote in their journals daily, which was highly therapeutic. Additionally, many blogged for CNN.com, and some even took pictures for *Time for Kids* magazine. All of these activities added to the richness of the program.

As you know, upon our return the children began their service as Journey for Change Global Ambassadors for one year. During this time, they will volunteer in Bushwick, Brooklyn, other boroughs in New York City, and around the country. They will also advocate on behalf of better resources in American inner cities and for orphaned and vulnerable children in Africa and raise funds for their African counterparts. I look forward to keeping you posted along the way and sharing all of the highlights of the year with you and your wonderful colleagues at South African Tourism.

Again, thank you so very much for all that you have done as a member of the Journey for Change family. We deeply, deeply appreciate it.

With warm and respectful regards,

Malaak Compton-Rock
Founder and Director
The Angelrock Project

How Can I Thank You? Let Me Count the Ways. . . .

*Y*ou can't necessarily thank all your donors the same way, or you'd never have time to do anything else. But you can thank everyone in some way. Here are some suggestions for how.

1. *For your largest donors:* Announce their name from the stage at a public event; offer a full-page ad in your program or journal; link their website to yours; put their name up on a sign or screen at your next event; mention them in any ads you take out.

2. *For middle-level donors:* List their name in your program; offer a quarter-page or half-page ad in your program or journal; call to thank them personally.

3. *For all donors:* Send a personal thank-you note and periodic updates about the group.

Going On with the Journey

Creating Journey for Change was an incredible journey in and of itself. The work involved in creating partnerships and sponsorships, the labors of fund-raising, and the sheer magnitude of organizing a fourteen-day international trip for thirty at-risk youths was a bigger undertaking than any I'd done yet.

It was also the most meaningful experience I've ever been involved with. To bring together the people of my two "homes" while helping a group of young people see themselves as global ambassadors for change felt like what my whole life had been leading up to. The fun was just beginning.

MY JOURNEY: FOUNDER OF (RED) BOBBY SHRIVER

Bobby Shriver is a businessman, politician, husband, father, and all-around good guy who is very, very special to me. He has founded three companies in the last ten years to help eliminate the financial and health emergencies threatening the people of Africa. These organizations include DATA (Debt, AIDS, Trade, Africa), ONE, and (PRODUCT) RED.

I met Bobby by chance in an airport lounge flying from New York to L.A., and we quickly delved into a conversation about our mutual love of Africa and made plans to meet. We became fast friends with a mutual respect for each other's work. As a businessman and humanitarian, Bobby is so out of my league, but boy, he has a way of making you feel special and letting you know that your work is meaningful.

Bobby immediately offered his assistance with Journey for Change. Along with his wonderful colleague Kate Cusick, he facilitated multiple donations of (PRODUCT) RED partner products, including Dell laptops, Converse sneakers, and Hallmark cards, for each participant. For me, this was not only a generous contribution but one that helped me to teach the kids about exercising their consumer power. I was able to explain that a percentage of all proceeds from the sale of (PRODUCT) RED products goes to Global Fund (RED) grants in Ghana, Lesotho, Rwanda, and Swaziland. To date, (RED) partners have generated more than $130 million for the Global Fund, which immediately translates into lives saved, and every life thus saved is accounted for. So prior to leaving for South Africa, my kids realized that you can look totally cool in Gap clothes and Converse sneakers and save lives at the same time. I was thrilled to get to chat with him recently about his global work.

Q. You are a major public servant. Where did your motivation come from?
A. Well, I owe that one to my mom and dad. You know, my parents practiced what they preached in our house. They expected us to

serve. My dad started the Peace Corps and my mom founded the Special Olympics. Their work is, of course, an inspiration for all that I do. And the cool thing is that though I have started a lot of my own businesses, I am still very involved in Special Olympics and really all that I do is based on my family and my need to serve others.

Q. We met in an airport. You were so nice to me and the minute I told you what I wanted to do with Journey for Change, you told me to call you. Why?
A. Hey, I love the idea of Journey for Change. I love what you are trying to do for these kids. And I told you, I think it is brilliant that you had them sign contracts to be Global Ambassadors for a year. That is my favorite part of the program. You are holding them accountable and making sure that they participate continuously when they return from South Africa. It's great.

Q. When we had our first meeting at the (PRODUCT) RED headquarters in New York City you showed me a video—the *Lazarus Effect* video—that really changed my life because I had never seen how fast a person's life can be saved when they have access to antiretroviral therapy medication.
A. Yes, that video is amazing and very powerful. It is something that I need to show to everyone so that they get what we are doing at (RED). It is very simple. You buy (RED), you save lives. The *Lazarus* video literally shows you how someone's life can be saved the moment they receive their antiretroviral therapy.

Q. During that meeting, I called (RED) a charity. You quickly corrected me and said that (RED) is a business, not a charity. Of course, this is true, but when a company is in the business of saving lives, it is hard to not think of it as a charity.
A. Yes, I am very passionate about correcting people who call (RED) a charity. We are not a charity. We are a business, period. We are about making money like any other company. The only difference is that we donate 100 percent of what we make to the Global Fund to

purchase antiretroviral therapy medication for people with AIDS in sub-Saharan Africa. We have a very different approach and have a business model designed to create awareness and a sustainable flow of money from the private sector into the Global Fund, to help eliminate AIDS in Africa. And this is the way to go. This is how you do it.

Q. How does (RED) work and who are your current business partners?
A. Every day 4,100 men, women, and children die from AIDS in sub-Saharan Africa. This is both preventable and treatable. We know that if people have access to drugs, they can live. To date, our partners have helped us raise over $130 million, which is the equivalent of providing more than 825,000 people with HIV with lifesaving anti-retroviral therapy for one year.

Currently, our (RED) partners are American Express, Apple, Bugaboo, Converse, Dell, Emporio Armani, Gap, Hallmark, Nike, and Starbucks. (PRODUCT) RED partners send a portion of the profits made on (PRODUCT) RED products directly to the Global Fund, to fight AIDS in Africa. The consumer does not pay extra for this. (RED) does not handle this money. It is sent directly to the Global Fund.

Q. When you are in the nonprofit field like me and you coordinate a program such as Journey for Change, you must ask for help. You literally cannot do it without the support of donors and companies. I always tell people that you just have to ask for what you need and hope for the best. Well, I asked and you and (RED) came through in such an important way. Why is this sort of partnership important to you and the company?
A. Like I said, I think the Journey for Change program is such a cool concept. And I understood what you were trying to do when you told me you wanted the kids to understand that they can exercise their consumer power. We also want to spread the word about (RED) and get our products into the hands of people who can help us deliver our message. I thought we would be a good match.

Q. We received donations from Dell, Converse, and Hallmark. Do you understand the impact that you made for our kids?
A. Yes, I think that I do. I am glad that it worked out. I was really excited for the kids to wear those Converse sneakers. We have such cool designs and it was great for the kids to know about them. Everyone really needs to see how cool our sneakers are. So many amazing people have designed shoes for us and you can purchase some one-of-a-kind designs and effect change at the same time. And our partnership with Dell is so important. Everyone nowadays buys a new computer every two to three years or so. Buy a (RED) Dell and you save a life. And our Hallmark cards are so unique and cool. And again, there are so many different designs. And you know, we all send cards to people. So send a (RED) Hallmark card.

Q. Each Journey for Change participant received a (RED) Dell laptop. You helped us to bridge the digital divide in the inner city. This is hugely important. And then you and your team joined Chris and me, Target, and AARRIS Architects to open a new computer lab and library at the Salvation Army Bushwick Community Center through the donation of eighteen (RED) Dell desktops. Hence, you furthered the goal by allowing hundreds of kids at the center to use the computers on a regular basis. What does this mean to you?
A. We know that being able to work on a computer and access the Internet on a regular basis is crucial for all of us. Kids in the inner city must have this option to compete. As a company, (RED) is happy to introduce our partners to worthy endeavors.

Q. Okay, let's chat about the iconic Gap (PRODUCT) RED campaign. It was amazing! The photos are so eye-catching and created such a sensation. It is just phenomenal that all those celebrities came together to help promote your message to buy (RED) Gap products.
A. Yeah, it was a very, very cool thing. Bono called on a lot of friends who he knew cared about the issue, and so did I. It is one of the perks of having friends who are in the public eye. You can call them and ask them to take part in something extraordinarily important. We asked and they came. We are grateful.

Chapter 9

Speaking Up and Taking a Stand

■

Our lives begin to end the day we are silent
about the things that matter.
—MARTIN LUTHER KING JR.

"I think I'm here because I'm supposed to change this world from how it is, to make a new beginning."

These words came from twelve-year-old Sydney Smart on our very first morning in South Africa. We were at the first of many morning devotionals that we would hold every day after breakfast, giving the children a chance to think about such concepts as commitment, faith, and friendship. Although Sydney was excited about this adventure in foreign travel, she was already focused on the service aspect of the trip. She had no idea *how* she could change the world—but she knew that she wanted to.

Not all the Journey for Change kids were as focused on service as Sydney, though. That's why I designed those first few days in South Africa as a chance for the children to get their bearings. I didn't want to plunge them into service work right away, before they even had the time to assimilate the sights, sounds, and tastes of this new country.

Our first full day in South Africa, we brought the children on a tour of Soweto, the historic Johannesburg township that is home to two Nobel Prize winners, Archbishop Desmond Tutu and anti-apartheid activist Nelson Mandela. Soweto was also known as the center of uprisings led by schoolchildren, whose courageous protests were an important aspect of the antiapartheid movement. Our tour therefore included a visit to the Hector Pieterson Museum, where our Journey for Change kids learned about children no older than themselves who risked their lives to demand freedom and protested against the Afrikaans Medium Decree of 1974, which forced all black schools to use Afrikaans and English, instead of their own mother tongue, such as Zulu, in a fifty-fifty mix as languages of instruction. The decree was resented deeply by blacks, as Afrikaans was widely viewed, in the words of Desmond Tutu, as "the language of the oppressor."

Many of the protestors commemorated by the museum were killed by the police, including twelve-year-old Hector Pieterson, who became the iconic face of the 1976 Soweto uprising in apartheid South Africa when a news photograph of the dying Hector being carried by a fellow student was published around the world. Our kids were moved but sobered and maybe a little shocked by the extent to which these children had taken part in such life-or-death struggles.

They soon recovered their spirits at Wandies Place, the famous South African restaurant and one of my favorite places to eat in Soweto. I'm not the only one who loves Wandies: Bill Clinton, Will Smith, Kofi Annan, Quincy Jones, and the O'Jays have also come to this tiny restaurant, the walls of which are plastered with pictures of the famous people who have eaten there.

At dinner, I chatted with thirteen-year-old Donovan Rogers, who wants to be a veterinarian and who has written a 116-page manuscript about how his life would have been different if he'd been able to be the kind of person he wants to be, someone who always lives up to his ideals. I asked him what he thought about the afternoon.

"It was depressing," he said. "Because if I'd been there, I would probably have been one of those kids, and then I probably would have gotten shot."

I asked him why he thought the kids had taken that action when their parents and older siblings hadn't.

"When you're thirteen," he said, "you want to go your own way."

What did he think people should do when they faced injustice? He thought about it and finally replied that people should "try to speak constructively, so that other people will listen, instead of throwing rocks and being angry."

Even though Donovan didn't agree with everything the Soweto students had done, he was certain that if he had been with them, he would have been part of their protest. Advocacy isn't always easy, and I was glad that Donovan could draw that conclusion from his visit to the Hector Pieterson Museum. But advocacy and protest can change the world, and I was glad that he had drawn that conclusion, too.

The next day was Sunday, and the children had the chance to attend a Salvation Army church in a working-class Johannesburg neighborhood that in many ways resembled their own communities in Brooklyn. One of my favorite moments of the whole trip happened at that church, when Jonathan, one of my shiest boys and one who initially did not want to come, went to the stage and played the drums with the gospel band, showing that he might not be able to communicate his feelings through words, but he can do it mightily through worship and music. That evening, we prepared them for the next day's activities, centering on visits to the shantytowns of Diepsloot, where the children would meet with the grannies and orphans I'd come to know and love.

We wanted our children to be prepared for these visits, which can be challenging even for experienced aid workers. The sight of so much poverty can be overwhelming, and it's easy to feel that no amount of help will ever be enough. We also wanted the children to have some idea of how to handle themselves in this new situation.

The first part of the orientation session was led by Dr. Mark Aguire, a physician who has dedicated his life to the HIV/AIDS crisis in Africa. After sharing the horrifying statistics about how HIV/AIDS has affected South Africa and other African countries, he asked the children why AIDS was *their* problem, too. Here are some of the answers they shouted out:

"It's our world."

"We could be at risk."

"Your family could be in danger of it."

"People in Africa are people, too, and if people are suffering anywhere, we're all suffering everywhere."

"We need to feel a sense of responsibility to handle the privileges that we've been given."

"We are our brother's keeper, and if we don't think that it *is* our problem, then there isn't any hope for *any* problem, anywhere in the world."

I was so moved as I watched them struggle with their doubts and fears. These feelings were addressed by the next speaker at the orientation, Zamalinda Xulu, a South African Journey for Change volunteer who was working with us. Her husband, Cornelius, is the Angelrock Project's coordinator in South Africa. With sensitivity and grace, she coached our children, preparing them for the next day's visits.

Zama acknowledged that it might be intimidating to visit a stranger's home, to try to communicate with people who might not speak your language, to realize that the children and babies you see might be suffering from HIV. But, she said, "the whole heart of service is that you are basically doing something that is beyond yourself."

The children nodded, some nervously, others with a growing enthusiasm. I watched them with pride, thinking that tomorrow, they'd begin their first big service trip. I knew that Journey for Change would change and empower them. But I had no idea how much.

Orphans and Grannies

We started the next day at the Salvation Army's Ethembeni Children's Home, an orphanage dedicated to children under three, many of whom had been orphaned because of AIDS and many of whom had been born infected. The Salvation Army officer who runs it with his wife told us, "If you think of a place where children can be left, we have a child who's been left there."

That was sad enough, but he followed it by telling us that he never even gets to know the infants on the second floor. "The worst thing I've ever had to do is pick up a three-month-old body," he said. It was easier, he told us, if he didn't even learn their names until they got old enough to have a real chance at life.

Our kids were nervous as the staff led them through the orphanage. But many of them have younger brothers and sisters, and all of them had at least some idea of how to relate to little children. Slowly but surely they began to respond to the children, holding and rocking the babies in the nursery, and at first gently and then more boisterously playing with the toddlers on the playground.

Antonio, a thirteen-year-old whose family comes from the Dominican Republic, was working very hard at holding Pulisa, whose name meant "Rose." He explained that he thought she was mad—"because she looked like I do when I get mad," he said—and indeed, she slapped him away the first three times he tried to hold her. But he persisted, and finally, she held on to him, and then she wouldn't let anyone else hold her; in fact, if someone else came near them, she often tried to slap the new person away. She didn't want Antonio to put her down or play with her—she just wanted him to hold her.

Our young people had a wonderful time throwing the children balls, helping them up and down the slide, and cheering for them on the monkey bars, but they were also super-aware of why these children were there in the first place. Dedicated as the orphanage staff clearly was, they never had enough time to hold the children or to give them much individual attention. At various points throughout the day, I heard our children discussing their complicated reactions to this experience. Was it better that the orphans had had at least this one visit? Or worse for them to miss us when we left?

Later, after we had returned to Bushwick, our children talked about the orphanage visit again and again. If you asked any of them what part of service they enjoyed most, most of them were pretty sure to mention this visit. Knowing that they were playing with kids who didn't get attention every day, our children loved the simplicity of just holding and rocking a baby, and the whole experience made them feel really useful.

After lunch, we went on to a community center where a group of boys danced for us in big rubber boots. The children later learned that this was a traditional gumboot dance, which is performed by dancers wearing Wellington boots. The dance originated among South African gold miners. Many of the steps and routines are parodies of the officers and guards who controlled the mines and workers' barracks. Later, I heard our children commenting on how amazing it was to see these dances performed halfway across the globe yet contain so many moves and gestures that they recognized from their own dancing. In fact, it was just like the dance movement called stepping—done by members of African-American fraternities and sororities.

Later, we finally made it to the shantytowns of Diepsloot. The poverty is shocking; it continues to be so even to me, and I've seen it so many times. But now I saw it through the kids' eyes. The houses cobbled together out of wood and corrugated metal, ceilings peeling away and dirt floors, dark windowless rooms with every single piece of material wealth that anyone in the family has ever been able to collect all jammed together somehow—high stools with the stuffing coming out of the seats, empty plastic bottles, broken picture frames, tiny metal cars, anything they might ever have had or found or been given or chosen not to throw away. This collection of broken and damaged items in some of the shacks existed side by side with evidence of domesticity and care: a wooden spice rack with some glasses carefully arranged on each shelf; a framed picture of a family member on a tabletop; flowered shower curtains and tablecloths hung in a doorway for some kind of privacy. A lot of the shacks are as clean as the residents can manage, some cleaner than others if the residents have household cleaning supplies available to them.

In one of the shacks, a young woman had painted a poem on the wall in deep red paint:

EACH DAY I DREAM BUT
IT NEVER END
EACH DAY I PLAN BUT
IT NEVER HAPPEN
BECAUSE MY MIND IS STILL
BLOWN FOR
WHAT I DREAMED ABOUT

DAYS ARE GONE
A YEAR GOES BY TIME SEEMS

TO GO BY SO FAST
I NEED WINGS TO FLY
SEE ANOTHER WORLD
AND FILL THE GREATNESS
BEING ME

I couldn't help thinking of Langston Hughes's famous question "What happens to a dream deferred?"

Becoming Global Ambassadors

Each of the children was assigned a Diesploot family to sponsor during the trip, and after they visited their families, they gathered into groups and began planning what to do next. Their goal was to determine what each family needed most and to prepare a shopping list that was within the budget we had given them. The next day, we'd all go to Makro—a South African store that reminded me of a Costco or Sam's Club—and buy what we could.

The kids struggled for quite a while with this part of their service. Having seen the poverty and need of the families they had visited, they understandably wanted to give these new friends *everything*—the food, clothes, medicine, and fuel that would make the families feel secure. But now that they were making their shopping lists, they realized that they could only do so much. However much they bought the next day, they wouldn't be getting—or giving—as much as they wanted to.

Seeing a degree of poverty that was beyond anything they themselves had ever known was one step in these kids' journey for change. Now, as they planned their lists, they took another. Instead of simply following instructions and making a shopping list in priority order, they began advocating for their families. Couldn't we give them more? Wasn't there room in the budget for an extra mattress, some more paraffin, a few more blankets? Didn't we understand that children were involved, children without toys or pencils or books or warm clothes? How could we fail to fund these needs?

This confrontation with the limits of service can be heartbreaking—but it is a key aspect of volunteerism, and it must be faced. I was struck by the fact that my friend Annie Hausmann was going through a similar struggle. The wonderful mother, organizer, and volunteer whom I had met through our common work on the Triple Negative Breast Cancer Foundation had come with Journey for Change at her own expense, helping me with the million and one tasks that I knew I might expect. She was heartbroken at the poverty she witnessed, the overworked mothers, the undernourished children. "Can't we help more?" she kept asking me. "How can we help some of these people and not others?"

"We can't help them all," I told her. "But if everyone would help *someone*, then we'd all have what we need."

I think the kids had started to figure this out for themselves, because the next day at Makro, they took yet another step on their journey for change. They started collecting their own money to supplement the budget we had given them, eking out enough to buy toys or extra socks or warmer blankets for the children they had met.

When we went back into the shanty we'd visited the day before, the one with the poem on the wall, Antonio made his usual extraordinary contact with one of the children. Antonio—who had told me that his hero was Nelson Mandela—had this wonderful way of just getting into a child's space and relating to him exactly where he was, very quietly and gently.

LaToya, the little girl whom you met in the introduction—the one who cried over not being able to do more—hugged the grandmother who headed this family several times. Later she told me she still felt sad, as she had the day before, "but mainly happy." I watched her smiling shyly as she hugged the elderly woman, and I listened closely as she told a friend how glad and proud she felt about able to help.

Antonio, too, told me as we left that he felt happy, mainly, but also sad. "Why?" I asked him. He said, "We had two mattresses, and one was softer than the other, and I wanted the old woman to have that one. But the younger woman had a baby, so . . ."

When the children returned to the States, I thought, they would take their next steps on their journey. They would start to figure out how to raise money for the families they had met, and they would also begin to think about how to lobby Congress for greater funding and international aid. With the motivation and knowledge that they had gained on this trip, they could truly fulfill their contract to become ambassadors for change.

Their Words

*B*efore, during, and after the trip to South Africa the children continued to reflect on what Journey for Change had meant to them. Here are some of the thoughts they shared.

This trip has made me a better person. Now I am more grateful for what I have and I learned to appreciate all the things that my parents do for me. When I hugged the granny from the house visits she was full of joy. The kids were playing and running around with stickers. I was watching them and saying, WOW!, I never knew it takes so little to make someone happy. I am going to continue to make a difference in people's lives because I feel that it is the right thing to do.   —Jenee Lawson, 15

I think the Journey For Change has made a big change in my life. I was able to leave my neighborhood and learned to stop complaining about what I eat. It also stopped me from complaining about how small my house or apartment is. The trip makes me feel like going back and living there so that I can continue to support the families and others that are not as fortunate as I am.   —Albert Brunn III, 12

Since I've come back from Jo'berg, I have changed a lot. One thing I noticed with my change process was how grateful I am now! I noticed that I am more eager to give money to others when they ask which I couldn't do ever before this trip. I don't complain when I don't get my way because I am so grateful now!   —Donovan Rogers, 13

After this trip I realized that if I just do something simple or even major to somebody it changes things. For instance if I were to give the most miserable person that no one liked, not even me, and I gave that person happiness, I and other people would feel a different way about that same person that was miserable just the day before. What I'm trying to say is basically what a lot of other people say, we can make the world a better place and we can make a difference we just have to take it one step at a time.
                                                            —*Dasia Carr, 12*

Becoming Advocates

When we got back to Brooklyn, our kids were more eager than ever to continue to help the families they had met in South Africa. One little girl in particular, Nobubele, had touched us all. She and her mother had been badly burned in a shantytown fire and when we left South Africa, her mother was in the hospital.

Our kids leaped into action, organizing a car wash within a month of their return. You've already heard about my kids being there, and Annie's. But the fund-raiser quickly became a community effort as well. Some of the parents sold barbecue and Caribbean food at the car wash, raising additional dollars for Nobubele. Some sold candy. Many encouraged their friends and neighbors to bring their cars in for a wash.

Meanwhile, two of our Journey for Change kids threw a fund-raiser of their own: Queen Clyde and Mariàh Ralph organized a bake sale. Before these middle school girls had gone to South Africa it would probably never have occurred to them that they had the power to touch someone's life, let alone to help a little girl pay her school fees and buy her lunches. But they had seen for themselves what dedication to service could do, and there was no stopping them now.

Soon after we returned, we learned that Nobubele's mother had died. Although we had originally intended to rebuild her shack, our goals had to shift as she went to live first with relatives and finally with Margaret Xaba, an aid worker with one of my South African partner organizations, the Olive Leaf Foundation. In December 2008, I was able to announce at a Journey for Change meeting that the money we had raised had been transferred to an account for Nobubele, which paid her school fees for the year, bought a new uniform, bought Christmas clothing, and even paid ahead for two months' worth of school lunches. The ambassadors have since planned and held their second car wash to raise additional monies for Nobubele and other orphans in need.

In order for the kids to continue to sow the seeds of activism, we organized a trip down to Washington, DC, in November 2008. The trip included the usual cultural events—the museums and monuments that no trip to Washington would be complete without, including the interactive Newseum and the Air and Space Museum, which receives more visitors than any museum in the nation. The kids particularly loved the Lincoln Memorial and taking pictures in front of the White House at night. They even had dinner at Busboys and Poets, where my mom hangs out, a bookstore-café for socially conscious readers, which seemed very fitting. While at dinner, three of the girls pointed out that they were sitting at a booth underneath a photo of Marian Wright Edelman!

We also visited Howard and Georgetown universities, which was extraordinary. I knew at the end of those visits that these children had seen their world open up to the point where college was a real possibility to them. We also met with an aide to New York senator Chuck Schumer and with Congresswoman Maxine Waters herself. During their session with Congresswoman Waters, they were able to tell her what they needed as inner-city schoolchildren and what they thought the United States should do for the children in South Africa. Since then, whenever they see the congresswoman on the news, they e-mail me about it. I know their sense of access to those in power and their sense of entitlement to voice their views has grown and will keep growing.

As you read in chapter 6, we also went to the Holocaust Memorial Museum and talked about the genocide in Darfur. I asked the kids to send me e-mails about how we could help Darfur's people, and I was so proud of the time and energy they put into their responses. I think my personal favorite blogging assignment of this trip was when we asked the kids where they saw themselves in five, ten, and fifteen years. Through their answers I knew that they saw themselves with good, productive lives. I saw that they had aspirations and dreams and were determined to make them happen!

Understanding Advocacy

To become an advocate is to take up the responsibility of influencing your government and your society in the direction you think best. By speaking out on issues that concern you, you are advocating for a particular vision of society. By joining with others to speak out, you are making everyone's voice more powerful.

Many of my heroes are people whom I would define as advocates: Martin Luther King Jr.; Nelson Mandela; Marian Wright Edelman; Robert F. Kennedy; Muhammad Yunus, pioneer of the microcredit movement to make affordable small loans available to individual entrepreneurs in developing nations; Jeffrey Sachs, the economist who advocates for sustainable development and more equitable economic solutions; Cornel West, who uses his academic position as philosopher to explore issues of race and African-American culture; and Dorothy Height, longtime head of the National Council of Negro Women. All of the people on that list have fought—and in many cases are still fighting—for a more just world in which everyone's voice can be heard.

Those are the great leaders, of course, the ones we've all heard of, the ones who devoted themselves to a cause full-time. But you shouldn't underestimate your own ability to effect change on a local, state, or even national level, even if so far, no one but your friends and family has ever heard of you. By writing a letter, making a phone call, attending a school board meeting, circulating a petition, or visiting an elected representative, you are advocating for *your* vision of society—and you have enormous power to make a difference.

Given that we live in a country that prides itself on being a democracy, I find it somewhat discouraging that so many people have become resigned to the idea that they don't really have a voice in the issues that affect them. However, given how things have been for the past several years, I can understand why this is so to some extent. For quite a while, it has looked to many people as though many of the politicians in power—whatever their party affiliation or position—seem less interested in listening to the people they represent than in talking to lobbyists, campaign donors, and one another.

Of course, whatever political party you are a part of or identify with, 2008 was exciting in many ways. We were living in historic and wonderful times, with Hillary Rodham Clinton becoming the first woman to run for president of the United States as a potentially electable candidate and our country's election of Barack Obama, the first African-American to become our nation's president. As I was wrote this book, Hillary Clinton was named our secretary of state, preparing to serve during very trying times around the world. For me, personally and as a mother, this is wonderful.

But we are also dealing with a barrage of corrupt politicians who keep getting caught doing the most ridiculous things. Our political cartoonists and the late-night comedians are having an absolute ball, but they are about the only ones. It is hard not to get frustrated with people who are supposed to be representing our best interests when it seems as if they are treating their offices as businesses instead of as trusts for the people and acting like "me, me, me" corporate executives instead of like dedicated public servants.

What I do know, however, and this keeps me sane and hopeful, is that there are lots of good people who still run for public office on the local, state, and national level who are truly committed to representing our best interests. These are people who really want to make this world a better place for all of us. And these are the people you want to call, write, and e-mail about your concerns.

Another hopeful factor is that we now live in this wonderful world of the Internet and e-mail, where it is so easy to search for a cause that you care about, find an organization that is dealing with the particular issue you want to advocate for, and follow its guidelines on how to make a difference.

True, the heads of big corporations and others try to persuade our leaders by hiring powerful lobbyists, whereas the ordinary individual—the working mother, urban teenager, rural dad, surburban stay-at-home mom, or young professional—does not have the money to do this. But guess what? You don't need to. We, the people, are so much more powerful than we think we are, and we have changed this nation many times through advocacy—marching, sit-ins, petitions, strikes, calls to Congress, leafleting, and rallies. There are also so many stories of "mother warrior" and "father warrior" advocates changing laws and policy because they were acting out of experiences that moved them to anger, determination, and a passion for justice.

Think of Megan's Law. This law was enacted because of the rape and murder of seven-year-old Megan Kanka, who was attacked by a neighbor who was a convicted sex offender. Megan's parents, Richard and Maureen Kanka, were outraged that a convicted sex offender had been living across the street from them without their knowledge, leading them to let their little girl travel freely through a community that had suddenly become dangerous. They started the Megan Nicole Kanka Foundation and gathered more than four hundred thousand signatures on a petition demanding immediate legislative action. Within three months, Megan's home state of New Jersey passed the first so-called Megan's Law, requiring convicted sex offenders to register so that their communities could be notified. The following year, federal legislation was passed, and on May 17, 1996, President Bill Clinton signed an amended Megan's Law.

Anyone who has children feels a profound gratitude toward Richard and Maureen Kanka. And anyone who wants to advocate for any cause has reason to feel inspired that two ordinary people found a way to transform public policy for an entire nation.

Time to Take Action!

I hoped to inspire the Journey for Change: Empowering Youth Through Global Service participants to believe in their own power to change our world, and I hope their efforts have inspired you to become an agent for change. Here are twelve ways that you can make a difference and some suggestions for how to put each of them into action.

1. Organize a Protest March

It's amazing how effective it can be to get a group of people out in the streets, raising their voices. "Raise a ruckus!" as Marian Wright Edelman likes to say. You'll discover that your march has at least three potential benefits: It puts people in power on notice; it inspires others to realize that there's something they can do; and it energizes you and your fellow protestors.

So if you're concerned about an issue in your community, figure out who has the power to solve the problem. Then get a permit to hold a march, ending at the offices of the people whom you want most to listen to your message.

It is great to have a short but powerful slogan that you can collectively call out as you march, and do not forget to make signs and posters to carry. In fact, there is something really wonderful about the leaders of the march and a group of volunteers assembling in advance at someone's home and making the signs and posters together.

2. Circulate a Petition

A petition is basically a letter identifying a problem and offering a solution. Its power comes from the many names at the bottom of the letter, which make it crystal-clear that an issue has wide support.

As with holding a protest march, circulating a petition has three effects. Most obviously, of course, it alerts people in power to the concerns of those who signed. But it also has an effect on those who circulate it as well as those who sign it. The very act of asking someone to put his or her name on a petition becomes an opportunity to have a conversation about an issue. The person who's circulating the petition gets the chance to explain a point of view; the person who's being asked to sign has the chance to think about a new idea and to realize that taking action is possible.

Make a goal of how many names you want signed on your petition. You can come up with this number if you think about who you are going to be presenting the petition to: Is it your local school board head, the county commissioner, your city's district attorney, a state legislator, a leader in the national Senate? How many people are in your town? Do you think you can get 20 percent to sign your petition? Or do you need to set up a website and send out mass e-mails asking people to sign electronically?

Whatever you decide, once you reach your goal, the most critical step is to turn your petition over to the right person and then demand an answer!

3. Write to Elected Officials—or Bombard Them with Phone Calls
A letter-writing campaign is another highly effective way of making your voice heard. Of course, even a single letter to a politician can have an effect. But asking a large number of people to bombard an office with letters, phone calls, e-mails, or a combination of the three can have an even greater impact. Recently, a legislative aide for a very powerful and effective senator told me that this was one of the best ways to get their office's attention.

4. Ask for Meetings with Elected Officials
Nothing moves an elected official like a face-to-face conversation, simply because you have the chance to speak directly to his or her concerns. Also, the fact that you've gone to the trouble of requesting the meeting tells your representative that you care about this issue deeply. If you can come into the meeting with a delegation from a larger group, so much the better: Now you're really reminding government officials that they're supposed to answer to voters like you!

Always remember that state and national politicians don't have offices only in state and national capitals. They often have local offices throughout their district, region, or state. When they're home they also often schedule time each week to be available to their constituents. So if you do want to speak with a representative, you don't necessarily need to travel any farther than across town. Just pick up the phone and make an appointment. As a voter, isn't that your right?

Speak Up and Listen Closely: Holding a Successful Meeting with a Government Official

• **Go as a group.** Ideally, you'll be there representing a formal organization or an informal group of concerned citizens. So why not show up as a group? Choose a small delegation—perhaps three to five people—to meet with the official. Then have the rest of your group wait nearby. It's empowering to remember that you're not alone, and it makes a statement to the politician as well.

• **Prepare your presentation.** Choose three key points you'd like to make, and divide them up among three group members. Each member should practice speaking for no more than two minutes on his or her point while the others give pointers. When you meet with your representative, you want to sound clear, concise, and on top of your topic—but not over-rehearsed or artificial.

• **Listen politely.** Why would you meet with someone if you didn't care what he or she had to say? Let your official ask you questions, express concerns, or explain objections. If he or she isn't saying much, you ask the questions: "What do you think of our position?" "You haven't supported this position in the past—why not?" And, most important, "Can we count on your support?" Ask in a respectful, interested way—and then really listen to the answers. Assessing where your representative stood when you left the meeting will be an important part of your next strategy session, so be sure you've gotten all the information you can.

5. Attend Meetings About Issues That You Care About

Going to meetings of your town government, your local school board, or a local planning commission can be critical in having a say about policy. Often, governmental agencies are required to hold hearings on important topics; often, too, they're required to conduct all business at meetings that are open to the public. Even if you don't have a place on the agenda, just showing up at a meeting makes a statement to officials that people are watching, listening, and forming opinions. And if you get a chance to speak, so much the better. You can usually find out what's scheduled for your local units of government by looking at their website, in the local paper, or in your local post office. Or call or visit your local city hall or town administrative office.

6. Join an Advocacy Group

Groups such as Amnesty International, the Sierra Club, or the National Organization for Women understand that there's power in numbers. Why not add your voice to theirs? By becoming a member of a large and respected advocacy group, your world will be opened to the many ways that they work to make a difference in this world and you will have access to many wonderful and innovative tools to make a difference, too. You will usually receive newsletters, mailings, e-mails, and other sources of information, keeping you informed about the issues that concern you and giving you ways to react.

Local groups, such as parent-teacher organizations or even a group you start, can have a tremendous impact on local politics. So if you need to go this route, do not be afraid. Just remember that none of the national advocacy organizations started out large and powerful. They started in a living room full of concerned people who wanted to make a difference.

7. Sign Up for Newsletters, E-mail Alerts, and the Like to Keep Yourself Up-to-Date

Even if you're not interested in joining a group, advocacy organizations often have the best and most up-to-date information about an issue. Go to an organization's website and sign up for its mailing list, action alerts, and the like. The website may also feature publications that the group recommends or books written by its officials.

This is actually something I do on a regular basis. Because my plate is pretty full already with the causes I work on full-time, I am not a full-time member of many advocacy organizations. However, I do go on websites that represent causes I care about, and I sign up for e-mail alerts and e-newsletters. I receive them from Save Darfur, the Children's Defense Fund, (RED), and many others.

8. Write Letters to the Editor of a Newspaper or Submit an
Op-Ed Piece

Publishing your thoughts is a time-honored American tradition, and it's one that many of us can still take advantage of, especially those of us who live in areas with relatively accessible local papers that accept op-ed pieces from "unfamous" people.

Even if you're in a major metropolitan area, however, you can still write a letter to the editor. Don't you always read those first anyway? I know I do!

Dear Editor: Making Your Letter Strong

- Organize your letter around a clear, strongly stated central idea. Usually, letters to the editor are limited to one or two paragraphs, so you'll really have time for only one point. Choose your point wisely and express it clearly.

- Follow the rules for submission. You can usually find these on the editorial page, but if necessary, call the publication or check out its website.

- Be respectful. Your letter is far more likely to be printed if it appears to be an objective statement of the facts—even if it also includes a strongly held opinion. Name-calling, sarcasm, exaggeration, or overly personal comments will likely weaken your credibility and may keep your letter from being printed.

9. Create a Leaflet and Give It Out

This is another time-honored American tradition, and I'm all for it. The wonderful thing about leafleting is how many different ways you can use it. I've seen families handing out homemade leaflets in front of the Starbucks by my office, raising awareness about Darfur. I've seen a wide variety of groups use leaflets to get people to come to an event, such as a rally, fund-raiser, or protest. I've also seen people give out leaflets to urge others to write a letter, to make a phone call, or simply to become informed.

Think about how you can use the written word to reach more people with your message of advocacy. Then stand in front of a popular business like a coffee shop or grocery store, on a busy street corner, or in front of a post office. Remember to ask for permission. A local business owner can give this to you, but if it is a governmental building, call city hall in advance or drop by your local administrative building.

10. Attend Rallies

Perhaps because of the way I was brought up, I tend to think of this as my default action: something I always do if I receive an e-mail, get a phone call, or read a notice in the newspaper about a rally. If I care about the issue, I show up. Think about it: What is the first thing they report on the news about a rally? How many people showed up! Sometimes the media and politicians measure the effectiveness of the rally by how many people show up. So by attending a rally, you are adding a powerful body to a collective group. As a group, you can garner effective media attention and force your elected officials to pay attention.

The other great thing about attending a rally is that you will meet like-minded people, you will usually receive additional handouts about fund-raisers and events related to the issue, and you will learn additional facts that you did not know. By attending a rally, you can feel a sense of accomplishment and you can also learn how to advocate on behalf of your cause in other ways.

Recently, I attended a rally in the Ninth Ward of New Orleans, taking a stand on the lack of progress being made in rebuilding this vital part of town. It made me feel really good to attend. I was not a speaker; I was not giving interviews to the press. I was just a concerned American citizen. I've also made it my business to go to any Save Darfur rally I possibly can, as my way to show concern for the genocide that continues to occur in Sudan. What issues move you to action? A rally might be a terrific way to show you care and an extremely powerful instrument in your advocacy tool kit.

11. Participate in an Electoral Campaign

If someone is running for office whose beliefs match yours and who has pledged to try to effect change, why not express yourself by working for that candidate? I know that both Chris and I found it extremely empowering to support Barack Obama in his pesidential campaign. I was thrilled to read in the many post–Election Day analyses of his efforts that on-the-ground organizing in many small locales made the difference between defeat and victory. Even in a big national race, every vote counts—and in such close calls as the 2008 Alaska and Minnesota Senate races, every vote counted as well.

Local campaigns can also be energizing, as you see the effect of your work in a very immediate way. If you're active in your local community, you might consider finding someone you like and urging him or her to run for office—or even running for office yourself!

12. Donate to a Campaign or Cause

When you give money to an organization or an electoral candidate, you are in a sense engaged in advocacy. Your donation says, in a very tangible way, "I believe in this cause [or this person], and I'm willing to put myself on the line to show my support."

Never underestimate the power of a small donation, either. I still remember those $10 and $25 donations I got from people who read about Journey for Change: Empowering Youth Through Global Service on my website and decided to send in a check. Those checks were just as important and, believe me, just as needed as any larger donation. And even if your political views do not match President Barack Obama's, no one can say that his political machine was anything less than genius. Small donations made by masses of people gave him the money to run a nationwide campaign that was so effective. It is my opinion that the people who made small donations to his campaign helped him to win the election.

Wear the Band:
Raise Awareness, Raise Money, Raise Your Voice

You've seen those elastic wristbands that people wear—but did you realize that they could be a powerful tool for advocacy? Buy a band in the color that represents a cause you support, or sell bands to raise money for the cause. It's a quick, easy, and effective way to make a contribution and take a stand. Not only are you helping to raise money, but you are literally promoting your cause every time you wear the band!

Color: Yellow (Livestrong)
Cause: Cancer awareness
Foundation: Lance Armstrong Foundation
Cost: 10 for $10, 100 for $100, 1,200 for $1,200
Website: www.store-laf.org

Color: Orange
Cause: Lung cancer awareness and antismoking
Foundation: The American Cancer Society
Cost: 5 for $5
Website: www.acswristbands.org

Color: Red (Courage)
Cause: AIDS research
Foundation: AIDS Research Alliance
Cost: $1 each
Website: www.aidsresearch.org

Color: Green
Cause: Support our troops
Foundation: Remind
Cost: 10 for $5
Website: www.remind.org/take_action/merchandise

Color: Pink (Imagine Life Without Breast Cancer)
Cause: Breast cancer awareness
Foundation: Susan G. Komen for the Cure
Cost: 5 for $5
Website: www.shopkomen.org

Color: Light Blue (Cultivate Peace)
Cause: Feeding the hungry in the Darfur region of Sudan through
   Mercy Corps
Foundation: The Hunger Site
Cost: 10 for $10 or 100 for $100 ($100 = 1,000 cups of food)
Website: shop.thehungersite.com/store

Color: White (Kids Matter)
Cause: Improving the health and well-being of children
Foundation: Ronald McDonald House
Cost: $3 each
Website: rmhc.org

Journey for Change: The Journey Continues

When I think about the first year of Journey for Change and what it's meant to the first batch of children, I come back to Jeremy and Jonathan. You recall how hard I had to work to get them to come with us, how much resistance they put up. But the moment they hit South African soil, they blossomed. You could see the joy in their faces as soon as they stepped out of the plane—the thrill of being somewhere new, the excitement that maybe this was *their* world after all, and it was wider than just a few blocks in Brooklyn.

The two of them absolutely *loved* volunteering, which I'm sure was just as much a surprise to them as it was even to me. I expected them to pitch in and be good sports, but they went far, far beyond that. Every volunteer opportunity that came up, they did it 100 percent, and they did it cheerfully, generously, in the most open and willing way. In Brooklyn, they had both done a lot of posturing around their friends, not wanting to seem uncool. But with their fellow JFC ambassadors, they were able to let go of that pose, to let those barriers down, to be more of who I now know they really are.

Jeremy in particular showed himself to be one of the most responsible young people I have ever met. When we got back from South Africa, he was at every single event, every single meeting, every single activity that Journey for Change sponsored. That level of commitment began in South Africa, where he was always the first one up, the first one in for breakfast, always sitting in the front of the room, asking some helpful question or making some insightful comment. Of course, he's the same boy I saw in the orientation—but magnified! His experiences have let him become a bigger Jeremy, a prouder Jeremy, a Jeremy who takes up more space. I couldn't wish better for him—and I know the world will benefit from his newfound pride and confidence.

One thing I'm very proud of is the way that he and Jonathan and the other four "rec boys" have worked to involve the other rec center kids in their experiences. In December 2008, the six guys from that program who went to South Africa gave a PowerPoint presentation to the seventy-five who stayed home. Jonathan, who barely spoke five words to me when I first met him, stood up in front of a roomful of people and did his part of the PowerPoint presentation. He had certainly come a long way!

We had let the other JFC kids know that this presentation was taking place and had invited them to come, if they could, to support their fellow ambassadors. Even though it was a Sunday afternoon—time to hang out with family and friends—about ten of them came, including, of course, LaToya. As the presentation ended, I could see her growing more and more impatient, and finally her hand shot up in the air. "Hey," she said, polite but determined. "You have to tell them about Nobubele!"

Leave it to LaToya to get to the heart of the matter. I couldn't believe we had forgotten to tell the story of the little South African girl who had been orphaned since we got back, whose school fees and uniforms our JFC kids had raised money for.

"Why don't *you* tell everyone about Nobubele?" I suggested. And she instantly burst into tears—but she told the story. That to me was LaToya all over, keeping her eye on what needed to be said, staying smart and rational—but moved to tears at the same time. I was so proud of her, I found myself crying, too.

When we first developed Journey for Change, I had the idea of getting the kids to sign a contract committing them to one year of service as Global Ambassadors. I had thought I would need the leverage of this signed piece of paper to get them to commit and participate after the trip was over. But I needn't have worried. Far from objecting to all the things I have planned, they're always objecting that I don't put enough on the schedule. They are eager for all three components of the program—advocacy, service, and cultural activities—which are all intended to make them into global citizens. My goal for this program is to make the kids feel like they are a part of this world, to make them feel like they have something to offer their world, to make them feel like they must serve in this world. And so far, at least, the program couldn't be more successful.

I'm certainly proud of the way individual children have stepped up to the plate. I was especially proud of the way Queen and Mariah organized their own bake sale to raise funds for South Africa, along with participating in the car wash that we all did together. They put together the whole bake sale: buying food, baking, making posters, spreading the word on their block. When they called me at the end of the day to inform me that they had raised $350, I was proud to tell them just what $350 could do in South Africa.

Another young man, Joshua Hall, organized a penny drive in his neighborhood. Joshua had his own family history of service because his mother, Denese Hall, runs a wonderful program that she founded, Clothed with Love, which collects backpacks and school supplies and other things that kids need to start off the school year. Often with her children's help, Denese distributes these things to neighborhood families who can't afford to buy their own new supplies. As a parent who sometimes had to struggle from paycheck to paycheck, Denese knew just how important it was for kids to have their own new things each year—and how hard it could be for families to provide them. Joshua's initiation into service came not with Journey for Change but from working with his mother on Clothed with Love. But the penny drive showed that he could act on his own, too.

I knew how much our donations meant to the people of Diepsloot because I stayed in touch with Cornelius Xulu, the youth minister and community outreach project coordinator working in

Johannesburg. I've known him for years and am delighted that he also works with me as the Angelrock Project South Africa coordinator. Using some of the funds I was able to donate, Cornelius took about eighty grannies Christmas shopping in December 2008. I asked him what happened on the trip, and he sent me the following e-mail:

> *I felt energized and humbled by the experience. It was so amazing to see the gratitude the grannies had at receiving their Christmas groceries. When the truck pulled into their meeting place in Diepsloot with their groceries, they started singing, praying, and crying. I found that experience to be quite emotional. They just kept talking about how grateful they are for you and the fact that you always keep your promises to them. I think that was probably the most impactful part of the day for me.*

So all of us—myself as well as the children—have been inspired by the difference we have been able to make in South Africa. But I think, upon reflection, that the truest meaning of Journey for Change actually came to fruition not in South Africa, but in Bushwick.

The children had agreed that we were going to ring in the New Year through our service, so on December 29, 30, and 31, we served. We got involved in a wide variety of projects: serving food at soup kitchens, helping the elderly, working in a homeless shelter, helping out at a nonprofit that serves abused children, working in a day-care center. We put in full days, too: from ten A.M. to five P.M. each of the three days. The kids were fine with all of those activities. The one they didn't want to do, though, was the one that turned out to be the most meaningful: cleaning up the streets of their own neighborhood.

I don't know why I insisted on including that in the list of activities, but somehow I felt it was important. The kids certainly hated the whole idea of it. They said they'd be embarrassed picking up trash and dog poop out on the street, that their friends and neighbors would laugh at them. I asked them whether the kind of people who would laugh at them for cleaning up their own community were the kind of people who could help them get where they wanted to go in life, and maybe that made an impression, because despite their complaining, every single one of our Journey for Change kids showed up, on time, to clean up. And guess what? We had a blast! People were so grateful to us, they were screaming out thank-yous from their stoops and shouting at us how proud they were, how grateful. The kids got into it, for themselves and with one another, scolding one another for missing a piece of paper or a stray branch, sending one another back along the street to scoop up any trash they might have missed. The kids got so into it, in fact, that we ended up staying out two hours longer than we thought we would, because everybody was having such a great time. And, as always seems to happen, the kids who were the most embarrassed beforehand ended up being the ones right up in front, marching down the street with their trash bags held high.

For the ambassadors' spring break in April 2009, we traveled to New Orleans to rebuild houses with the nonprofit St. Bernard Project in St. Bernard Parish. Our kids stayed at Camp Hope, a converted school that now serves as a humble but effective place for volunteers from around the world to stay when they come to New Orleans to help rebuild the city that is still so devastated by Hurricane Katrina four years after the storm. We were blessed to be able to help rebuild three different homes in a parish that had 100 percent devastation. Though our site coordinators were a little worried that our kids might not be up to snuff based on their ages, we have been told that our group was one of the most determined, hardworking, and effective groups they have ever had. And during our stay at Camp Hope, I was so fulfilled by watching our kids interact with college students, retirees, and others from across our nation who all had the same mission in mind: to serve, to build, and to uplift the residents of the great city of New Orleans. (I would be remiss if I did not thank JetBlue Airways for flying us to New Orleans!)

And my heart sings with pride because in commemoration of the Journey for Change Ambassadors completion of the program, we held a graduation ceremony on Thursday, September 17, 2009, at the Time Warner Center overlooking Central Park courtesy of Time

Warner. Our ambassadors were given certificates from leaders from the fields of education, arts, media, and business as a way of introducing them to the plethora of career opportunities open to them through continuing their education. But what made the evening even more special—what really brought our group full circle—is that the great African-American critical thinker Henry Louis Gates Jr., Alphonse Fletcher University Professor at Harvard University as well as director of the W. E. B. DuBois Institute for African American Research, agreed to take DNA samples of all our participants so that we could provide them with their genetic family tree, tracing their ancestry in this country and beyond, as Dr. Gates did in his acclaimed PBS series *African American Lives*. With the assistance of Bennett Greenspan of Family Tree DNA and African DNA, as well as Gina Paige and Dr. Rick Kittles of African Ancestry, Dr. Gates told each ambassador what country and tribe his or her ancestors hailed from. I found out that my ancestors are from Nigeria and I am a member of the lbo tribe. It was an emotional and memorable evening for all of us, and I truly cannot think of a greater gift to give these children—my children—who I dearly love.

We've traveled all the way around the globe to South Africa. We've gone to Washington, DC, and rebuilt houses in New Orleans. We've talked with members of Congress, and we've thought about how to help the people of Darfur. We ended up on the streets of Brooklyn, cleaning up the kids' own community, and toured the United Nations, the world's forum for maintaining international peace and security and promoting social progress, better living standards, and human rights, and we will give them a piece of their past so that they can have a complete road map for their future.

It's been an absolute privilege to watch these kids become agents for change in their world. Their inspiration and commitment to serve nourishes and reinforces my own and set me on the path to write this book. My hope is that their story and my story, along with the advice in these pages, might ignite in others—in you—a spark to make this world we share a better place, to build the village. Join us!

Building the Village
Even More Resources and Ideas
to Help You on Your Way

∎

CHAPTER 1: EACH ONE, TEACH ONE

In this chapter we talked about creative ways to give. Here are some other fun and easy ways to give back.

Donate Your Foreign Currency

American Airlines supports UNICEF's Change for Good Program, which allows travelers on select flights to donate unused U.S. and foreign currencies to flight attendants or make donations in Admirals Clubs and Flagship Lounges. Change for Good has generated over $90 million that UNICEF has used to provide a healthier, happier future for millions of children. And Virgin Atlantic operates Change for Children, a program that works the same way. Change for Children raises an average of $80,000 each month, which goes toward nonprofits and organizations such as Save the Children. For more information, see www.virgin-atlantic.com.

Donate Your Old Car

There are many organizations that can use your old car for a good cause or to give to a needy family. Check out these websites for more information.

America's Car Donation Center: www.donateacar.com
Cars for Causes: www.carsforcauses.net
Charity Cars: www.800charitycars.org

Donate Your Car Now: Help Protect Missing Kids: www.donate
carnow.org
Purple Heart Cars: Help Our Veterans: www.purpleheartcars.org
The Salvation Army: www.salvationarmy.org

Donate Your Used Cell Phones and Computers

Even a deactivated cell phone can be used to call 911, which means it
can be given to someone who needs a reliable way to call for emergency help. You can often donate your deactivated phone to a local
police station, battered women's shelter, or domestic violence organization. Likewise, desktop computers can often be used by nonprofits
and local schools. If you can't think of an organization to give to, try
talking to a local United Way, Red Cross, or YMCA/YWCA for ideas.

Donate Your Extra Frequent-Flier Miles

Make-A-Wish Foundation uses frequent-flier miles to help sick children achieve a cherished wish (www.wish.org). And Operation Hero
Miles uses them to support our injured service members and their
families (www.heromiles.org).

You can also give your miles to auctions. Often, charitable organizations offer air travel and a stay in a hotel room as an auction
prize. You can help by donating your miles to a specific destination.
Check in with organizations or friends involved in charity events
and ask if your miles are needed.

Online Auctions

A fun and exciting way to help raise money for nonprofit organizations is by bidding on one-of-a-kind experiences via online auction
websites. These virtual marketplaces raise millions of dollars for
charity by packaging memorable auction lots for people who want
to support nonprofit organizations and have loads of fun at the
same time. Two of my favorite auction websites are Charity Buzz
(www.charitybuzz.com) and Charity Folks (www.charityfolks.com).
In fact, I have raised over $22,000 for Journey for Change: Empow-
ering Youth Through Global Service by using Charity Folks!

Start a Giving Circle

A giving circle is a group of people that commits to raising and donating money. Some groups are small and informal: A handful of friends has dinner at someone's house once a month and donates the money they would have spent on a restaurant meal to a charitable group instead. Other groups are larger and more organized: They collect monthly or yearly pledges and solicit grant applications from local groups. You can learn more about these wonderful groups from the Giving Circle Network, www.givingcircles.org.

Unique UNICEF Ideas

Some ideas from the UNICEF website for even more creative ways to give:

• **Cards and gifts:** If you and your kids want to help children around the world, consider purchasing UNICEF cards and gifts for holidays and other special occasions. UNICEF sells tribute cards, arranges for donations to be made as wedding gifts or favors, and accepts stocks, securities, and corporate matching grants. To shop for UNICEF cards and gifts, visit www.unicefusa.org/shop/.

• **eBay:** When you sell something on eBay, you can designate 10 to 100 percent of your profits to go to UNICEF or to some other worthy cause. For more information, go to pages.ebay.com/givingworks/faq.html.

• **PayPal:** You can donate to UNICEF or to another worthy cause through PayPal. Just go to www.paypal.com and enter "donate" in the search box.

Something to Keep in Mind: Directing Your Aid to the Right Cause

When you're giving aid to any large organization, such as UNICEF, the International Red Cross, or the Salvation Army, you must stipulate where you want your money to go, or your donation may go to the organization's general fund and not necessarily to support a particular effort. Be sure to write the name of the effort you're supporting in the memo section of your check and/or attach a letter.

CHAPTER 2: ME TO WE: FINDING MYSELF BY SERVING OTHERS

In this chapter we discussed how you could find ways to give of your time. Here are some great websites to help you and your family find just the right volunteer opportunity for you.

For Kids

Youth Volunteer Corps of America, www.yvca.org
This group operates in locations across the country, offering young people ages eleven through eighteen a chance to become involved in community service.

DO Something, www.dosomething.org
Using the power of *online* to get teens to do good stuff *offline*. When you log on to this website, you get a menu asking you, "What's your cause?" who you want to work with, where you want to work, and how long you want to work. Then you get a menu of choices that fit the parameters you've requested. Going on this website is a great way for kids to learn that they have a wide variety of options for service in a fun and creative way. Fun fact: Nancy Lublin, the founder of Dress for Success, is the CEO of DO Something!

Kids Korps, www.kidskorps.org
Kids Korps USA is committed to making children "more aware of their environments" and providing them with opportunities "to contribute to the positive welfare of their communities." Kids Korps's model is the Peace Corps: a volunteer-based group that organizes service projects in communities across the nation.

Roots and Shoots, www.rootsandshoots.org
Roots and Shoots is a program of the Jane Goodall Institute, a global network of more than eight thousand groups in almost a hundred countries. This organization's mission is to engage and empower youths with service learning projects. Youths of all ages take action to improve the world through projects that promote care and concern for animals, the environment, and the human community.

Invisible Children, www.invisiblechildren.org
Invisible Children is helping to bring an end to the Lord Resistance Army's plague of capturing children to fight as soldiers and to build schools to educate former child soldiers and a new generation of Ugandans.

Invisible Children is a social, political, and global movement using the transformative power of stories to change lives. The organization inspires youths to value creativity, idealism, and sacrifice. The movement fuels the most effective, adaptable, and innovative programs in the world and is made up of a tireless staff, hundreds of full-time volunteers, and thousands of students and supporters. The coalition is made up of young citizens of the world, who are students, artists, activists, and entrepreneurs. Invisible Children is using its voice to ask President Obama to spearhead efforts to bring peace to Northern Uganda. The members are mobilizing a generation to capture the attention of the international community and make a stand for justice in the wake of genocide.

For Professionals

Financial Services Volunteer Corps, www.fsvc.org
This amazing organization was founded by the late Cyrus Vance, former U.S. secretary of state, and John Whitehead, former cochair of Goldman Sachs and former U.S. deputy secretary of state. The group uses volunteers to build financial systems that enable developing countries to take advantage of economic opportunities.

International Executive Service Corps, www.iesc.org
The International Executive Service Corps (IESC) includes more than eleven thousand experts in more than fifty-five countries. The IESC funds experts who work with groups on a range of useful projects "to assist the growth of free enterprise and democracy."

Taproot Foundation, www.taprootfoundation.org
This foundation recruits highly skilled professionals to help make local nonprofits more effective.

For Seniors
Experience Corps, www.experiencecorps.org
If you're over fifty-five and you'd like to tutor urban youths, Experience Corps may be just the group for you. With over two thousand members, the organization reaches some twenty thousand students in twenty-three cities.

Executive Service Corps Affiliate Network, www.escus.org
This national network of nonprofit consulting agencies offers "high-impact volunteer activities to executives and professionals who have had senior-level experience in business, government, or nonprofits."

CHAPTER 3: RAISING CHILDREN WHO GIVE
This chapter dealt with how we can prepare the next generation to become good citizens. Here are some books and organizations that provide useful information about how to empower your children to become lifelong humanitarians.

> *The New 50 Simple Things Kids Can Do to Save the Earth* by Sophie Javna, Andrews McMeel Publishing, 2009
>
> *Teaching Kids to Care: Nurturing Character and Compassion* by Bettie B. Youngs, Ph.D., Ed.D.; Joanne Wolf, Ph.D.; Joani Wafer; and Dawn Lehman, Ph.D., Hampton Roads Publishing, 2007
>
> *The Teen Guide to Global Action: How to Connect with Others (Near and Far) to Create Social Change* by Barbara A. Lewis, Free Spirit Publishing, 2007
>
> *The Kid's Guide to Service Projects: Over 500 Service Ideas for Young People Who Want to Make a Difference* by Barbara A. Lewis, Free Spirit Publishing, 1995
>
> *The Kid's Guide to Social Action: How to Solve the Social Problems You Choose and Turn Creative Thinking into Positive Action* by Barbara A. Lewis, Free Spirit Publishing, 1998
>
> *It's Your World—If You Don't Like It, Change It: Activism for Teenagers* by Mikki Halpin, Simon Pulse, 1994

I Can Make a Difference: A Treasury to Inspire Our Children by
    Marian Wright Edelman, Amistad, 2005
A Kid's Guide to Giving by Freddi Zeiler, Innovative Kids, 2006

Here are some of my favorite organizations that help kids to help
other kids.

Do Something, www.dosomething.org
Global Youth Action Network (GYAN), www.youthlink.org
TakingIT Global, www.tigweb.org
Free the Children, www.freethechildren.org
One World Youth Project, www.oneworldyouthproject.org

CHAPTER 4: WHEN A CAUSE FINDS YOU: ONE PERSON AT A TIME CHANGING THE WORLD

In this chapter we talked about fund-raising, which may seem daunting at first. Here are some additional resources that will tell you everything you need to know about how to raise money for a worthy cause.

Books

*The Zen of Fundraising: 89 Timeless Ideas to Strengthen and Develop
    Your Donor Relationships* by Ken Burnett, Jossey-Bass, 2006
Nonprofit Kit for Dummies, second edition, by Stan Hutton and
    Frances Phillips, For Dummies, 2005
How to Start a Non Profit by Quick Easy Guides, 2008

Websites

Network for Good Learning Center: www.fundraising123.org
As the website explains, the group's mission is simple: "to provide
nonprofits with free access to the best available online fundraising
and nonprofit marketing resources."

eTapestry, www.etapestry.com
eTapestry helps you track current or prospective funders while

managing gifts, pledges, and payments. To find out more, call these numbers: 1-888-739-3827 (1-888-739-ETAP) or 1-317-336-3827.

Foundation Center, www.foundationcenter.org
As the website explains, "the Foundation Center is a national non-profit service organization recognized as the nation's leading authority on organized philanthropy, connecting nonprofits and the grantmakers supporting them to tools they can use and information they can trust. Those who use the organization include grantseekers, grantmakers, researchers, policymakers, the media, and the general public. The Center maintains the most comprehensive database on U.S. grantmakers and their grants; issues a wide variety of print, electronic, and online information resources; conducts and publishes research on trends in foundation growth, giving, and practice; and offers an array of free and affordable educational programs."

CHAPTER 5: WHEN CATASTROPHE STRIKES: FINDING STRENGTH AND CONFRONTING CHALLENGES

As we discussed in this chapter, sometimes it can be hard to know how to help out in a crisis. When you want to take action on an international problem or respond to a catastrophe you've witnessed on the news, your first stop may be the Red Cross (www.redcross. org), which has been a first responder to disasters around the world. But here are some other great organizations I enthusiastically recommend.

The Salvation Army, www.salvationarmyusa.org
This venerable group has been collecting donations for the needy for decades, and they're often one of the early responders in a disaster area. Contact your local branch to find out about making donations or volunteering.

American Friends Service Committee, www.afsc.org
A mainstay of the civil rights movement and many other movements for justice, the AFSC can be an invaluable resource if you're looking to give back.

Concern Worldwide, www.concern.net
This international group focuses on "the ultimate elimination of extreme poverty in the world's poorest countries," according to its mission statement. Its programs include campaigns for children's education, against child labor, and against runaway climate change. In addition to long-term development work, Concern engages in emergency response.

Doctors Without Borders/Médecins Sans Frontières, www.doctors withoutborders.org
This Nobel Prize—winning international medical humanitarian organization was created by French doctors and journalists in 1971. Today the group helps people in nearly sixty countries, most often in response to armed conflicts, natural disasters, epidemics, malnutrition, and exclusion from health care.

Oxfam International, www.oxfam.org
Oxfam focuses on supporting development, advocating for justice, and raising international awareness of poverty and injustice. The group also responds to emergencies in a variety of developing nations.

Save the Children, savethechildren.org
"Providing communities with a hand up, not a handout" is the group's slogan. Save the Children works with families to improve the lives of children through a number of key campaigns.

UNICEF, www.unicef.org
During emergencies, children are especially vulnerable to disease, malnutrition, and violence. In the last decade, more than 2 million children have died as a direct result of armed conflict, and more than three times that number have been permanently disabled or seriously injured. An estimated 20 million children have been forced to flee their homes, and more than 1 million have been orphaned or separated from their families. An estimated three hundred thousand child soldiers—boys and girls under the age of eighteen—are involved in more than thirty conflicts worldwide. UNICEF focuses on these

children and their families—on the essential interventions required for protection, to save lives, and to ensure the rights of all children everywhere. The chaos and insecurity of war threatens or destroys access to food, shelter, social support, and health care, and results in increased vulnerability in communities, especially for children.

CHAPTER 6: CITIZENS OF THE WORLD

In this chapter, we discussed how impactful our generosity can be on a global level. Charity may start at home but it can also reach very far. Here are some more ways that you can help with the crisis in Darfur, an issue that is a particular passion of mine, and also some great suggestions and information about global fair-trade products. Check this list for ideas every time you need to purchase a birthday, holiday, or anniversary present.

Darfur: Never Again
If you care about the genocide in Darfur, act now! The resources below will help you to educate yourself and get involved.

Darfur Relief Organizations
Air Serv International, www.airserv.org
Donate online for humanitarian flights carrying vital cargo.

AmeriCares, www.americares.org
AmeriCares is one of the few relief agencies delivering airlifts of medicine into Darfur, thus greatly increasing the odds of this critical aid reaching the people who desperately need it. Donate online by choosing "Help the People of Darfur."

Lutheran World Relief, www.lwr.org
Designate donation to Darfur/Sudan Crisis, P.O. Box 17061, Baltimore, MD 21298-9832; 1-800-597-5972.

Medical Teams International, www.medicalteams.org
Donate online by choosing "Sudan Emergency Relief."

Relief International: www.ri.org
Donate online by choosing "Sudan: Darfur and South Sudan."

Darfur Advocacy Groups
>   American Refugee Committee, www.arcrelief.org
>   Genocide Intervention Network,
>   www.genocideintervention.net/index.php
>   Save Darfur, www.savedarfur.org
>   1-800-Genocide, the Anti Genocide Hotline,
>   www.1800genocide.com

Books on Darfur
>   *Darfur: A New History of a Long War (African Arguments)* by Julie
>   Flint and Alex de Waal, Zed Press, 2008
>   *Darfur Diaries: Stories of Survival* by Jen Marlowe, Aisha Bain,
>   and Adam Shapiro, Nation Books, 2006
>   *The Devil Came on Horseback: Bearing Witness to the Genocide in
>   Darfur* by Brian Steidle and Gretchen Steidle Wallace, Public
>   Affairs, 2008
>   *Not on Our Watch: The Mission to End Genocide in Darfur and
>   Beyond* by Don Cheadle and John Prendergast, Hyperion, 2007

Products and Gifts That Make a Difference
There are so many fair-trade products and crafts that you can enjoy
or give as gifts and know that the money is going to support a great
cause. Here are some of my favorite fair-trade retailers.

Bath and Beauty
>   A Better Footprint, www.abetterfootprint.com
>   Anti-Body, www.anti-body.com

Coffee
>   Bucks County Coffee Company., www.buckscountycoffee.com
>   Higher Grounds Trading Company, www.highergroundstrading
>   .com
>   The Coffee and Tea Exchange, www.coffeeandtea.com

The Fair Trade Coffee Company, www.fairtradecoffee.org
Fresh Coffee Now, www.freshcoffeenow.com
Organic Products Trading Company, www.optco.com

Chocolate

Divine Chocolate, www.divinechocolateusa.com
Cocoa Camino, www.cocoacamino.com
Yachana Gourmet, www.yachanagourmet.com

Handicrafts

Be Sweet, www.besweetproducts.com
A Better Footprint, www.abetterfootprint.com
Global Exchange Fair Trade Online Store,
    www.globalexchangestore.org
Laga Designs International, www.laga-handbags.com
Watabaran, www.watabaran.org
Ten Thousand Villages, www.tenthousandvillages.com
7 Loaves, www.7loaves.com

Where to Learn More About Fair Trade

To learn more about fair trade, check out the quick, easy, and informative book *50 Reasons to Buy Fair Trade* by Miles Litvinoff and John Madeley, Pluto Press, 2007. You might want to check out a very useful handbook called *The Better World Shopping Guide: Every Dollar Makes a Difference,* second edition, by Ellis Jones, Ph.D., New Society Publishers, 2008. Here's a brief excerpt from that book showing you how they've rated some popular products to help you make responsible choices.

Coffee

A+ Thanksgiving Coffee
A Equal Exchange, Cafe Campesino, Cafe Mam, Elan, Pachamama, Caffe Ibis, Green Mountain, Peace Coffee, AlterEgo, Grounds for Change, Higher Grounds, Adina for Life
A- Local Coffee Shops
B Peet's

B- Starbucks, Seattle's Best

C+International Delight

C- Continental, Eight O'Clock, Hill Bros., MJB, LaVazza, illy, Chock Full o'Nuts

D+Millstone, Folgers

D- Nescafe, Nestle, CoffeeMate

F Maxwell House, Gevalia, Sanka, General Foods, Yuban

Eggs

A+Organic Valley

A Eggology

A- Humane Harvest, Veg-a-Fed, Mother's, Chino Valley, Clover Stornetta, Judy's Family Farm

B Horizon Organic

C+Rock Island

C Gold Circle Farms, Eggland's Best, Land-O-Lakes, Second Nature

C- Nulaid

D+Lucerne

F Egg Beaters

Electronics

A- Apple, Sony, Aiwa, Toshiba, Kodak

B+ Texas Instruments

B- Hitachi, 3M

C+Fuji, Panasonic, Plantronics, Sanyo, Pioneer, Koss

C TDK, Haier, Apex, JVC, Magnavox, Eveready, Kenwood, Energizer, RCA, Duracell

D+Nintendo, Radio Shack, Samsung, Goldstar/LG, Emerson, Phillips

D Mitsubishi

D- Circuit City, Daewoo, Microsoft

F GE

CHAPTER 7: SPREADING THE SEEDS:
THE POWER OF THE MEDIA

In this chapter we discussed how to work with others and the media to bring attention to the causes you care about. Here are some resources to help you work with the media and take your charity to the next level.

Books

How to Form a Nonprofit Corporation by Anthony Mancuso, Nolo Press, 2007

How to Write Successful Fundraising Letters, second edition by Mal Warwick, Jossey-Bass, 2008

The Fundraising Planner: A Working Model for Raising the Dollars You Need by Terry and Doug Schaff, Jossey-Bass, 1999

Successful Fundraising: A Complete Handbook for Volunteers and Professionals by Joan Flanagan, McGraw-Hill, 2002

Event Planning: The Ultimate Guide to Successful Meetings, Corporate Events, Fundraising Galas, Conferences, Conventions, Incentives, and Other Special Events by Judy Allen, Wiley, 2000

An Editor's Guide to Perfect Press Releases: The Key to Free Publicity for Your Organization or Business by Penny Fletcher, BookSurge Publishing, 2004

How to Write a Press Release by Quick Easy Guides, 2008

How to Start a Non Profit, first edition, by Quick Easy Guides, 2008

Websites and Digital Downloads for Help with Press Releases

• wikihow, www.wikihow.com/write-a-Press-Release

• eHow, www.ehow.com

• PRWeb, www.prweb.com/pressreleasetips.php

• *How to Write Eye-Catching Headlines for Your Press Releases and Articles* by Joan Stewart, digital PDF download, 2003, www.amazon.com

• *Free Publicity 101: How to Write Press Releases and Get Your Story in the Media* by Cathy Stucker and IdeaLady.com, digital PDF download, 2006, www.amazon.com

CHAPTER 8: IF IT TAKES A VILLAGE, BUILD ONE

In this chapter, we talked about the importance of getting individuals and corporations to support your humanitarian efforts. Here's some more information about angelrock.com, an online community I started. Come on by or use this as a model and inspiration to start your own movement.

I felt a very personal need to build an online village because of the thousands of letters and e-mails that I receive letting me know that people really want to give back but do not know how to access the tools to do so. Responding to this call, I started the Angelrock Project, an online e-village promoting volunteerism, social responsibility, and sustainable change. The Angelrock Project includes valuable information on how to volunteer, advice on making monetary or in-kind donations, and links to life-changing nonprofit organizations. In addition, one can regularly read inspirational Angel stories about people whose lives are dedicated to helping others and find lists of recommended Angel organizations, books, and websites of the month.

I welcome you to visit and read the information we offer under the links "Angel Rock Projects," "Angel Shop," "Angel Service," "Angel Giving," "Angel News," "Angel Talk," and "Angel Rock Information," as well as view our photo gallery of service activities and trips, our videos, and our weekly blog, among many other inspirational and educational elements. The site can be found at www.angelrockproject.com.

CHAPTER 9: SPEAKING UP AND TAKING A STAND

In this chapter we talked about how important it is to advocate for causes we believe in. Here are some resources to help you stand up and speak out.

Books

> *Introducing Advocacy: The First Book of Speaking Up: A Plain Text Guide to Advocacy* by John Tufail and Kate Lyon, Jessica Kingsley Publishers, 2007

Rules and Standards: The Second Book of Speaking Up: A Plain Text Guide to Advocacy by John Tufail and Kate Lyon, Jessica Kingsley Publishers, 2007

Listen Up! Speak Up! The Third Book of Speaking Up: A Plain Text Guide to Advocacy by John Tufail and Kate Lyon, Jessica Kingsley Publishers, 2007

Advocacy in Action: The Fourth Book of Speaking Up: A Plain Text Guide to Advocacy by John Tufail and Kate Lyon, Jessica Kingsley Publishers, 2007

Special Needs Advocacy Resource Book: What You Can Do Now to Advocate for Your Exceptional Child's Education by Rich Weinfeld and Michelle Davis, Prufrock Press, 2008

Advocacy and Empowerment: Mental Health Care in the Community by Bruce L. Black, Taylor and Francis, 2007

Healthy Voices, Unhealthy Silence: Advocacy and Health Policy for the Poor by Colleen M. Grogan and Michael K. Gusmano, Georgetown University Press, 2007

Refugee Rights: Ethics, Advocacy, and Africa by David Hollenbach, Georgetown University Press, 2008

Organizations

Institute for Sustainable Communities, www.iscvt.org

This organization sponsors community-driven projects in the United States and around the world. It focuses on a number of issues, including community-building, justice, health, education, sustainable development, and advocacy. At its Advocacy and Leadership Center, leaders teach advocacy-related skills and inspire students to create new programs for justice and reform.

Websites

The Advocacy Group, www.advocacy.com
World Advocacy, www.worldadvocacy.com

Here are four important issues to consider advocating for.

I. Hunger: A Growing Problem in America

As I was preparing this book, I was shocked to read a CNN story on November 11, 2008, reporting that 691,000 American kids went hungry in 2007. The USDA found that during 2007, we had hit a ten-year record for the number of children who "suffered a substantial disruption in the amount of food they typically eat." The number of hungry kids had risen by more than 50 percent since the year before.

The situation was made far worse by the economic crises of 2008. Already, food pantries are reporting that donations are down while the number of people who need their help is skyrocketing. And it's not only in economically depressed areas that people go hungry, either. Even in affluent areas, folks are going without food, as evidenced by the existence of such groups as Table to Table, a hunger-relief organization in my own prosperous home of Bergen County, New Jersey.

In my opinion, allowing people to go hungry in our wealthy country is simply not acceptable. If you agree, check out www.thehungersite.com or www.hungeractioncenter.org to see how you can help. Or go to www.feedingamerica.org to find a food pantry in your own area and make a donation.

2. Children's Rights

A wonderful and important way to advocate for the rights and protection of the world's children is by advocating for one or more of the fifty-four articles of the Convention on the Rights of the Child. Read the full range of human rights that each child should be afforded and lobby your legislature on behalf of the world's children. You will help give a voice to the voiceless and ensure that this world is a better place for our most precious resource—children. To read all of the fifty-four articles, please visit the Office of the United Nations High Commissioner for Human Rights at www2.ohchr.org/english/law/crc.htm.

3. World Poverty

Global poverty is one of the most challenging issues we face today. Consider advocating to reduce extreme poverty by supporting the UN Development Millennium Goals to End Poverty by 2015.

In September 2000, world leaders came together at the United Nations to adopt the United Nations Millennium Declaration, committing their nations to a new global partnership to reduce extreme poverty. The group identifed eight Millennium Development Goals:.

Goal 1: Eradicate extreme poverty and hunger
Goal 2: Achieve universal primary education
Goal 3: Promote gender equality and empower women
Goal 4: Reduce child mortality
Goal 5: Improve maternal health
Goal 6: Combat HIV/AIDS, malaria, and other diseases
Goal 7: Ensure environmental sustainability
Goal 8: Develop a global partnership for development

To learn more about the UN Millennium Goals, visit www.un .org/millenniumgoals/.

4. Child Labor

The term "child labor" is often defined as work that deprives children of their childhood, their potential, and their dignity, and is harmful to physical and mental development. It refers to work that is mentally, physically, socially, or morally dangerous and harmful to children; interferes with their schooling by depriving them of the opportunity to attend school; involves children being enslaved, separated from their families, exposed to serious hazards and illnesses, and/or left to fend for themselves on the streets. It is thought that there are 218 million child laborers worldwide. (Information from International Programme on the Elimination of Child Labour.)

Rugs and Rescue

One industry that is known to misuse children as workers is the handmade carpet industry, which exploits nearly three hundred thousand children. You can help advocate against this horrific practice by supporting the Rugmark Foundation, a group that is working to end illegal child labor in the carpet industry by convincing factories to agree to employ only adult labor and then monitoring those factories with regular inspections. The group also rescues children from illegal rug factories and offers them much-needed educational opportunities as well as working to end all child labor in South Asia.

You can help this group in three very important ways:

1. Purchase only rugs that carry the Rugmark seal of approval.
2. Use the group's website to find a retailer in your area that sells rugs with the Rugmark seal.
3. Donate to the cause of ending child labor.

Visit the organization at www.rugmark.org.

Other resources to use to help advocate for the eradication of child labor include:

Child Labor Coalition, www.stopchildlabor.org
Child Rights Information Network, www.crin.org
Global March Against Child Labour, www.globalmarch.org

I hope the one-hundred-plus ideas and suggestions throughout this book give you all the tools and inspiration you need to write that check, go to that march, work at that soup kitchen, or otherwise "pay your rent." Good luck and enjoy!

Acknowledgments

■

For me, as you can imagine, this is the hardest part of writing this book. How can I ever thank everyone who has helped me to lead a life of service? How can I thank every member of my collective village? I have come to the conclusion that I cannot even come close in the number of pages that has been allotted to me, so please know that if we have crossed paths and connected in any way, big or small, I not only thank you, but I honor you. The blessings that you have bestowed upon me or the people I serve through your generous spirit live inside my heart each and every day.

I must start by thanking my mother, Gayle Fleming, for her expectation that I lead a life of service. To my husband, I thank you not only for your constant support, but for your unyielding acceptance of me as a human being and for encouraging me to follow my dreams. I am most grateful that you understand that my work takes me far away from our home and that you hold the fort down when I am gone. Basically, you let me do my thing and that is why this book is even possible. To my daughters, Lola Simone and Zahra Savannah, thank you for being my constant companions as we give back to society together. Mommy also thanks you for flying from pillar to post, for making friends with the children you meet worldwide, and for allowing me to hold, love, and hug so many other babies and children. And to the newest addition to our family, Ntombifuthi Samantha, God has had a plan for us from the beginning of your life and though I do not know where it will ultimately lead us, I do know that I love you as much as I do the children who came from my womb. You are my Zulu angel and a lasting bond to my adopted country of South Africa. I thank my mother-in-law, Rose Rock, for her son, Chris, and for sending him to the Bushwick Salvation Army Community Center. I owe so much to my beautiful grandmother Homizelle "Gan Gan" Alexander. Thank you for teaching me about forgiveness and how to be a lady. To the rest of my family, brothers, sisters, aunts, uncles, cousins, nieces, nephews, and in-laws, I love and thank you all for your support. Thank you to Patricia "YaYa" Cadette for helping me to care for my children, joining me on the road, and donating to my causes. Lastly, thank you to Uncle Guy-O, Auntie Michelle, Uncle Dwight, and

Auntie LaLa, my children's God parents, who show them such love and guidance and help Chris and I to raise our girls with security and a deep spiritual foundation.

My friends help me to breath and support my nonprofit endeavors in so many ways. They are listed in no particular order but I thank them all equally: Lisa Mabry, Lauren Pemberton, Erica Reid (and hubby L.A. Reid), Holly Robinson-Peete (and hubby Rodney Peete), Benita Nall, David Chin, Soledad O'Brien, Deleon Sheffield, Annie Hausmann, Lori Stokes, Deborah Roberts (and hubby Al Roker), Gayle King, Tonya Lewis Lee, Star Jones, Stacy Morrison, LaTanya Richardson Jackson, Veronica Webb, Iman, Lenora Klein, D'Angelo Thompson, Derrick Rutledge, Angela Burt-Murray, Wendy Williams, Sthu Zunga, Colin Cowie, Stuart Brownstein, Frederica Stines, Deirdre Gary, Nancy Sharp-Zickerman, Emme, Jackie Sandler (and her hubby Adam Sandler), Michelle Kydd-Lee, Shannon Rotenberg, Charisse Webster, Katie McGrath Abrams, Timothy White, Ruthann Huvane, Tanya Young, and all the Freedom School girls.

To my mentors, both near and far, I am indebted to you: Terrie M. Williams, my first boss and constant supporter. Thanks for giving me a job right out of college and for instilling the best work ethic in me. I am grateful to call you a friend and continue to learn from you; Marian Wright Edelman, my inspiration and guiding light. I am so honored to work beside you to protect our planet's most precious resource. Thank you for asking me to serve on the board of the Children's Defense Fund and for writing such a beautiful foreword for this book. I will always call you Ms. Edelman because calling you "Marian" would be like calling Mother Theresa "Ms. T!"; Charles "Chip" J. Lyons, the former president of the U.S. Fund for UNICEF and my boss while I worked there. You were at my side the first time I stepped foot on African soil. As someone who loves the continent probably even more than I do, I know you realize how special this is to me. You continue to inspire me and change the trajectory of my life every few years. By setting up my UNICEF-assisted visit in South Africa long after I left the U.S. Fund, you helped to give my life new meaning; I owe a debt of gratitude to Oprah Winfrey. First and foremost, *The Oprah Winfrey Show* was the first national media outlet to promote styleWORKS. As you can imagine, this helped to solidify my small grassroots nonprofit. And after all of these years, you have continued to single out my work in a multitude of ways, and I am so honored and grateful. I will never forget the night you called me to take part in *Oprah's Big Give*. With this opportunity, you made me realize that I could use my voice on television to encourage others to serve, and you gave me the "bug" to do so. However, your greatest gift to me was to encourage Chris and I to visit South Africa to meet Madiba. I honestly cannot imagine what my life would be like if I did not say, "Honey, we are going to South Africa for Christmas" four years ago. For one thing, I know that Lola would not have said to you that she wanted to go to Capetown instead of Nairobi, as if she was talking about Disney World! Thank you for being such a powerful force in my life and in the lives of women and girls worldwide.

And to my nonprofit posse—the people who are in the trenches saving and enriching lives each and every day—thank you and know that you are my inspiration: Bobby Shriver of (RED); Lynn Stratford of the U.S. Fund for UNICEF; Pam Cope of Touch A Life Foundation; Margaret Xaba of the Olive Leaf Foundation; Keith Norris of Brooklyn Ballers Sports Youth & Education; Sang Ng of UNICEF; Dr. Steve Perry of Capital Preparatory Magnet School; Ric Ramsey of the LEAD Program; Kevin Powell of Black and Male in America; Deborah Koenigsberger of Hearts of Gold; Sarah Culberson of the Kposowa Foundation; Jeanne Middleton Hairston of the Children's Defense Fund Freedom Schools; all the girls of the Triple Negative Breast Cancer Foundation; and the staff of the Salvation Army Bushwick Community Center and the Salvation Army of Greater New York.

Thank you to the staff, volunteers, partners, friends, and interns of the Angelrock Project, especially Cecelia Falls, Regina Lauricella, Cornelius Xulu, Zamalinda Xulu, Margaret Xaba, Tiara Francis, Julia Fishman, Ken Fredman, Charles Kliment, and Richard Menage. Thank you also to my assistant, Lea Delgado Cohen, for her incredible work ethic, fun sense of humor, and amazing organizational skills.

To each and every one of the Journey for Change ambassadors, thank you for being a part of this incredible journey and for allowing me to be a part of your lives. To every sponsor, donor, partner, and supporter of the program, words cannot express how grateful I am to you. Dr. Henry Louis Gates Jr., Bennett Greenspan, Gina Paige, and Dr. Rick Kittles, you all blessed the Journey for Change participants beyond belief by tracing their lineage and providing them with the keys to their ancestral past. Thank you to the CNN team, including Soledad O'Brien, Jon Klein, Mark Nelson, and Michelle Rozsa, for coming on the journey with us and showcasing our story in *Black in America 2*.

To the grannies and orphans of South Africa, thank you for accepting me into your lives and for teaching me the true meaning of resilience, respect, and gratitude. You have made my life fuller and much more blessed than I could ever imagine. A very special thank you to Gogos Skhosana and Nkosi.

I want to thank my ICM team led by Esther Newberg, who is not only a hoot and a holler, but is whip smart and fun to work with. And thank you to my husband's ICM boys Steve Levine and Eddy Yablans who introduced me to Esther. Of course, I must thank my editor, Christine Pride, for guiding me and telling me throughout the whole writing process that she wants to volunteer on one of my projects. And thank you to Rachel Kranz for helping me organize and chronicle my many thoughts and ideas for this book.

To all the grass-root volunteers and service providers worldwide, I revere you, I honor you, and I wrote this book so people could learn from you.